FREEDOM
ON THE
ALTAR

FREEDOM
ON THE
ALTAR

———

The UN's Crusade
Against God & Family

———

William Norman Grigg

American Opinion Publishing, Inc.
Appleton, Wisconsin

First Printing .... March 1995

Published by
American Opinion Publishing, Inc.
Post Office Box 8040
Appleton, Wisconsin 54913
(414) 749–3783

Printed in the United States of America
Library of Congress Catalog Card Number: 95–75907
ISBN: 0–9645679–0–3

To my parents,
Richard and Angie Grigg,
with love, gratitude, and respect.

Contents

1. Welcome to the "Global Neighborhood" 1

2. UNESCO: School Board of the New World Order 33

3. Whose Children? 55

4. "Empowerment" or Enslavement? 91

5. A Covenant With Death:
   Population Control in the Brave New World Order 105

6. Multiculturalism and the UN Assault
   on American Nationhood 131

7. One World Under Gaia 157

8. The Coming Persecution of the Faithful? 181

9. Ending the "Experiment on our liberties": Get *US* Out! ... 207

Notes 217

Index 235

Personal Acknowledgements 261

About the Author 263

Recommended Reading 264

CHAPTER 1

Welcome to the "Global Neighborhood"

[T]he empire of the Romans filled the world.... [T]he world became a safe and dreary prison for [Caesar's] enemies.... To resist was fatal, and it was impossible to fly.... "Wherever you are," said Cicero to the exiled Marcellus, "remember that you are equally within the power of the conqueror."
— Edward Gibbon[1]

[W]e have ceased to be the world of nation-states that we once were.... I don't believe that the world is going to retreat into a situation where people are going to run away from this global neighborhood we've become, because there are no sanctuaries left — there's no place to run to.
— Shridath Ramphal, co-chairman of the Commission on Global Governance[2]

For 50 years, the United Nations and its supporters have insisted that the body represents "the last, best hope of mankind." One recent expression of this sentiment was offered by the *Deseret News*, Utah's largest-circulation daily newspaper, which editorially insisted that "Despite its dismal recent showing, the United Nations remains the world's best hope for cooperation and peaceful coexistence."[3] During the UN's 50th anniversary, the institution's founders and founding events will be presented through a haze of nostalgia, and the world body's present undertakings will be depicted as the selfless labors of heroic idealists seeking to summon a peaceful future.

But there are many people who have seen that future, and who

1

want no part of it. Survivors and witnesses of the UN's 1961 "peacekeeping" massacre in Katanga, a province of the former Belgian Congo, regard the "Blue Berets" as something less than heroic. Religious scholar Thomas Molnar, who has ample first hand experience with UN "peacekeeping" activities, testifies: "I have often walked in the footsteps of United Nations troops 'intervening for peace' and seen pillage, rape, and injustice. In the ex-Belgian Congo, Indian UN soldiers were feared like the plague; 30 years later, Russian UN troopers [returned] to Bosnia after demobilization to continue ravaging land and population. Meanwhile, active Blue Berets, stationed in the Balkans, deal in drugs."[4] Nor has the UN endeared itself to the productive and responsible business classes of Haiti, who have been strangled by UN sanctions and blackmailed by the "international community" into accepting the return of Marxist psychopath Jean-Bertrand Aristide.

Although Americans are justifiably proud of the valor and skill of the American troops who fought in the 1991 Gulf War, it must not be forgotten that the armed conflict with Saddam Hussein's forces was fought to "empower" the UN, not to protect American interests. Therefore, the Americans who perished in that war should be numbered among the UN's victims. Furthermore, the Iraqi civilians who remember the UN-supported terror bombing of Baghdad, and the Iraqi children who have undergone hideous privations because of the UN's post-war embargo — to say nothing of the hapless conscripts who served as cannon-fodder for Saddam Hussein — are less than impressed with the UN's "humanitarian" pretensions. The only real winners in the Gulf War were the curiously indestructible dictator Saddam Hussein and the UN.

Christian and Moslem pro-life activists who attended the 1994 International Conference on Population and Development in Egypt can testify of the colonialist condescension of UN officials. That condescension curdled into bitter anti-Catholic hostility when the Church attempted to moderate the anti-family elements of the Cairo Programme. Chinese women compelled to undergo compulsory abortion and sterilization under Red China's UN-supported population control program undoubtedly look upon the world body as something other than a family-friendly institution. Tibetans, whose culture is being effaced from the earth by Red Chinese occupation forces, must be aware of the support which the Chinese communist government is receiving through UNICEF, the United Nations Fund for Population Activities, and the UN Development Program.[5]

Africans also have reason to dispute the UN's humanitarian pretensions. In 1994, UN "peacekeeping" troops in Mozambique purchased sexual favors from impoverished children.[6] In 1988, the director of the Belgian UNICEF committee was convicted of participation in a child sex and prostitution ring; the organization's Brussels office was used to manufacture child pornography, much of it involving children of North African descent. (See chapter 3.) Somalians will recall that during the UN's "Operation Restore Hope," civilians were massacred indiscriminately by Pakistani "peacekeepers." They may also recall the beating death of 16-year-old Shidane Arone at the hands of a Canadian "peacekeeping" regiment which treated Somalians to scornful racist abuse.[7]

There are numerous other examples of this sort which could be used to illustrate the character of the UN. However, such objections shatter harmlessly on the impregnable prejudices of the UN's devoted supporters, who — borrowing a theme which was often played by apologists for Soviet communism — insist that the world body should be judged by its professed ideals, rather than by its actual performance. Defenders of a UN-administered new world order insist that the triumph of their position is a historic inevitability, and many of them dismiss their opponents as deluded at best and psychologically infirm at worst. Those who defend the new world order skate effortlessly across the surface of glistening cliches: After all, they contend, the nations of the world are inextricably *interdependent*; a true *global culture* has emerged that makes all of humanity the inhabitants of a common *global village*; we must recognize that problems such as pollution, crime, warfare, ethnic conflicts, poverty, and disease *know*

3

no boundaries; and so on.

Others contend that the UN is a harmless distraction — a sinecure for the developed world's bureaucrats and a playpen for Third World malcontents. A variation of this argument was used by some members of the triumphant 1994 Republican majority. Rep. Sonny Callahan (R-AL), chairman of the House Appropriation subcommittee on foreign operations, insists that "We have got to have some kind of international organization that we have a strong voice in." Bud Nance, staff director for Senator Jesse Helms (R-NC), sought to placate press concerns over his employer's conspicuous criticism of the UN: "One of the real good reasons for the United Nations is to talk to each other.... [The UN] keeps the little boys from fighting among themselves, it provides stability."[8]

It is significant that the most common defense offered on behalf of the UN is that it is inconsequential. However, even if the depiction of the UN as the equivalent of a global coffee klatsch were reliable, the body would remain a financial imposition upon American taxpayers and thus constitute a tangible offense. It is also untrue that the body offers a forum in which the "peoples" of the world can talk to each other: The body is a forum for governing elites, most of which remain almost entirely unaccountable to the peoples they supposedly represent. It is also indefensible to maintain that a global body is "necessary" for communications among governments in an era of teleconferences, fax machines, and E-mail. Furthermore, is it not reasonable to believe that disagreements among nations are best dealt with through bilateral discussions, rather than through public confrontations in an international body?

Writing in 1987, *The New Republic*'s Charles Krauthammer — an internationalist who is not opposed to the UN in principle — pointed out that "the U.N. has failed in its principal role, which is keeping the peace. In fact, it has degenerated to the point where its actions exacerbate the few conflicts it still influences...."[9] Since that time, the UN has been "empowered" to take more assertive actions to "enforce" peace — with the lethal results described above.

American involvement in the UN has been associated with an unprecedented entanglement in military ventures which have nothing to do with our national security. Significantly, since the ratification of the UN Charter in 1945, Congress has not issued a single declaration of war; however, this does not mean that peace has prevailed — quite the contrary. Citing a Congressional Research Service study entitled "Instances of Use of United States Armed Forces Abroad, 1798-1993," researcher Thomas R. Eddlem observes that since the Senate ratified the UN Charter in 1945, American military conflicts abroad have consistently increased: There were six such conflicts during the 1950s, seven during the 1960s, nine in the 1970s, 22 during the 1980s, and 18 in the first three and a half years of this decade. Although it is true that not every such engagement has been a UN initiative almost all of them have been justified by a reference to UN guidelines. This is *stability*?

Despite this record, the UN's advocates insist that the organization needs to be further "empowered" in order to carry out its mission. This reflects an old axiom of politics: When a government initiative fails, blame inadequate funding, not mistaken premises. Several "working papers" for UN reform in the body's 50 year anniversary have been proposed, and all of them envision an increased imposition upon overburdened American taxpayers and greatly enhanced powers for the organization.

Shridath Ramphal has presented a "Global Human Security" blueprint on behalf of the Commission on Global Governance (CGG). Co-chaired by Ramphal and socialist Ingvar Carlsson of Sweden, the CGG has presented ten "clusters of reform," which include:

• "Acceptance and evolution of the concept of planetary security, including mandates for custodianship of the global commons [the ocean, the atmosphere, and anything else the UN sees fit to designate as such]...." This custodianship would be exercised by the UN in cooperation with the "international civil society" — governing elites, tax-exempt foundations, and UN-associated Non-

Governmental Organizations (NGOs).

• The establishment of an "apex global economic body within the UN system but reaching beyond governments in its functioning," what Ramphal has referred to as a UN "Economic Security Council" which would be able to raise "global revenues for global purposes through international charges and taxes agreed upon and imposed by treaty."[10]

Another, and arguably even more audacious outline for UN reform, is the "Global Security Programme" (GSP) put forth by the Gorbachev Foundation. Mikhail Gorbachev, an erstwhile Soviet dictator, is an unpunished mass murderer whose policies killed millions of innocent people in the Soviet Union, Latin America, Africa, and Asia. In other words, he is exactly the sort of person whose policy recommendations would find a receptive audience at the United Nations.

Gorbachev's GSP calls for the disarmament of all nations, the strengthening of UN law enforcement authority, the involvement of UN officials in "diversity" initiatives and "conflict resolution," the development of UN-directed initiatives in history revision to "revise incorrect or tendentious versions of the history of inter-group relations," and the creation of a "United Nations General Assembly Commission for the Prevention and Resolution of Conflicts" — a 10-15 member elitist body, presumably composed of august personages like Gorbachev himself, which would "keep a worldwide watch on potentially conflictual situations" and supervise preventative intervention.[11]

Gorbachev has also been assigned the task of writing an "Earth Charter" for the UN, which will set forth a definitive set of enforceable environmental guidelines for the earth's inhabitants. (See chapter 6.)

Why is a gangster like Gorbachev given such moral credibility by the UN? Totalitarian thugs who have killed far fewer people and inflicted far less misery than Gorbachev have rightly perished in prison or on the gallows. What is the mechanism whereby a proponent of a murderous, discredited ideology can achieve such influence upon the UN?

Collaboration, Collusion or ... Conspiracy?

Many decent and honorable people who observe the tenacity of collectivist ideas and programs can be heard giving voice to some variant of this frustrated remark: "Why are intelligent people following policies which have been discredited? Haven't we learned anything from the experience of modern totalitarianism?" Well, why do some intelligent people pursue criminal enterprises, in spite of the fact that crime is disreputable? The answer, of course, is that crime pays — either in a material sense or in the form of some psychological reward. Despite the fact that nobody seriously disputes the idea that criminal conspiracies exist, the idea of political conspiracies is considered suspect. Yet politics, which is essentially the process of organized compulsion, should be considered the most fertile ground for conspiracy.

In his work *The City of God*, Augustine wrote: "Justice being taken away, then, what are kingdoms but great robberies?"[12] Politics has historically been an exercise in collusion and conspiracy in which privileged insiders seek illicit advantage through the power of the state. Noted novelist Taylor Caldwell observed, "There is indeed a 'plot against the people,' and probably always will be, for government has always been hostile to the governed. It is not a new story, and the conspirators and conspiracies have varied from era to era.... But it was not until the era of the League of Just Men and Karl Marx that conspirators and conspiracies became one, with one aim, one objective, and one determination."[13] That determination was — and remains — the desire to create a global socialist order.

Pedigree of a Conspiracy

Socialism* did not emerge fully-formed from the brow of Karl Marx with the publication of *The Communist Manifesto* in 1848, nor was it a natural product of misguided idealism. The so-called

* "Socialism" and "communism" refer to essentially the same political doctrine. These terms refer to systems of political and economic collectivism, as do the terms National Socialism and fascism. The key difference between socialism and communism is a question of methods, not substance or objectives.

"League of Just Men" which retained Marx's dubious literary services was a remnant of earlier groups which had pursued the objectives contained in the *Communist Manifesto,* namely the destruction of Biblical religion, the patriarchal family, private property, and the independence of nations — in short, the creation of a socialist world government.

The concept of a world government which would pacify all disputes and supervise the perfection of mankind is literally centuries old. Arguably, the first modern thinker to conceive of this project was an apostate French priest named Charles Irénée Castel, also known as Abbé de Saint-Pierre (hereafter Saint-Pierre). In 1712, Saint-Pierre published a "Plan For Perpetual Peace" which could be considered the first recognizable draft for what is now called the new world order. Under Saint-Pierre's design, the ruling elites of Europe were to foreswear warfare, submitting instead to the jurisdiction of a "European Union," according to historians Will and Ariel Durant, which would be "armed with force to compel the acceptance of its decisions."[14]

Nor was Saint-Pierre content merely to sketch out the architecture of a continental government; he also sought to extend the reach of the state into the lives of its subjects, in order to remedy their "defects." In 1737 Saint-Pierre composed a tract entitled "Observations on the Continuous Progress of Universal Reason," in which (as the Durants summarize) he outlined "the indefinite perfectibility of mankind through the agency of reason in scientists and governments."[15] This was followed in short order by another pamphlet, "A Project to Perfect the Governments of States," in which Saint-Pierre suggested the creation of a special class of Platonic Guardians — what the Durants called a "Political Academy" taken from among the ranks of the most capable governing elites — "to act as an advisory body ... in matters of social or moral reform."[16]

Among the specific reform proposals offered by Saint-Pierre, according to the Durants, were "universal education under governmental (not ecclesiastical) control, religious toleration [which Saint-Pierre defined as a secondary role for the Church in public life] … the promotion of public welfare by the state, and the enlargement of national revenues by progressive taxes on incomes and inheritances." Does any of this sound familiar? The Durants observed, with some satisfaction: "Most of the basic ideas of the philosophes [18th century secular intellectuals] appeared as a prelude in Saint-Pierre, even to the hope for an enlightened king as an agent of reform."[17]

Of course, any political template in which political and intellectual elites are granted unlimited power to reshape the lives of the "lesser breeds" will find an eager audience among those elites. Jean-Jacques Rousseau was among those who eagerly devoured Saint-Pierre's writings.[18] Rousseau, who was arguably the most influential statist philosopher of the 18th Century and the apostle of political revolution, believed in the terrestrial perfectibility of mankind. In a letter written on January 12, 1762 to Malesherbes, Rousseau recorded an epiphany he had experienced while walking from Paris to Vincennes to visit Diderot:

> All at once I felt myself dazzled by a thousand sparkling lights. Crowds of vivid ideas thronged into my mind with a force and confusion that threw me into unspeakable agitation; I felt my head whirling in a giddiness like that of intoxication…. Ah, if ever I could have written a quarter of what I saw and felt under that tree, with what clarity I should have brought out all the contradictions of our social system! *With what simplicity I should have demonstrated that man is by nature good, and that only our institutions have made him bad!*[19] [Emphasis added]

This experience could be called "The Road to Damascus in Reverse"; rather than being convinced of his sinful nature and need for divine redemption, Rousseau came to believe that he was by nature good and entitled to re-arrange mankind's "sinful" institutions. Of course, this belief is utterly incompatible with the Biblical view of mankind as a fallen race in need of God's grace and intervention. Unlike those who hold to the Christian tenet that man must be redeemed by God, disciples of the Enlightenment maintain that man must be "rehabilitated" or "empowered" by the state. As world history since July 14, 1789 has compellingly illustrated, the struggle to bring about the terrestrial "perfection" of man always results in murderous assaults upon traditional institutions.

As noted above, Rousseau was among the most enthusiastic supporters of Saint-Pierre's plan for "perpetual peace." In his critique of the plan, Rousseau declared that "once there is a society it is necessary to have a coercive force to organize and coordinate the movements of its members so that the common interests and reciprocal ties are given the solidity they would not be able to have by themselves."[20] This is a recognizable formula for totalitarianism. Furthermore, Rousseau believed that it would be necessary (in Shakespeare's words) "to reap the harvest of perpetual peace by ... [the] bloody trial of sharp war"[21]: According to Rousseau, perpetual peace "can only happen by means that humanity might find violent and fearful.... We will not see federative leagues [of the sort envisioned by St.-Pierre] except by revolution...."[22]

A revolutionary battering ram was needed — and one materialized: The subversive network of the Illuminati.

"Perfection" Through Revolutionary Violence

The story of Illuminism is a familiar one to many; some regard it as historical gospel, others as hysterical gibberish. Among the former group we can find Librarian of Congress James H. Billington,* who has written: "The story of the [18th and 19th-century] secret societies can never be fully reconstructed, but it has been badly neglected — even avoided, one suspects — because the evidence that is available repeatedly leads us into territory equally uncongenial to modern historians in the East and in the

---

* Mr. Billington's credentials to address these subjects are impeccable. He is a former Rhodes Scholar, a member of the Council on Foreign Relations and a scholar-in-residence at the Aspen Institute for Humanistic Studies. His vita is studded with prestigious academic positions with various internationalist groups. His book *Fire In the Minds of Men: Origins of the Revolutionary Faith* (1980) remains one of the most convincing studies regarding the influence of Illuminism and its kindred cabals on the modern "revolutionary faith."

West." Billington has documented that it is from "romantic occultism" in general, "and Bavarian Illuminism in particular" that "the modern revolutionary tradition as it came to be internationalized under Napoleon and the Restoration" descends.[23] To understand the UN's objectives and aspirations, it is necessary to review its pedigree in the "modern revolutionary tradition," beginning with the UN's occultist ancestor, the Bavarian Illuminati.

The Durants offer a concise description of the origins of the Illuminati:

> In 1776, Adam Weishaupt, professor of canon law at Ingolstadt, organized a ... secret society, which he called Perfektibilisten, but which later took on the old name of Illuminati. Its ex-Jesuit founder, following the model of the Society of Jesus, divided its associates into grades of initiation, and pledged them to obey their leaders in a campaign to "unite all men capable of independent thought," make man "a masterpiece of reason, and thus attain the highest perfection in the art of government."[24]

The Illuminati's platform called for — among other things — the abolition of private property, patriotism, the family, and religion.[25] One commentator sympathetic to the Illuminati explains that "The teachings of the Illuminati hold that all is material, that all religions are of human invention, that God is man, and man is God, and the world is his [that is, man's] kingdom."[26] Thus man's perfection would be supervised by other men — the "illuminated ones" who are supposedly destined to preside over human evolution.

At the time of the Illuminati's founding, its doctrines had been well established and expounded by anti-Christian intellectuals such as Rousseau, Diderot, Voltaire, d'Alembert, and others, who are known collectively in history as illumines, philosophes, and encyclopedists. Although they were given to quarrels among themselves (Rousseau and Voltaire in particular enjoyed a memorable feud), this group of elitists shared a common goal — the destruction of Christian society and the creation of a new society

11

under the direction of "enlightened" — that is, *illuminated* — despots. In outlook, Weishaupt's society was the distillate of the anti-Christian worldview championed by the philosophes.

Charles William Heckethorn, a 19th century historian of esoteric and occultic groups, pointed out that Weishaupt used the hierarchical structure of his society to winnow out potential rebels. "If [a candidate] was found unreliable," records Heckethorn, "he was not allowed to go beyond" the preliminary degrees of Illuminism; however, "if he proved an apt scholar, he was gradually initiated into the latter [degrees], where all that he had been taught before was overthrown, and radical and deistic theories and plans were unfolded...."[27]

Thus it was at its highest degrees that the revolutionary character of illuminism was revealed, and initiates were placed under covenant to carry out the wishes of The Order (as the society referred to itself). Reports Heckethorn, "[A]ccording to statements found in the writings of Weishaupt, the Magus degree was to be founded on the principles of [philosopher Benedict de] Spinoza, showing all to be material, God and the world One, and all religions human inventions." Furthermore, at the Rex degree existing social structures would have to be abolished and the world would have to be remade.[28]

Heckethorn, who was sympathetic toward the Illuminati, recounts that before the exposure of the cabal, "The Order made considerable progress, including among its members priests, prelates, ministers, physicians, princes, and sovereign dukes," although relatively few of them were initiated into the higher degrees.[29] There are two significant points to be recognized here: First, the effort to subvert Christian society was directed from *above*, by the elite; it was not a spontaneous uprising from the struggling proletarian masses *below*. Second, Weishaupt's conspiracy included many who were genuinely unaware of the movement's ultimate objectives, people who had joined for social reasons or perhaps out of a misplaced idealism.

Although the Bavarian Illuminati organized by Weishaupt was outlawed in 1784, it survived in the form of "reading societies" and other front groups.[30] Billington writes that the illuminist "diaspora" brought about "a posthumous impact that was far greater throughout Europe than anything the order had been able to accomplish during its brief life as a movement of German intellectuals."[31] Specifically, what Billington describes as "Weishaupt's Rousseauian vision of leading humanity to a new moral perfection freed from all established religions and political authority" found plentiful converts among the French philosophes[32].

The various strands of anti-Christian thought coalesced around Weishaupt's organization, and it was largely through the illuminist network that the French Revolution was brought about — a "violent and fearful" revolution intended to summon a new order in which man would be perfected through the state. The illuminist network infiltrated France in the early 1780s, including among its first inductees such dubious historical notables as Count Mirabeau and Talleyrand.[33] Count Mirabeau was a significant connecting link through which the illuminist designs were imported into France from Germany.[34]

Mirabeau, whose most notable accomplishments came in the fields of agitation and propaganda, invented the revolutionary vocabulary which still haunts political discourse — terms and phrases such as "revolutionary," "counter-revolutionary," and "revolution of the mind." Furthermore, his propaganda took on an unambiguously religious cast: He referred to the French National Assembly as "the inviolable priesthood of national policy" and baptized the revolutionary ideology as "a political gospel" and a new religion "for which the people are ready to die."[35]

The rites of this "new religion" were macabre. According to an account provided by Heckethorn — who was, it must be remembered, sympathetic to the Illuminati — the initiation rituals of the French branch of The Order were a satanic burlesque, in which a naked, tormented, and sexually degraded neophyte was compelled to repeat an oath which included this asseveration:

I swear to sever all bonds uniting me with father, mother, brothers, sisters, wife, relations, friends, mistress, king, superiors, benefactors, or any other man to whom I have promised faith, obedience, gratitude, or service."[36]

Once committed to The Order, the inductee was told that he may be called upon to rid "the earth, by death or stupefaction, of those who revile truth [as defined by the Illuminists], or seek to wrest it from our hands."[37] Those who joined The Order were permitted the indulgence of every carnal impulse; one contemporary account testifies that the meetings of the French Illuminist lodge were scenes of the grossest debauchery.[38]

This combination of political conspiracy and moral debauchery throve at the Palais-Royal between the years 1788-1792 under the supervision of Phillip, the Duke of Orleans, an illuminist who was the king's cousin. According to Billington, "the Palais provided a living link with the underworld of Paris and with the new social forces that had to be mobilized for any revolutionary victory." Those "new social forces" were represented by depraved political theatre, prostitution, pornography (including De Sade's works), and narcotic and sexual dissipations of every conceivable variety.[39]

By elevating the basest impulses of the human character, the *illumines* brought about the pure Democracy of abject bestiality. Billington writes that the "Temple of voluptuousness" (as the Palais-Royal became known) was able to "mobilize mass emotions" by offering "the intoxicating ambience of an earthly utopia. Distinctions of rank were obliterated, and men were free to exercise sexual as well as political freedom."[40]

Amid the corruption of pre-Revolutionary France, at least one author offered advance warning of the coming cataclysm. Eleven years before the Revolution began with the storming of the Bastille, Louis-Sebastien Mercier, a chronicler of the Palais-Royal social revolution, predicted that a "republican" revolution would begin with *that very event.*[41] The Revolution was not the product of abstract, impersonal forces; it was an event which was carefully planned as the inauguration of a "new religion" and a new world order. That the French Revolution was the product of a malignant design was recognized by Lord Acton in his *Lectures on the French Revolution*:

> The appalling thing in the French Revolution is not the tumult, but the design. Through all the fire and smoke we perceive the evidence of calculating organization. The managers remain studiously concealed and masked; but there is no doubt about their presence from the first.[42]

As de Tocqueville and others would later observe, the French Revolution was perhaps the first political revolution without borders — a global crusade on behalf of a messianic political idea.[43]

Many Americans of the era, including some of the most notable figures of the founding generation, were aware of illuminism and the threat it posed to freedom. George Washington was aware of the organization and warned about "the nefarious, and dangerous plan, and doctrines of the Illuminati...."[44] Early Federalist leader Fisher Ames, a member of the first Congress, condemned the illuminist ideology as "visions of bedlam [which] have visited some famous heads"[45] and explained that illuminists "manifest a strange heat in the heart, but no light in the brain," seeking "to kindle every thing in the state that is combustible, into a blaze."[46]

Furthermore, Ames understood that illuminism was not an affliction confined to France, but was intended to foster upheaval throughout the European continent and beyond. He wrote that the "slender hope" afforded by a gauzy, vaporous vision of world brotherhood "is all that the illuminists have proposed as the indemnity for all the crimes and misery of France, and all the horrors of the new revolutions that they wish to engender in Europe from the Bosphorous to the Baltic."[47]

Ames warned Americans of an illuminist-oriented pro-French faction in America.[48] That faction was involved in the creation of "Democratic Societies" which sought to propagate illuminist ideas among struggling American citizens.[49] Other prominent Americans who warned of the Illuminati's designs on the infant American republic included the Rev. Seth Payson,[50] and the Rev.

Jedediah Morse, a noted geographer, textbook author and father of inventor Samuel Morse.

But America's Constitutional foundations held firm because they were set in the bedrock of sound principles. Perhaps the most incisive critique of the Rousseauist/illuminist design for "perpetual peace" was that written by James Madison and published in *The National Gazette* on February 2, 1792. Madison summarized Rousseau's plan as a scheme to create "a confederation of sovereigns, under a council of deputies, for the double purpose of arbitrating external controversies among nations, and of guarantying their respective governments against internal revolutions." He pointed out that the plan would "perpetuate arbitrary power wherever it existed"; in addition, it would extinguish "the hope of one day seeing an end of oppression [and] cut off the only source of consolation remaining to the oppressed."[51]

For those who sought an end to the scourge of war, Madison prescribed the American constitutional formula: Compel the government to protect the rights and interests of the people. "Were all nations to follow the example" set forth in the U.S. Constitution, Madison proclaimed, "the reward would be doubled to each." It is the embrace of true republican principles, according to Madison, that is "the only hope of Universal and Perpetual Peace."[52]

The Idea Survives

Although the Illuminati's objectives were not fully consummated, the Revolution and the subsequent Napoleonic campaigns did result in a partial application of the design for "perpetual peace," and an unwelcome partial vindication of Madison's predictions. The Congress of Vienna, which was blessed by the influence of statesmen like Metternich and Castelreagh, created a "Holy Alliance" which was intended to prevent another outbreak of revolutionary violence and aggression. However, the policies pursued in the name of preserving the "Concert of Europe" were not entirely uncontaminated by the 18th-century notions of "Perpetual Peace" promoted by Saint-Pierre, Rousseau, and the illuminists. British historian Paul Johnson notes that although the system devised by the Congress of Vienna had broken down by the 1820s, while it lasted it was "the golden age of the political police."[53]

One English observer at the Congress wrote with horror that the delegates were devising "all sorts of wild schemes of establishing a general police over all Europe and sending the troops of one country to keep order in another...." In a letter written to an acquaintance, Beethoven recalled that "Before the French Revolution there was great freedom of thought and political action." However, lamented Beethoven, that event — which had promised "Liberty, Equality, and Fraternity" — had produced instead "the present policy of repression." Taxation and regulation also flourished as a result of the Congress. One critic of the system sarcastically remarked that "The Congress is working on a law that will lay down how high birds may fly and how fast hares may run."[54]

Of course, the system created by the Congress did not endure, nor did peace become perpetual. The remnants of the Illuminist network re-emerged in the communist revolutions of 1848.[55] Although defenders of the Revolution of 1848 have insisted that the uprising was spontaneous on the part of the oppressed, the Revolution was an event fostered by, and sustained by, elites.

Enter Marx

Until the late 1840s, Karl Marx had been an obscure figure whose writings — particularly his poetical and dramatic offerings — suggested membership in occultic organizations.[56] In November 1847, Marx was approached by the *Bund Der Gerechten* or the "League of Just Men," which was a descendant of the Illuminist network.[57] The League wanted Marx to compose "a confession of faith" which would be used to unite the world-wide revolutionary network into an instrument of terror.

Marx's *Communist Manifesto* was completed in January 1848; by February 1848 — a few days before the communist uprising began — Marx received a downpayment of 6,000 gold francs from the "impoverished" proletarian League.[58] On February 22, 1848, as if a switch had been thrown, the revolution prophesied by Marx materialized. As had been the case with Mercier's predictions of the French Revolution, advance warning had been given.

Amid the chaos and bloodshed which anticipated and attended Louis Blanc's 1848 revolution in France, Frederic Bastiat, a member of the French house of deputies and one of the most eloquent defenders of the free market, noted that there appeared to be a natural affinity between the socialist radicals and the governing elites: They agreed on the premise of a government directed by "forward-looking" elites, but disagreed as to the specifics of the government in question. Furthermore, the supposedly anti-socialist policies implemented by the French government had the effect of enriching the socialist cause. The government, wrote Bastiat, was busy "concocting the antidote and the poison in the same laboratory."[59]

Once again, the failure of the 1848 revolution did not destroy the illuminist design. Writing in 1897, Heckethorn declared that the views of the Illuminati, which were considered radical and subversive in 1776, "at the present day, are held by many men of just and enlightened views."[60] Following the bloody cataclysm of World War I — a conflict which decisively overturned the political and religious institutions which had prevailed in Europe for centuries — one such "just and enlightened" man resurrected the illuminist faith in a regimented society presided over by a "forward-looking" elite. He also presented a revised design for "perpetual peace." The concept — and indeed, even the name — for this updated version of the "perpetual peace" concept was offered by an enigmatic figure known as "Colonel" Edward Mandell House, an advisor to U.S. President Woodrow Wilson.

Wilson and His Doppleganger

The relationship between Wilson and House was roughly identical to that which existed between the Corsican Brothers: If one was cut, the other would bleed. Wilson confided to an associate:

> Mr. House is my second personality. He is my independent self. His thoughts and mine are one. If I were in his place I would do just

as he suggested.... If any one thinks he is reflecting my opinion by whatever action he takes, they are welcome to the conclusion.[61]

House was Wilson's "silent partner" and was referred to by the President as "the only person in the world with whom I can discuss everything."[62] Thus it is of no small historical importance that House, President Wilson's alter ego, was an unabashed and unapologetic socialist.

Like Marx, who had written the communist "confession of faith," House turned to literature as a vehicle for socialist evangelism. In 1912, seeking for a way to popularize an ideology which had fallen into deserved disfavor with the American public, House published a "political romance" entitled *Philip Dru: Administrator*. House later explained that "unless it was known [as a novel] its audience would be reduced at least ninety-nine percent. If it was called what I really mean it to be, only those who think pretty much as I do would read it, and those I am trying to reach would never look at it."[63] A perusal of the book proves that like most "forward-looking" elitists, House entertained a very low opinion of the tastes and intellectual capacity of the "common" people. The book was less a novel than a recital of socialist themes. Ineptly plotted and larded with contrived and emotionally overripe prose, the book was described by House as the definitive expression of "my ethical and political faith."[64]

That faith, noted Charles Seymour, a Sterling professor of history at Yale University, was essentially a form of "social democracy reminiscent of Louis Blanc and the [communist] revolutionaries of 1848...."[65] The volume's epigram was a quote taken from Giuseppe Mazzini, one of the most significant revolutionists of the 19th century who advanced the illuminist program in Europe via a network of secret societies.[66] The novel was dedicated "to the unhappy many who have lived and died lacking opportunity, because, in the starting, the world-wide social structure was wrongly begun." As with those who had been initiated into the highest ranks of the Illuminati, House aspired to nothing less than the power to remold the world closer to his heart's desire.

Like the 18th century *illumines*, House dreamed of a nation —
and ultimately, a world — united under the dictatorial rule of an
enlightened despot. House describes Dru, his fictional political
savior, as having a "quivering heart" as he contemplates injustice. After leading a putsch against America's constitutional government, Dru arrives in Washington "panoplied in justice and
with the light of reason in his eyes.... the advocate of equal opportunity ... with the power to enforce his will."[67]

Dru's will was to pursue "Socialism as dreamed of by Karl Marx
... [with] a spiritual leavening...."[68] Yet his first priority was diligently to cultivate the support, both financial and intellectual, of
the wealthy and well-born: "[I]t will be the educated and rich, in
fact the ones that are now the most selfish, that will be in the
vanguard of the procession. They will be the first to realize the
joy of it all, and in this way they will redeem the sins of their
ancestors."[69]

The "negative" government created by the Constitution —
which protects the rights of individuals from the power of the
State — was replaced by Dru with an omnicompetent "positive"
government in which "the property and lives of all were now in
the keeping of one man."[70] A corporate oligarchy was created in
which government would favor preferred economic concerns in
exchange for political support. A "League of Nations" was created,
and the American Hemisphere was joined under a single political
authority administered by the quivery-hearted political savior,
Philip Dru.

Immediately after Wilson won the 1912 election, House set
about putting his political faith into practice. As Dru had done,
House recruited the conspicuously wealthy into his vanguard, including mega-bankers Paul Warburg, Frank Vanderlip, and J.P.
Morgan.[71] An ambitious package of Dru-style "reforms" was assembled. Prof. Seymour observed in the mid-1920s that "The specific measures enacted by Philip Dru as Administrator of the
nation [in House's novel] indicated the reforms desired by
House."[72] In a letter to an associate, Franklin K. Lane, Wilson's
Secretary of the Interior, stated: "All that book has said [sic]

should come about... The President comes to Philip Dru in the end."[73]

However, the fondest desire of both Wilson and House — the creation of a League of Nations which incorporated the United States — was not fully realized. The Senate's refusal to ratify the League of Nations Covenant caused the organization to sink into deserved oblivion. Accordingly, House and his vanguard had to adopt a different strategy in pursuit of a socialist world government.

The oligarchy which surrounded House included a group called "The Inquiry" — 100 "forward-looking" social planners who drew up the peace settlement after World War I. This group understood that it would be necessary to change American public opinion — particularly elite opinion — before the nation could be eased into a global superstate. Accordingly, in 1919, House hosted an assembly of globalist notables which resulted in the Institute of International Affairs, which would have branches in New York and London — the Council on Foreign Relations (CFR) and the Royal Institute of International Affairs (RIIA), respectively. The RIIA was intimately linked to the Round Table, a British cabal organized by Cecil Rhodes. Once again, following the *Dru* formula, most of the founding members of the CFR (according to the account of the organization's official historian) "were bankers and lawyers" associated with J.P. Morgan.

The founding President of the CFR was John W. Davis, Morgan's personal attorney and a millionaire in his own right; Paul Cravath, the founding vice president, was also allied with Morgan interests; Russell Leffingwell, a business partner of Morgan, would later become the Council's first chairman. Other luminaries from Morgan's financial constellation filled out the CFR's early membership rolls.[74] Through its interface with Wall Street finance, the CFR had the resources to conduct its "educational" offensive on behalf of globalism. And of course, this arrangement paid immediate dividends for Insiders as well. One illustration of its rewards can be found in this observation from Ron Chernow, the former director of financial policy studies for the Twentieth Century Fund: "Between the wars [WWI and WWII], the mysterious troika of the Bank of England, the New York Fed, and the Morgans had largely governed the international monetary order."[75]

Foreign Affairs, the flagship publication of the CFR, has been a reliable retailer of globalist nostrums and socialist policy recommendations. The CFR spent the period between the World Wars creating what historian Charles Howland referred to as "an outpouring of books" and other "scholarly" studies intended to create an intellectual hegemony on behalf of the globalist worldview.

As had been the case with Col. House's socialist soap opera *Philip Dru: Administrator*, the effusion of "scholarly" ink inspired by the CFR — and financed by financial elites and tax-exempt foundations — was intended to "cure" America of its "isolationist" tendencies. The deliberate cultivation of "internationalist" opinion between the wars is a splendid illustration of the chief function served by the CFR today: The organization seeks to create a globalist monopoly on public discussion by establishing the parameters of "respectable" debate.

Many of the quasi-fascist policies inaugurated through FDR's New Deal represented a continuation of the *Dru* blueprint. Furthermore, what House was to Woodrow Wilson, the CFR was to Franklin Delano Roosevelt. Through the influence of its members, the organization essentially ran FDR's State Department, and at its doorstep must be left the responsibility for the Roosevelt Administration's incredible appeasement of the Soviet Union. It was this same cabal which began drafting plans for a United Nations organization during WWII. The U.S. delegation to the UN's founding conference in San Francisco in June 1945 contained 47 members of the CFR; the Secretary-General of the conference, Alger Hiss, was both a member of the CFR and a secret Soviet agent who was later convicted of perjury.

A Bizarre Union

As William F. Jasper documents in his definitive study *Global Tyranny ... Step by Step*, the United Nations is the perverse progeny of the seemingly unlikely — yet essentially incestuous — marriage between big money in the west and totalitarian Marxism in the east:

> The creation of the United Nations ... was the culmination of an intensive campaign begun in the early days of this century by those who could only be described as the pillars of the American Establishment. Names like Carnegie, Morgan, Warburg, Schiff, Marburg and Rockefeller headed the list of those promoting "world order."
>
> It is interesting then, though a source of confusion to many, to learn that not only were the ideas of world government in general and the League of Nations and United Nations in particular especially fond goals of these "arch-capitalists," but they were also the ultimate objects of desire for world socialists and communist movements.[76]

For this reason, the "Cold War," despite its very real human cost, was the intellectual and geopolitical equivalent of a professional wrestling match: It was essentially a choreographed display conducted by "opponents" who (as then-Secretary of State Cyrus Vance said of President Jimmy Carter and Soviet dictator Leonid Brezhnev) "share the same goals and aspirations." American assistance preserved Stalin's regime during WWII; after Stalin devoured Eastern Europe, the West adopted a policy — first ventilated in *Foreign Affairs* — called "containment," which permitted the peaceful digestion of Soviet conquests. Various periods of "detente" offered periodic infusions of Western aid and capital to keep the Soviet Union and its empire alive. In all of this, the Establishment was simply continuing the strange symbiosis which began when the same business interests which eventually clustered around the CFR helped underwrite the Bolshevik Revolution.[77]

Once again we see the syndrome described by Bastiat — the creation of the poison and the antidote in the same laboratory. But to what end? Political analyst Edith Kermit Roosevelt (a grand-daughter of Theodore Roosevelt) offered this explanation:

What is the Establishment's view-point? Through the Roosevelt, Truman, Eisenhower and Kennedy Administrations its ideology is constant: That the best way to fight Communism is by a One World Socialist state governed by "experts" like themselves. The result has been policies which favor the growth of the superstate, gradual surrender of United States sovereignty to the United Nations and a steady retreat in the face of Communist aggression.[78]

Those who are unconvinced of the conspiratorial character and background of the CFR could usefully regard the group's headquarters at Harold Pratt House in New York City as an incubator for ruinous policies. Are all CFR members conspirators? Of course not. (As we have seen, not all of Weishaupt's Illuminists were aware of that group's genuine objectives.) But at the heart of the CFR can be found a group of individuals who aggrandize themselves by pursuing power in ways injurious to the public good — in other words, a conspiracy.

It is not necessary to describe or document the decisive influence of the CFR — and of its sister organization, the Trilateral Commission — on the political, business, and media worlds since 1919, as this has already been done elsewhere.[79] It is sufficient for our needs to understand that the CFR brackets policy questions between false alternatives. For instance, with respect to the question of foreign aid, the CFR will "authorize" discussion regarding amounts of aid, or of specific beneficiaries; however, it will rule out of bounds any discussion of the basic unconstitutionality of foreign aid. In this way, political debate remains a safe and harmless distraction, not unlike a football game which is played entirely within the forty-yard lines.

Regarding the CFR's domination of American politics, one need look no further than this description, which was offered by *Washington Post* ombudsman Richard Harwood in 1993. Referring to *Foreign Affairs*, Harwood writes:

The quarterly is published by the Council on Foreign Relations, whose members are the closest thing we have to a ruling Establishment in the United States.

The president is a member. So is his secretary of state, the deputy secretary of state, all five of the undersecretaries, several of the assistant secretaries and the department's legal adviser. The president's national security adviser and his deputy are members. The director of Central Intelligence (like all previous directors) and the chairman of the Foreign Intelligence Advisory Board are members. The secretary of defense, three undersecretaries and at least four assistant secretaries are members. The secretaries of the departments of housing and urban development, interior, health and human services and the chief White House public relations man ... along with the speaker of the House [are members]....

This is not a retinue of people who "look like America," as the President once put it, but they very definitely look like the people who, for more than half a century, have managed our international affairs and our military-industrial complex.[80]

Which Side are They On?

The forty-yard lines which the CFR and its allied elites have constructed around the UN favor totalitarian assumptions over the values cherished by America's Founders. Thus it should surprise no one that a man like Gorbachev would enjoy prominent standing within the CFR-led Establishment and be a trusted architect of UN "reform." Nor should it be considered surprising that Gorbachev presented his plans for UN reform during a meeting of the CFR at the Harold Pratt House.[81]

In a December 1988 speech before the UN General Assembly, Gorbachev declared: "Two great revolutions, the French Revolution of 1789 and the Russian Revolution of 1917, exerted a powerful impact on the very nature of history.... those two revolutions shaped the way of thinking that is still prevalent...."[82] This is the "way of thinking" which has inspired collectivist oligarchs like Saint-Pierre, Rousseau, Weishaupt, and House, and which permeates the CFR-influenced governing Establishment today — a "way of thinking" which is irreconcilable with the Spirit of 1776.

Nevertheless, the UN's "way of thinking" was emphatically endorsed by President George Bush during a speech before the UN General Assembly on September 23, 1991. In that address, President Bush — a former member of the CFR and Trilateral Commission, declared:

> [Y]ou may wonder about America's role in the new world that I have described. Let me assure you, the United States has no intention of striving for a *Pax Americana*. However, we will remain engaged. We will not retreat and pull back into isolationism.... [W]e seek a *Pax Universalis* [universal peace] built upon shared responsibilities and aspirations.... [We must] [i]nspire future generations ... to say, "On the ruins of conflict, these brave men and women built an era of peace and understanding. They inaugurated a new world order...."[83]

Relatively few Americans grasped the implications of this address, which expressed a complete apostasy from the constitutional concepts explained by Madison — and an unabashed embrace of the "perpetual peace" design which has created untold tragedy over the course of more than two centuries. The UN's vision of "peace" and the communist vision of "peace" are identical — a fact which was candidly recognized by no less an authority than former UN secretary-general U Thant. In a message sent to a 1970 UNESCO symposium on Lenin held in Finland, Thant declared:

> Lenin was a man with a mind of great clarity and incisiveness, and his ideas have had a profound influence on the course of contemporary history.... *[Lenin's] ideals of peace and peaceful coexistence among states ... are in line with the aims of the U.N. Charter....*"[84] (Emphasis added)

A Satanic Design

The adjective "satanic" is properly used when describing the hideous bloodshed which has resulted from the centuries-old campaign to bring about the terrestrial perfection of mankind. But there is a deeper sense in which this crusade has earned that description. In his drama *Faust*, Goethe captured the essence of the satanic design. As Mephistopheles tempts Dr. Faust, the Doctor suddenly understands the tempter's intentions toward him: "You can't achieve wholesale annihilation, [a]nd now a retail business you've begun"![85] Of course, this is not to say that Mephistopheles would neglect an opportunity to inflict wholesale misery — and there is only one route through which this may be accomplished.

Although misery and tragedy can come in individualized allotments, it is only through the state that *wholesale* annihilation or misery can be achieved. Individuals kill each other; clans feud; gangs conduct hit-and-run raids on each other's "turf." However, only governments fight wars, and it takes the power of a totalitarian state to commit genocide. A world government would traffic in wholesale misery, either by requiring all subordinate institutions to retail its policies (the fascist alternative) or by establishing a direct monopoly on political power (the communist alternative).

The satanic design inspires the tactics used in pursuit of the total state. One of the titles by which Satan is known is "The Accuser." The Holy Bible's book of Job describes Satan's attempt to ruin Job by provoking him to sin — and then accusing him before God. In a similar fashion, tyrannical governments create or exacerbate "problems" or "crises" which serve as rationales for enriching their own power. As we will see, the UN excels at this diabolical game, inventing or exaggerating "global crises" which are cited as pretexts for global government. Always it is humanity — more specifically, human liberty — which is indicted by the UN as the cause of "problems" for which a global state is the prescribed "remedy."

Marxists and other radical socialists have made use of the tactic of satanic accusation. Marx himself was an informant for the Austrian police, betraying his revolutionary "comrades" for money.[86] Stalin was particularly adept at this game: He denounced minor Communist party members to the Czarist police, thereby gaining access to police files which he turned over to party leaders.[87] A variation on this tactic was used by the Illuminist revolutionary government of France in July 1791, when it invoked martial law to deal with the menace to public order created by the mob it had incited.[88] Perhaps the most famous use of this tactic was that made by the German National Socialist regime, which used the arson attack on the Reichstag in 1933 to pass an "Enabling Act" permitting Adolf Hitler to rule by decree. Once more we see the familiar strategy of "creating the poison and the antidote in the same laboratory."

Some who find the conspiratorial concept acceptable may take issue with the term "satanic." They should consider the following. Anton LaVey, the founder of the Church of Satan, has explained his organization's objectives in the following terms: "We advocate a benign police state, feeling that in a few short years the public will have become sick of ensuing [sic] anarchy to the point that they will welcome a cop on every corner."[89] The UN's apologists insist that some form of world government is the only alternative to anarchy and mass bloodshed, and among the official policy objectives of the United Nations — and the United States government — can be found the comprehensive disarmament of all nations (and individuals) and the creation of a militarily omnipotent "planetary police."[90] In short, the creation of a planet-spanning, "benevolent" police state which will put an end to the "anarchy" of independent nation-states.

Webster's Dictionary defines the adjective "satanic" as "characterized by extreme viciousness or cruelty" — a description which certainly applies to the communist, fascist, and Nazi dictatorships of this century. The burden upon this book is to demonstrate that the UN-administered world regime which is under construction shares the assumptions of those previous dictatorships and will thus rival them in "extreme viciousness [and] cruelty."

Perpetual Peace or Eternal Tyranny?

To understand the wages of "perpetual peace" as envisioned by the UN, we will illustrate the continuity of assumptions, values, objectives, and tactics which has characterized an identifiable ruling elite over the course of more than two centuries. Upon examining this evidence, readers should ask themselves, once again, if it is ignorance which leads otherwise intelligent people to pursue discredited, tyrannical policies, or if it is deliberate, premeditated, and organized — that is to say, conspiratorial — malice.

The UN is intended to be more than a meaningless debating society or an intellectual sandbox for the political elite. The question which Americans should ask themselves is this: What would life be like if the UN's ambitions were realized? There are those who are uneasy over the growing involvement of the UN in America's affairs, particularly with regard to military "peacekeeping" ventures, but somehow manage to console themselves with the thought that such impositions are relatively minor and not yet unbearable. Such people should consider the wisdom contained in Edward Gibbon's observation that "A nation of slaves is always prepared to applaud the clemency of their master who, in the abuse of absolute power, does not proceed to the last extremes of injustice and oppression."[91] It is not enough to think in terms of the relatively innocuous burdens which the UN presently inflicts; rather, we must discern the potential abuses which reside within the body's stated objectives.

There are many who contend that the UN is not, nor was it ever intended to be, a world government. Such a statement cannot be reconciled with the body's founding texts or the pronouncements of its contemporary representatives. Shridath Ramphal, co-chair of the Commission on Global Governance, insists that "This is not the time to be talking about world government" and that his UN-affiliated commission deals with "issues of governance — not issue of world government ... but of government in its broadest sense." But in the same address Ramphal announced the end "of the world of nation-states that we once were."[92] Ramphal's commission seeks the creation of a world in which nation-states would act as administrative units of a central political authority — in other words, retail outlets for political tyranny. Irrespective of the label Ramphal uses, the substance of what he describes is a world government.

This book seeks to demonstrate that, if the UN-supervised new world order is allowed to proceed, the "last extremes of injustice and oppression" which result will include:

• Mandatory indoctrination of children in the "values" embodied by the UN, which indoctrination may include compulsory "volunteer" service;

• Dictatorial control over family affairs, including compulsory birth control, parental "licensing," and the summary seizure of children from parents who are found to be "incompetent" by UN-approved authorities;

• The effective eradication of America's distinctive institutions of liberty and the Western biblical culture which produced those unparalleled institutions;

• The creation of a world religion and an unprecedented campaign of persecution against those who profess and practice traditional Biblical religion.

Denying the Abuses in Principle

James Madison taught that we must "take alarm at the first experiment upon our liberties", and that such "prudent jealousy [is] the first duty of citizens.... The freemen of America did not wait till usurped power had strengthened itself by exercise, and entangled the question in precedents. They saw all the consequences in the principle, and they avoided the consequences by denying the principle."[93] The "experiment upon our liberties" is well advanced.

As this book will document, the UN intends to regiment all aspects of human existence, including our modes of worship, our family relationships, and decisions relevant to the birth and upbringing of children. In matters of "peacekeeping" and social policy, the UN is "[strengthening] itself by exercise, and [entangling] the question in precedents."

But it is not impossible to stop that diabolical experiment. The solution begins with the understanding that the principles upon which the UN was founded have had murderous consequences in this century; we can only avoid those consequences *if we deny those principles*. Thus it is to an examination of those principles which we will turn in the chapters that follow.

CHAPTER 2

UNESCO: School Board
of the New World Order

*"We are not content with negative obedience, nor even with
the most abject submission. When finally you surrender to us,
it must be of your own free will. We do not destroy the heretic
because he resists us ... We convert him, we capture his inner
mind, we reshape him."*
— Big Brother's agent O'Brien in George Orwell's *1984*[1]

*It may be hoped that in time anybody will be able to per-
suade anybody of anything if he can catch the patient young
and is provided by the state with money and equipment....
When the technique has been perfected, every government that
has been in control of education for a generation will be able
to control its subjects securely without the need of armies or
policemen....*
— Bertrand Russell, Humanist/Socialist philosopher
(and UNESCO adviser)[2]

Shortly before the 104th Congress began its work, the Clinton
Administration announced that the United States would delay its
re-entry into the United Nations Education, Scientific, and Cultural Organization (UNESCO), despite earlier assurances that
U.S. membership would resume in October 1995. Presidential
Counselor Timothy Wirth (CFR) explained to a group of UNESCO
supporters that "We would like very much to rejoin UNESCO.
But we need $65 million to rejoin. We don't have $65 million in
that account. We would have to take it away from the United Nations Development Programme or the Population Fund."[3]

Although the lack of direct U.S. involvement in UNESCO has created some financial hardship for the institution, unofficial contacts have continued. UNESCO collaborated with the U.S. Agency for International Development (AID) to rebuild Haiti's educational system during the UN/U.S. occupation of Haiti.[4] Furthermore, UNESCO was a major coordinating player in the UN World Summit on Social Development, which was held in Copenhagen in March 1995. The purpose of that event was to foster "social integration" and "global human security" — that is, to extend the UN's dominion over all human activities. UNESCO has also retained its links with UN-aligned Non-Governmental Organizations (NGOs), including prominent tax-exempt organizations. For example, the Virginia-based Millennium Institute received funding from UNESCO to produce *Studies for the 21st Century*, a summary of 40 separate versions of "21st Century Studies" which are used in educational and religious programs.[5]

It is significant that the Clinton Administration depicted America's continued absence from UNESCO as a question of money, rather than a matter of political philosophy. If $65 million is all that separates the U.S. from UNESCO, America's descent into socialism is all but complete.

Socialism and Scandal

UNESCO has never been a popular entity in the United States, and various UNESCO-related educational initiatives in the late 1950s and 1960s shattered upon the determined resistance of the American public. By the time of Ronald Reagan's election in 1980, American public opinion had turned decisively against the UN and all of its works. Something had to be sacrificed to placate the electorate, and UNESCO was chosen as the organizational scapegoat.

Under the leadership of Director-General Amadou Mahtar M'Bow of Senegal, the stench of socialism emanating from UNESCO became unbearable. One British commentator described M'Bow's UNESCO as a "Third World kleptocracy"[6]. The body swilled enormous amounts of money — one-quarter of which was taken from American taxpayers — to fund M'Bow's opulent lifestyle and to underwrite an incessant stream of anti-American and anti-Western rhetoric. Under M'Bow, the body devoted itself to advancing a "New World Economic Order" which would radically redistribute wealth from the prosperous "North" to the undeveloped "South." However, the final outrage for most Americans came when the organization announced a "New World Information Order" which would require all journalists to be licensed — presumably by a global body — in order to report on world affairs. This proposal decisively alienated the "mainstream" press, which was uncharacteristically quiet when the Reagan Administration announced the U.S. withdrawal.

Speaking at a December 1983 press conference about UNESCO, State Department spokesman Alan Romberg declared that the body had "Politicized virtually every subject it deals with," had displayed a "hostility toward the basic institutions of a free society, especially a free market and a free press," and had "Demonstrated unrestrained budgetary expansion." Notwithstanding all of this, however, the Reagan Administration made it perfectly clear that the withdrawal was temporary. Secretary of State George Shultz (CFR) pledged undiminished support for the UN and stated that the 12-month notice was intended to give UNESCO "a potential opportunity to respond to the serious concerns that have caused our withdrawal." The clear implication was that UNESCO could use its time in the "penalty box" to rehabilitate its reputation and make it more palatable to a distracted public.[7]

Apparently, the rehabilitation campaign is almost complete. In August 1993, a Clinton Administration task force under the direction of Assistant Secretary of State Douglas Bennet (CFR) recommended that the United States resume its dues-paying membership in UNESCO in October 1995. This followed the introduction of a House resolution by Congressman Esteban E. Torres (D-CA), a former ambassador to UNESCO, which urged American re-entry into the body.[8] In late 1994, The *New York Times* editorialized that the Reagan Administration's decision to withdraw from UNESCO until at least 1995 made "political as well as fiscal sense." Of course, as long as America was coughing up one-quarter of the annual bill for a third-world kleptocracy, the political opposition to UNESCO was intense. However, the *Times* assured us, UNESCO Director-General Federico Mayor "has cut the payroll and generally returned Unesco to its original mission as a promoter of literacy, a protector of cultural monuments and a champion of a freer flow of education."[9]

As is usually the case, the *Times* presented the public with only half of the truth — the wrong half, as it happens. UNESCO is indeed ready to resume its "original mission"; however, that mission was better illustrated by M'Bow's socialist evangelism than by Mayor's tactical retrenchment. Simply put, UNESCO was designed to function as both the school board and the propaganda ministry of the new world order. This was candidly conceded in a pro-UNESCO editorial published in *The Saturday Review* in 1952:

> If UNESCO is attacked on the grounds that it is helping to prepare the world's peoples for world government, then it is an error to burst forth with apologetic statements and denials. Let us face it: the job of UNESCO is to help create and promote the elements of world citizenship. When faced with such a "charge," let us by all means affirm it from the housetops.[10]

UNESCO's Origins

When the charter for the United Nations Educational, Scientific and Cultural Organization (UNESCO) was drafted in 1945, the document proclaimed that "since wars begin in the minds of men, it is in the minds of men that the defenses of peace must be constructed."[11] The body apparently believed that war-weary populations would be so anxious to secure "peace" that they would support the creation of a global body with a self-assigned mandate to reconstruct the minds of men.

Founded in London in November 1945, UNESCO was both a continuation of and an expansion upon the Paris-based International Institute for Intellectual Cooperation, which was affiliated with the League of Nations.[12] The National Education Association (NEA) was also among the earliest advocates of a global school board, and in 1920 the NEA created an International Relations Committee for the purpose of facilitating education for "world understanding." In 1942, amid an orchestrated euphoria regarding the World War II U.S.-Soviet "alliance," NEA head Joy Elmer Morgan penned "The United Peoples of the World," a psalm to world government which was published in the December *NEA Journal*. According to Morgan, "To keep the peace and insure justice and opportunity we need certain world agencies of administration such as: A police force; a board of education...."[13]

The campaign for a world "board of education" began in earnest in 1943, with the creation of an NEA "war and peace fund" which collected donations for such a body.[14] Across the Atlantic a similar campaign was being undertaken in London under the direction of the Conference of Allied Ministers of Education (CAME). A formal proposal to create a United Nations Bureau of Education was considered at the Ninth Meeting of CAME, which was held in London during April 1944. The U.S. sent a high-profile delegation to the event, which produced a draft for an interim UN educational organization.[15]

Even in its embryonic state, UNESCO was devoted to radical social engineering. Pro-UNESCO authors Walter Laves and Charles Thomson note that "[T]he delegates at [the founding UNESCO conference in] London called for better education to fashion better men for a new life in a democratic society." The Yugoslav delegate to the meeting candidly urged the embryonic body to embark on a campaign to re-educate the world's population.[16] Of course, the objective of re-education for the creation of a new man found a ready-made constituency among Marxists. Former communist Joseph Z. Kornfeder later explained that "UNESCO corresponds to the agitation and propaganda department in the Communist party. This department handles the strategy and method of getting at the public mind, young and old."[17]

Founding UNESCO Director-General Julian Huxley angered some American officials by appointing communists and communist sympathizers in key posts. For example, the chief of the Soviet Ministry of Education served as an early director of UNESCO's secondary education department. In 1956, a subcommittee of the Senate Judiciary Committee concluded that "by far the worst danger spot, from the standpoint of disloyalty and subversive activity among Americans employed by international organizations, is UNESCO...." The report recalled that Pierre Gerety, a former chairman of the International Organizations Employees Loyalty Board, had testified that "there existed in UNESCO a clique of people who placed the interests of the Communists and Communist ideology ... above their own country."[18]

The World's "Philosophical" Vanguard

Such is the background of the entity which presumes to act as the world's intellectual vanguard. According to Julian Huxley, UNESCO's first Director-General, "The world today is in the process of becoming one, and ... a major aim of UNESCO must be to help in the speedy and satisfactory realization of this process...."[19] Huxley defined the body's governing philosophy as "a scientific world humanism, global in extent and evolutionary in background."[20] Huxley declared that "political unification in some sort of world government will be required for the definitive attainment" of the next stage in human evolutionary progress.[21]

Furthermore, according to Huxley, UNESCO would assist in the process of "values clarification" on a global level. Because none of the religious traditions were adequate to the needs of a world government, a new world morality would have to be summoned into existence, and it would be UNESCO's task to do the summoning: "It will be one of the major tasks of the philosophy division of UNESCO to stimulate ... the quest for a restatement of morality that shall be in harmony with modern knowledge and adapted to the fresh functions imposed on ethics by the world of today."[22] Instilling this new world morality in schoolchildren would be UNESCO's most important task.

The preamble to the UN convention on "Children's Rights" demands that children be "brought up in the spirit of the ideals proclaimed in the Charter of the United Nations." The most substantial obstacle to this objective consists of parents who choose to raise their children to appreciate and defend Biblical morality and America's institutions of constitutional government. Thus it is not surprising that the thrust of the "educational" efforts undertaken by UNESCO and its supporting elites has been to usurp parental prerogatives regarding education in order to mold children into "world citizens."

Parents who are beguiled by the winsome idealism expressed in some portions of the UN's founding documents — the UN Charter and the "Universal Declaration of Human Rights" — should acquaint themselves with the world body's perspective on the origins and purposes of "human rights." Under the American concept of rights, the individual possesses God-given rights which the state must protect. However, the UN embraces a collectivist worldview in which "rights" are highly conditional concessions made by an all-powerful government: Individuals enjoy the "freedom" to serve the purposes established by the almighty state, and their "rights" are therefore granted or rescinded at the whim of the ruling elite.

In 1951, while the language of the Universal Declaration was fresh and the UN's prestige was at its zenith, a telling exposition of the UN's concept of "rights" was presented by Lin Mousheng, who was then the secretary of the UN Commission on Human Rights. According to Mousheng, "The procedural, civil, and political rights on the one hand, and the economic, social, and educational rights on the other, were to a large extent developed under the inspiration of the liberal movement of the eighteenth century and the socialist and communist movement of the nineteenth century respectively..... [This] represents a new synthesis of human thought and may well be the harbinger of a new epoch in human evolution."[23]

As we saw in the first chapter, the "liberal movement" referred to by Mousheng is best embodied by the militant secularism which created the French Revolution, not the Biblically-inspired movement which led to American independence and the creation of the U.S. Constitution. The "liberals" of that era aggressively sought not only to subvert established churches, but to de-Christianize entire societies in order to make room for a new secular religion of the state. The desired result was not a morally accountable individual who could live as a free man, but rather a deracinated political subject whose actions and beliefs were to be regimented according to the "general will" as it was interpreted by an omnipotent government.

The UN's debt to the doctrine of the "general will" is recognized by Mousheng in his interpretation of Article 29 of the UN Declaration: "Article 29 contains two ideas: On the one hand, everyone has 'duties to the community in which alone the free and full development of his personality is possible.' On the other hand, the community may impose such limitations on the exercise of rights and freedoms 'as are determined by law.'"[24] In other words, from the UN's point of view, the individual is "free" to do exactly as he is told to do by the "community's" rulers. This concept of "citizenship" is, in a specific sense, anti-American — and it is this perspective which is promoted by UNESCO and its allies.

Attitude Reconstruction

In order to bring about the "new synthesis of human thought" referred to by Mousheng, it would be necessary to expunge "improper" attitudes among would-be world citizens. Accordingly, one of the early concerns of the UNESCO network was to conduct an "educational offensive" against nationalist and traditionalist attitudes. Early supporters of UNESCO minced no words in describing the body's functions. In an editorial entitled "The Teacher and World Government," in the January 1946 issue of *NEA Journal*, Joy Elmer Morgan wrote:

> In the struggle to establish an adequate world government, the teacher has many parts to play. He must begin with his own attitude and knowledge and purpose. He can do much to prepare the

hearts and minds of children for global understanding and cooperation.... *At the very top of all the agencies which will assure the coming of world government must stand the school, the teacher, and the
organized profession.*[25] [Emphasis added.]

In December of that same year, Morgan returned to this same
theme in another editorial entitled "Fundamentals of Abiding
Peace": "The organized teaching profession may well take hope
and satisfaction from the achievements it has already made toward world government in its support of the United Nations and
UNESCO. It is ours to hold ever before the people the ideals and
principles of world government until practice can catch up with
those ideals."[26]

In 1948, seeking to advance the ideal of world government,
UNESCO produced a ten-volume series of pamphlets entitled *Toward World Understanding* which was designed to help educators foster a sense of "world citizenship" within schoolchildren.
(During the same year the NEA published a similar guide entitled
Education for International Understanding in American Schools.)
In the first pamphlet of the series, UNESCO recommended that
schools seek to develop in students "an attitude of mind favorable
to international understanding, which will make them conscious
of the ties which unite the people of the world, and *ready to accept the obligations which an interdependent world imposes* [Em-
phasis added.]"[27] To that end, history, geography, cultural
studies, and related subjects were to be taught with a specific objective: "... to stress the interdependence of the modern world, the
development of international cooperation and the need for a world
community...."

But UNESCO was not content merely with the manipulation
of the cognitive aspects of conventional education. Director-General Huxley urged the organization to exploit "affective" — feel-
ing-based — avenues to "regulate" schoolchildren. He maintained
that such an approach was necessary in order to cure the "repression" associated with traditional concepts of guilt and sin, thus
"emancipating" the individual from outmoded moral attitudes.

41

Wrote Huxley: "One other item which UNESCO should put on its program as soon as possible is the study of the application of psycho-analysis and other schools of 'deep' psychology to education.... If we could discover some means of regulating the process of repression and its effects, we should without doubt be able to make the world both happier and more efficient."

In an ironic echo of *Brave New World* — a cautionary tale written by his younger brother, Aldous Huxley — Director-General Huxley insisted that the application of psychological methods to schoolchildren "would mean an extension of education backwards from the nursery school *to the nursery itself."* [Emphasis added][28] Although this element of UNESCO's program has yet to be implemented world wide, it has seen use in totalitarian countries such as Communist China and Romania. Furthermore, psychological intervention of a less expansive variety has been openly advocated by UNESCO in the war against patriotism.

UNESCO's Eleventh International Conference on Public Education, which was held in Geneva from June 28 to July 2, 1948, concluded that "one of the chief aims of education to-day should be the preparation of children and adolescents to participate consciously and actively in the building up of a world society" and that "this preparation should include not only the acquisition of skills, but *more particularly the formation and the development of psychological attitudes favorable to the construction, maintenance and advancement of a united world....*"[29] [Emphasis added]

That conference created 12 recommendations for globally oriented public education, which were submitted to "the Ministries of Education of the various countries." One recommendation was that "the educational authorities of different countries exchange views and information on the nature and results of this teaching in order to make the best use of their experience...."[30] One result of that "exchange of views" was Volume Five of the 1948 UNESCO series, which was entitled "In The Classroom With Children Under Thirteen Years of Age." The booklet, which was produced during a month-long UNESCO seminar held in Podebrady, Czechoslovakia in 1948, was primarily targeted at attitudinal "problems" which impede "world-mindedness."

The UNESCO panel declared that "Before the child enters school his mind has already been profoundly marked, and often injuriously, by earlier influences" — specifically, by insufficiently "world-minded" parents. Parents are criticized in the report for "infecting" their children with "nationalism," "chauvinism," and "sclerosis of the mind."[31] To overcome these supposed handicaps, UNESCO recommended that "whether in the home, the social environment or the school, our children should be educated ... to prepare themselves for citizenship in a world society."[32] Of course, this will require early and persistent efforts to "correct many of the errors of home training," which may "cultivate attitudes running directly counter to the development of international understanding."[33]

The "experts" summarized their indictment in these terms: "As long as the child breathes the poisoned air of nationalism, education in world-mindedness can produce only precarious results."[34] Dangling from this brazen declaration was a tacit endorsement of Huxley's statement that global education will eventually have to begin in "the nursery itself."

Curing "Improper" Attitudes

In the 1950s and 1960s, the American educational establishment was carefully knit together with UNESCO in order to bring about the globalization of curriculum in U.S. schools. Beginning in 1950, the UN required its member states to conduct a quadrennial audit of UN indoctrination programs in their respective educational systems. In the United States, this task was coordinated by the Department of Health, Education, and Welfare (HEW). The 1964 HEW report *Teaching About the United Nations* exulted that such an audit of global education in the U.S. "is invariably incomplete and outdated almost as soon as published."[35]

Predictably, there was a natural convergence between America's increasingly socialized educational establishment and UNESCO. According to the 1964 HEW report, "[The] epitome of the work of the United Nations could be applied as well to the task of teaching about it. The development of new structures of thought, erosion of misconceptions and prejudices, and elaboration of new tools for analyses leading to intelligent action is the major function of all education."[36]

Among the key American institutions used to transmit the UNESCO party line to the U.S. educational establishment was the Teachers College at Columbia University, whose leading lights included humanist John Dewey and sundry Fabian socialists. Writing in a pro-UNESCO compilation shortly after the organization was founded, Otto Klinberg, a professor of psychology at Columbia University, sketched out a set of recommendations for a campaign for the "symptomatic treatment of attitudes" which impeded world unity. According to Klinberg, "an attack should be made on the social and environmental conditions which support hostility to international understanding" as embodied in the UN and "the deeper psychological components and motives related to attitude formation must not be neglected."[37] In short, mass psychoanalysis of the American public would be a necessary prelude to world government.

In 1950, a group of social scientists led by Marxist Theodor Adorno published a study entitled *The Authoritarian Personality*. Adorno and his associates, using a system which they admitted was not based on a "strictly empirical" approach,[38] devised an "F" scale which attempted "to measure the potentially antidemocratic personality."[39] Not surprisingly, the Adorno group "discovered" that the "authoritarian personality" was more or less identical to the conventional, middle-class American personality. Accordingly, a government-directed program of attitude reconstruction would be necessary in order to protect "Democracy" from the people. As the late social commentator Christopher Lasch observed, the approach favored by the Adorno report dictated that America's social problems "could be eradicated only by subjecting the American people to what amounted to collective psychotherapy — by treating them as inmates of an insane asylum...."[40]

This malign assumption was enlarged upon by social scientist Daniel Bell in his 1955 work *The New American Right* (which was re-issued in 1963 as *The Radical Right*). Citing Adorno's "enlight-ening" study, Bell traduced conservatives as psychologically dis-turbed individuals whose conservative views were merely camouflage for "rather a profound if largely unconscious hatred of our society and its ways...." One token of this mental dysfunc-tion, according to an essay in Bell's compilation, was "the incred-ibly bitter feeling against the United Nations....[41]

In short, those who opposed the UN, or who were "excessively" concerned about the advance of domestic socialism, weren't merely misguided; they were *sick* and could be "cured" only through state intervention.

Sex-Ed Subversion

The prevalence of sex education in America's government school monopoly is another little-recognized effect of UNESCO's influence. Julian Huxley instructed UNESCO to deploy the tech-niques of psychoanalysis to fight "repression" — a term generally used in the context of sexual behavior. The campaign to free chil-dren from the "repressive" sexual mores of their parents is argu-ably the most effective means of subverting the home.

In 1964, UNESCO sponsored an International Symposium on Health Education, Sex Education and Education for Home and Family Living in Hamburg, Germany. That conference produced a set of "findings" which have since entered the common parlance of sex education. For instance, delegates were told that "[c]hildren learn about sex elsewhere ... rarely in the home," that formal sex education is made necessary by the fact that "sex is emphasized commercially in the mass media," that "sex education should be-gin at an early age," and so on. The educators who attended the conference were introduced to various methods of affective in-struction, including "discussion techniques, role-playing, psycho- and socio-drama....[42]

Most importantly, the conference attendees endorsed a tem-plate for universal sex education which had been presented by two Swedish delegates. In addition to explicit discussions of sexual practices and anatomy, the UNESCO model sex ed program dealt with abortion, birth control, and the practice of "sexual deviations" — all of which were banned in many or most American states at the time of the conference.

Three months after the UNESCO conference, the Sex Information and Education Council of the United States (SIECUS) was chartered. Within a very short time, SIECUS became the country's most influential sex education "clearinghouse," providing materials for hundreds of school districts throughout the United States. As author Claire Chambers observes in her definitive work *The SIECUS Circle*, "the SIECUS concept of sex education [was] a carbon copy of the Swedish program, as adopted by UNESCO."[43] According to Chambers, "the SIECUS orbit ... expanded to envelop publishing houses, film producers, governmental and private agencies, foundations, medical societies, educational institutions, and religious bodies."[44]

Perhaps better than any other subversive organization, SIECUS has perfected the art of creating the poison and the antidote in the same laboratory. The organization's approach has been to encourage the normalization of sexual perversions and then invoke the crisis of sexual decadence in order to curry support for government-funded "educational" initiatives.

In its quest to normalize perversion, SIECUS has even attacked the "incest taboo." In 1979, the organization published a "scholarly" report by Paul Ramey which urged Americans to revise their moral attitudes regarding incest. The report also distinguished between "positive" or "consensual" incest and "abusive" incest.[45] (This could be considered another Swedish import: The socialist Swedish government legalized father-daughter incest as a means of "democratizing" the family.[46]) Despite the predictable negative public reaction, SIECUS refused to abandon its pro-incest initiative; in fact, it expanded the crusade to include other forms of child molestation.

During a 1985 conference of the Society for the Scientific Study of Sex (SSSS, a SIECUS front), Dr. Mary Calderone, the first executive director of SIECUS, participated in a panel discussion on child sex abuse. Some of the participants were probably startled when Calderone contributed a kind word for pedophilia: "I ... have a question that is ... almost the reverse of what we've been talking about. What do we know about situations in which young children and older people, stronger people, have had a sexual relationship of one kind or another that has been pleasant, and the child feels good about it because it's warm and seductive and tender?... If the child really enjoys this, it may be the only time the child ever gets a loving touch."[47]

Significantly, SIECUS's pro-incest campaign began at roughly the same time that concern over child abuse became a national obsession. Most states require the same public schools which dispense SIECUS-inspired sex education to report suspicions of child abuse to law enforcement agencies. The 1992 SIECUS publications catalog listed Ramey's 1979 pro-incest paper, which was surrounded by newer offerings dealing with sex abuse prevention. Furthermore, the SSSS, which follows the SIECUS approach on most sexual matters, has been active in the effort to combat "sexual harassment" in schools — an epidemic of which is the predictable result of adolescent exposure to SIECUS-derived "educational" pornography.

Wherever it has had a substantial impact, the effect of the schizoid SIECUS sex ethic is to leave parents and children morally perplexed and dependent upon the ministrations of "experts." The increasing acceptance of that ethic can be seen in contemporary America — a society in which parents cannot govern their homes without government-approved instruction in "parenting skills" and professional individuals cannot negotiate the business world without receiving instruction in the latest doctrinal revision regarding "sexual harassment." In short, a society of a sort favorable to UNESCO's first constituency — government.

"Service Learning" or Slavery?

For most people, the most recognizable attribute of tyranny is a government's ability to compel its subjects to perform unremunerated labor — that is, slavery. For this reason it should be of great concern to Americans that an increasing number of school districts are enacting mandatory "community service" requirements for high school graduation. Although the programs vary, they all require unpaid "service" as a means of teaching students about their "community responsibilities" — that is, their supposed debt to the state.

No subject has been dearer to the heart of President Bill Clinton than his national service program, which includes the "AmeriCorps," the Corporation for National and Community Service, Volunteers In Service to America, the Peace Corps, and the Civilian Conservation Corps. *Newsweek* correspondent Steven Waldman, who has covered Clinton's National Service program from gestation to infancy, observes that Bill Clinton, who had grown up "during that brief, astonishing moment in history when government was considered an effective — even noble — way to change society," sought to create a program which "would help re-establish faith in government."[48] In the same way that Bill Clinton's program seeks to make converts on behalf of an activist federal government, UNESCO-approved international "service" programs once sought to evangelize on behalf of global government — and a revival of those programs may be a possibility.

In 1951, David S. Richie, the executive secretary of the Friends Social Order Committee, wrote an essay describing the history of the "volunteer labor camp movement." Initiated during World War One as an alternative to compulsory military service, the concept migrated to America during FDR's New Deal, where it became a showcase of egalitarian social engineering.[49] According to Richie, the New Deal mass-labor programs were the inspiration for similar UNESCO-related efforts involving youth. He explained that the work camps were "primarily directed toward socializing the attitudes of the participants, awakening in them ... a deep devotion to the struggle for social justice by nonviolent means."[50]

In 1946, American and European work camp activists began to consolidate their efforts. The next year, recorded Richie, "[T]he leadership of UNESCO recognized the potential contribution of international work camps to reconstruction and education for international understanding, and offered their assistance with educational aids and joint sponsorship."[51] In 1948, UNESCO convened an international work camp conference which included representatives of the "World Federation of Democratic Youth (WFDY)," a Communist organization which helped coordinate "large camps for tens of thousands of young people in the eastern European countries."[52] At that conference UNESCO established an international work camp Coordinating Committee which, until 1950, included WFDY representatives.

Although UNESCO was strongly supportive of the international youth labor camp concept, the idea failed to take root in the United States and Western Europe. This fact was not lost on Richie, who lamented the curious lack of enthusiasm among American youth for manual labor as a means of "socializing attitudes," noting that "in certain Eastern European countries, governments have enrolled hundreds of thousands of volunteers ready to work without pay on projects financed by the government."[53] Ah, if only the United States were more like Soviet-dominated Eastern Europe! As it happens, the Clinton Administration's desire to enroll hundreds of thousands of youth in nationally directed service programs suggests that the cultural convergence longed for by Richie is nigh upon us — and, significantly, the UN appears to be ready to undertake new initiatives in "community service" at the global level.

According to the prospectus for the UN's 1995 Social Development Summit in Copenhagen, one proposal dealing with the "mobilization of human resources" in the interest of creating global "solidarity" is a service program for youth: "A Youth Voluntary Service to the community at the world level should be considered to instill in young people a sense of service to the community ... and to create a sense of solidarity at the world level."[54]

A revival of the "international labor camp" program would take on a rather frightening aspect, should UNESCO and its comrades succeed in defining manual labor as a "responsibility of global citizenship." It should be remembered that the most active supporters of the Clinton Administration's national service program would make "voluntarism" mandatory by law. If present trends continue, it is not inconceivable that in the near future some American students may confront a UNESCO-inspired "global service" graduation requirement.

Continuing Links With UNESCO

Notwithstanding its occasional setbacks, UNESCO has never relented in its efforts to become the school board to the world, nor have its American allies ceased to promote educational schemes designed to teach schoolchildren their "obligations as world citizens." The most recent amalgam of the various elements of the UNESCO agenda — "affective" learning, indoctrination in collectivism, "service" learning, and the like — can be found in the various outcome-based education (OBE) programs which afflict school districts nationwide.

"Transformational" OBE programs lock an individual student into a computer-driven behavioral loop intended to "remediate" improper attitudes in pursuit of approved "outcomes." Accordingly, the kinship between the OBE design and the "transformational" pedagogy supported by UNESCO is patent. Like the comprehensive approach envisioned by *Toward International Understanding*, OBE seeks to uproot traditional attitudes which impede political consolidation — first at the national level, and then eventually at the global level. OBE is the latest bid to realize Bertrand Russell's vision: A completely socialized education system which will "catch the patient young" and use "money and equipment" provided by the state to create a passive, controlled population.

OBE is the descendant of the disastrous "mastery learning" approach, a pilot program of which, the Continuous Progress-Mastery Learning (CP-ML) project, utterly destroyed the Chicago public school system in the late 1970s. According to educator James T. Guines, who helped design the Chicago program, the CP-ML approach was based on the behaviorist approach favored by psychologist B.F. Skinner. Like Bertrand Russell, Skinner believed that the human behavior could be shaped by "experts" in much the same way that "a sculptor shapes a lump of clay."

An appreciation of Skinner's essential philosophy can be obtained through a perusal of his 1971 book *Beyond Freedom & Dignity*, which was financed by a federal grant (number K6-MH-21, 775-01) through the National Institutes of Mental Health.[55] Skinner asserted that "we need to make vast changes in human behavior" and specified, "What is needed is a technology of behavior" which will permit ruling elites to address problems such as "overpopulation," environmental destruction, war, and so on.

According to Skinner, "Freedom and dignity illustrate the difficulty. They are the possessions of the autonomous man of traditional theory, and they are essential to practices in which a person is held responsible for his conduct and given credit for his achievements. A scientific analysis shifts both the responsibility and the achievement to the environment."[56] Globally minded elites have chosen this Skinnerian approach, which would deprive humanity of freedom and dignity, as a means to bring about the triumph of the "scientific world humanism" sought by UNESCO's Julian Huxley.

Through the "scientific design" of culture, according to Skinner, human evolution could be advanced and human survival insured. Of course, this would provoke opposition from traditionalists: "A technology of behavior is available ... but defenders of freedom oppose its use. The opposition may raise certain questions concerning 'values.' Who is to decide what is good for man? How will a more effective technology be used? By whom and to what end?" Skinner proposed that a "true 'fourth estate,' composed of scientists, scholars, teachers, and the media" would be a reliable custodian of the social "controllers"[57] — thus insuring that "change agents" would be monitored by an elite which shares their radical ambitions. This arrangement is dreadfully familiar to those parents who have opposed Skinnerian OBE schemes.

James Guines, the Skinnerian disciple who helped design Chicago's proto-OBE program, explained its guiding philosophy to the *Washington Post*: "If you can train a pigeon to fly up there and press a button and set off a bomb [as Skinner had done during WWII], why can't you teach human beings to behave in an effective and rational way? We know we can modify human behavior. We're not scared of that. This is the biggest thing that's happening in education today."[58]

OBE would be an extraordinary threat to American liberty if it were a purely domestic endeavor. However, the program is an American branch of a world-wide initiative intended to bring about the consummation of UNESCO's original mission: The creation of a world government which "will be able to control its subjects securely without the need of armies or policemen."

Re-Education For All

In March 1990, UNESCO co-sponsored the World Conference on Education for All (WCEFA) at Jomtien, Thailand. That conference, which attracted representatives from more than 150 nations, created two documents: *The World Declaration on Education for All*, and *The Framework for Action to Meet Basic Learning Needs*. The *Framework* lists six goal areas that intimately parallel the Goals 2000 legislation enacted by Congress and signed by President Clinton in the spring of 1994.

The Jomtien conference produced the World Conference on Education For All (WCEFA), the American branch of which is United States Coalition for Education For All (USCEFA), an organization whose sponsors include the American Federation of Teachers and the National Education Association. USCEFA defines its mission as "taking this worldwide consensus [created at Jomtien] and bridging between the initiatives for reform in other countries and the goals for education reform in the United States" — in short, its mission is one of "bringing Jomtien home." The Coalition held its first national conference in Alexandria, Virginia on October 30, 1991, an event which attracted nearly 300 "leaders in education, business and media from over 28 countries." Out of the Alexandria meeting came a conference report entitled "Learning For All: Bridging Domestic and International Education."

The "Learning For All" document states that "Schools are at the center of the current social and economic transformation"; accordingly, they are given the task of imparting to school children "higher order skills such as creativity, critical analysis, [and] *global thinking*...."[59] [Emphasis added] The document illustrates the kinship between America's national education goals and UNESCO's global proposals in this passage: "The need to define readiness for schooling is especially critical, since it is the cornerstone of the goals of both the *America 2000* [now called Goals 2000] and Education For All declarations."[60]

Another key player in the effort to implement the UNESCO agenda for "social integration" is the Academy for Educational Development (AED), which is chaired by CFR member Cassandra A. Pyle and whose honorary chairman is Sol M. Linowitz, a CFR member who was co-negotiator of the Panama Canal Treaties. The AED develops and helps to implement educational programs in 30 states and health programs in all 50 states. According to *Linking Progress to People*, an AED policy paper for the 1995 UN Copenhagen Summit, "The Road from Cairo to Copenhagen to Beijing" runs through Jomtien.[61] In other words, the "Education For All"/Goals 2000/OBE enterprise is to be the means whereby the UN's population control agenda (which was outlined in Cairo) and social reconstruction designs (which were set forth in Copenhagen) will be implemented.

How Far Have We Gone?

Whether or not the U.S. ever formally rejoins UNESCO, the cancer of socialist internationalism within the U.S. educational establishment has metastasized to incurable proportions. This was clear to informed observers more than three decades ago. Speaking of the internationalization of America's educational culture during his January 10, 1964 Dag Hammarskjold Memorial Lecture, Secretary of State Dean Rusk (CFR) observed, "Few people seem to realize how far this movement has gone.... [W]hile nations may cling to national values and ideas and ambitions and prerogatives, science has created a functional international society, whether we like it or not. And that society, like any other, must be organized."[62] That is to say, the global society would have to be regimented in harmony with the designs of an intellectual elite.

Now that America's increasingly nationalized education system is being rapidly "harmonized" with UNESCO's EFA guidelines, we can expect a renewed, expanded, and intensified campaign to make the public school monopoly an indoctrination appendage designed to create "world citizens" who will submit to the state of their own free will and earnestly love Big Brother.

Chapter 3

Whose Children?

We must remove the children from the crude influence of their families. We must take them over and, to speak frankly, nationalize them. From the first days of their lives they will be under the healthy influence of Communist children's nurseries and schools. There they will grow up to be real Communists.
— Instructions given at a congress of Communist Party educators in 1918[1]

We really don't know how to raise children. If we want to talk about equality of opportunity for children, then the fact that children are raised in families means there's no equality.... In order to raise children with equality, we must take them away from families and communally raise them.
— Dr. Mary Jo Bane
Assistant Secretary of Administration
for Children and Families, U.S. Department
of Health and Human Services[2]

Every child is our child.
— UNICEF motto

In 1987, it was discovered that a group of people associated with the Belgian committee of the UN Children's Fund (UNICEF) had an interesting perspective on the UNICEF motto. In that year, UNICEF official Jos Verbeek and 17 others were arrested by Belgian police on charges of "inciting minors to debauchery." The organization's Brussels office building had been used to develop pornographic photographs of children, many of them of North African descent. More than 19,000 such photos were eventually collected by Belgian police, along with a mailing list of 400 names in 15 countries which had been prepared on the UNICEF office computer.[3]

The central figure in the UNICEF-linked child pornography and prostitution ring, which called itself the "Centre for Information on Children and Sexuality" (CRIES), was UNICEF worker Michel Felu, who had been repeatedly prosecuted for pedophilia. During his trial, Verbeek admitted that he had known of Felu's pedophilia since 1986, but had kept him on staff at UNICEF in order to "rehabilitate" him.[4] In 1988, Verbeek was convicted of involvement in both child pornography and prostitution. However, his two-year suspended sentence was later vacated by the same Belgian appeals court that increased the sentences of Felu and other members of the CRIES child sex ring.[5]

Dr. Judith Reisman, a world-renowned anti-pornography activist, recalls: "While an indignant pedophile press in Amsterdam insisted 'the supposed involvement of UNICEF with a child pornography case was sensationalized by the press,' the USA press ignored UNICEF's 'supposed involvement'...."[6] The custodians of approved opinion were undoubtedly concerned that the significance of the UNICEF child porn/prostitution scandal would not be lost upon the American public: If *every child* belongs to UNICEF, why shouldn't UNICEF officials use them as they see fit?

UNICEF at large has been guilty of other forms of child exploitation. In May 1975, *Detroit News* columnist Robert Heinl revealed that UNICEF had contributed almost $9 million to communist regimes in Indochina. Most of the aid, according to Heinl, "consisted primarily of trucks, bulldozers, heavy engineer construction equipment, and construction tools and materials [which were] precisely the materials most needed for support of continued warmaking."[7] Some portion of the money which went to enrich Hanoi's war effort against the U.S. and non-communist Vietnamese had been collected by idealistic American children as they went trick-or-treating for UNICEF.

According to the late James P. Grant, a long-time director of

UNICEF, the organization uses women and children as a "trojan horse" — something which the organization's subsidy of communist aggression in Southeast Asia demonstrates quite tidily.[8] But UNICEF is not the only UN entity which has exploited the plight of children for disreputable ends. In 1994, Graca Machel, the widow of Samora Machel, the late dictator of communist Mozambique, was appointed by Boutros-Ghali to chair a panel studying the impact of armed conflict on children.[9] Mrs. Machel is an expert on that subject, having been party to countless acts of violence against children as a participant in the Soviet-supported "war of national liberation" in Mozambique. Before Mrs. Machel's husband died in 1986, the regime over which he presided killed an estimated 75,000 men, women and children in a campaign of political terror. Thus when the UN was looking for an expert to study the question of violence against children, Machel was an irresistible choice.

Although many other such outrages could be cited, they merely serve to underscore the point that the UN is not a trustworthy custodian of *anyone's* children. But the larger and more important point to be made is that *no* government is a worthy steward of children. Yet the UN will not be satisfied until it has exclusive control over all children, and in this quest the world body is receiving a great deal of help from this country's social-work elite.

Empowering the "Experts"

For millennia, political elites have sought to destroy the social primacy of the family as a means of aggrandizing the state. Within the warm fuzziness of the catch-phrase "It takes a whole village to raise a child"[10] resides the malignant ambition to destroy the divinely ordained family as an independent source of social authority. This ambition has reached its logical consummation in the various UN instruments which presume to define the "rights" and "responsibilities" of parents and children — The Covenant on the Rights of the Child, and the Convention on the Elimination of All Forms of Discrimination Against Women — and the activities of UNESCO and UNICEF.

The UN's Convention on the Rights of the Child, which was signed amid great fanfare by the heads of state of more than 70 nations in September 1990, has been described as a "magna carta for children." Although the measure has yet to be ratified by the U.S. Senate, the Clinton Administration — led by self-designated "children's rights" crusader Hillary Rodham Clinton — has repeatedly stated its support for the document. While offering the eulogy at the funeral for former UNICEF director James Grant,* Mrs. Clinton declared that the Clinton Administration would sign the document and send it to the Senate for ratification.[11]

Because of concerns regarding the Convention's effect upon state and local policies in the U.S., the Clinton Administration issued assurances that the Convention could be modified with reservations to "make sure that it will not interfere with states' rights or the federal criminal justice system," according to a *Boston Globe* news account.[12] But if the Convention presents a danger to traditional American institutions and concepts of government, why ratify the measure at all? Furthermore, the Administration's assurances did not deal with the most important problem posed by the Convention: Unlike the actual Magna Carta, which was designed to limit the claims of government upon individuals, the UN "children's rights" convention is a blank check for government intervention within the home.

Article 3 of the Convention states that "In all actions concerning children, whether undertaken by public or private social welfare institutions ... the best interests of the child shall be a primary consideration"; Article 4 instructs the national governments which have signed the Convention to "undertake all appropriate legislative, administrative, and other measures for the implementation of the rights recognized in the present Convention."

The phrase "best interests of the child" and the directive that states enact binding measures to act in the name of those inter-

---

* Grant's funeral was held at the Cathedral Church of St. John the Divine in New York City — a facility which generates some of the most radical, anti-Christian religious initiatives associated with the UN. These will be discussed in Chapters Seven and Eight.

ests acquire an ominous meaning in light of the first section of Article 9: "States Parties [to the Convention] shall ensure that a child shall not be separated from his or her parents against their will, *except when competent authorities subject to judicial review determine, in accordance with applicable law and procedures, that such separation is necessary for the best interests of the child,"* [emphasis added]. Section 3 of the same Article states that children thus separated from one or both parents will have the right to maintain personal contact with them — "except if it is contrary to the child's best interests."

Throughout the entire document, vast and often unspecified powers are given to the "competent authorities" mentioned in Article 9 regarding the arbitration of matters dealing with the rights and "best interests" of children. Furthermore, as Article 9, section 3 of the Convention illustrates, these "competent authorities" would be empowered to intervene should a child seek to exercise his rights in a fashion which the experts decide is contrary to his "best interests." What government, no matter how brutal or corrupt, has not justified interventions into the family on the basis of "the best interests of the child?" As we shall see, Hitler and Stalin used this same pretext. The Convention should thus be considered a James Grant-style trojan horse intended to extend the reach of government into the home, using affected solicitude for children as camouflage.

The Perennial Conflict

It is important to understand that when UNICEF designates every child to be "our" child, and when the UN's "children's rights" convention seeks to make government the primary custodian of children, we see the world body acting in harmony with a statist tradition of great antiquity.

G.K. Chesterton, one of the most eloquent defenders of Biblical civilization and one of the most perceptive critics of the modern state, observed that "The ideal for which the family stands ... is liberty. It is the only ... institution that is at once necessary and voluntary. It is the only check on the state that is bound to renew itself as eternally as the state, and more naturally than the state."[13]

Perhaps better than any other early 20th century commentator — at least on the pro-family side — Chesterton understood the implacable hostility of the state toward the family. While modern collectivism was yet in embryonic form, Chesterton predicted the rise of the modern social welfare state and the decline of the autonomous family. Projecting from trends which were visible in his era, he predicted the following dismal results:

> The baby is to be left on the door-step of the State Department for Education and Universal Social Adjustment. In short, these people mean ... that the place of the Family can now be taken by the State.... The Hospital has been enlarged into the School and then into the State; not the guardian of some abnormal children, but the guardian of all normal children.[14]

The trends discerned by Chesterton in Europe were less pronounced in the United States of that era, thanks in no small measure to the resiliency of America's traditions. The traditional American perspective on the family is rooted in the Biblical principle of stewardship: Children belong to God, but they are the primary responsibility of the parents. John Locke, whose writings greatly influenced America's founding fathers, referred to "The power .. that parents have over the children ... to take care of [them] during the imperfect state of childhood." He maintained that this was a "duty which God and Nature has laid on man ... to preserve their offspring till they can be able to shift for themselves" as free and responsible individuals. "The society betwixt parents and children, and the distinct rights and powers belonging respectively to them," according to Locke, are endowments of God, not artifacts of the state:

> God [has] made the parents instruments in His great design of continuing the race of mankind and the occasions of life to their children. As He hath laid on them an obligation to nourish, preserve,

and bring up their offspring, so He has laid on the children a perpetual obligation of honouring their parents... From this obligation no state ... can absolve children.[15]

But throughout history, the state has sought to relieve parents of their divine appointment and "absolve" children of their duties toward their parents.

Pedigree of a Despotic Idea

The idea that "it takes a whole village to raise a child" arguably began with Plato's blueprint for a totalitarian "republic." Citizens of this "ideal" society would be authorized by the state's supervisors to "bear children to the state" during a limited period.[16] The ideal, according to Plato, would be a society in which "no parent is to know his own child, nor any child his parent,"[17] thus bringing about a "community of property and community of families...."[18] The most obvious defects in this utopian scheme were dissected in Book II of Aristotle's *Politics*, in which he pointed out that "Each citizen will have a thousand sons who will not be his sons individually, but anybody will be equally the son of anybody, and will therefore be neglected by all alike."[19] This prediction, which was made two and a half millennia ago, perfectly describes the modern welfare state. This leads one to ask: If the defects in the concept of a "community of families" were known that long ago, why are similar schemes still alive? The answer: Those who desire a planned society know that the destruction of the autonomous family will create a society of atomized individuals who are easier to control.

In the modern era, Jean-Jaques Rousseau adapted the Platonic model to serve the total state. Rousseau, as we have seen, was a humanist who craved the power to reconstruct society. Chief among the institutions targeted by Rousseau was the traditional family. He maintained that "instead of saying that civil society is derived from parental authority, we ought to say rather that the latter derives its principal force from the former."[20] This reversed the Biblical hierarchy: Rather than the family delegating some limited powers to the civil state, the state would impart some limited authority to the parents.

This idea is developed even further in Rousseau's work *On Political Economy*. In this essay Rousseau pioneered many aspects of the modern socialist worldview. He explained that "It is certain that all peoples become in the long run what the government makes them"[21] — an assumption basic to all totalitarian societies. The state was the agent of the "general will," and it was the state's task to "bring all the particular wills into conformity with [the general will]" and thus "establish the reign of virtue"; further, according to Rousseau, "every man is virtuous when his particular will is in all things conformable to the general will...."[22]

In order to bring about the triumph of "virtue," it was necessary to subordinate the individual family to the "general family." Rousseau wrote that the state was "the common mother of her citizens."[23] Where Chesterton — speaking for the Biblical tradition — taught that the family is "bound to renew itself as eternally as the state, and more naturally than the state," Rousseau — speaking on behalf of despotism — wrote that "Families dissolve, but the State remains." Accordingly, it was the duty of parents, as Rousseau saw it, to instruct their children in their State-appointed duties, "to regard their individuality only in its relation to the body of the State...." [24]

For this reason, Rousseau was adamant that "there ought to be laws for infancy" and that "government ought [not] indiscriminately to abandon to the intelligence and prejudices of fathers the education of their children, as that education is of still greater importance to the State than to the fathers...." The role of public education, he declared, was to imbue children with a reverence for the state as a "tender mother" and teach them "to will nothing contrary to the will of society...."[25] Appropriately, Rousseau's 1762 educational opus *Emille* presented Plato's totalitarian blueprint as an ideal guide for the education of children.[26]

Rousseau's ideas immediately bore murderous fruit during the French Revolution. Bertrand Barere, one of the most bloodthirsty members of the revolutionary Committee on Public Safety, offered this digest of Rousseau's family philosophy: "Children belong to the general family, to the Republic, before belonging to private families. Without this principle there can be no republican education."[27]

Socialism vs. the Family

When Marx and Engels composed the *Communist Manifesto*, they advanced the Platonic/Rousseauist anti-family concept, candidly demanding the "Abolition of the family!" They contended that with the coming of socialism "The bourgeois family will vanish as a matter of course...." They urged the replacement of "home education" with "social" education, the effective abolition of marriage, and state intervention in the home in the interests of "emancipating" children: "Do you charge us with wanting to stop the exploitation of children by their parents? To this charge we plead guilty."[28]

The socialists of Chesterton's era (the late 19th and early 20th centuries) eagerly promoted schemes to subvert and ultimately to supplant the family. All of them, Chesterton observed, began by elaborating upon the plight of "abnormal children" as a means of generating public sympathy for the state guardianship of all normal children. None was more emphatic in this regard than Fabian socialist H.G. Wells, who promoted the socialization of family responsibilities in his 1919 book *New Worlds for Old* (a forerunner of his 1940 *New World Order*).

After summarizing a variety of poignant domestic problems and family crises, Wells urged his reader to "get quite out of his head the idea that the present system maintains the home and social purity."[29] Assailing critics of socialism who (correctly) objected that collectivism would destroy the family, Wells declared that "Socialism comes not to destroy but to save" the family through government intervention: "Socialism regards parentage under proper safeguards ... as 'not only a duty but a service' to the state; that is to say, it proposes to pay for good parentage — in other words, *to endow the home*." [emphasis in original][30]

The Fabian program was to provide direct government subsidies to mothers — not fathers — and thus make mothers dependent upon, and accountable to, the state; of course, this proposal prefigured the contemporary Aid to Families with Dependent Children program. This assistance was highly conditional, of course, and mothers who found themselves raising their children in a way which the state did not approve would face severe penalties: "Neglect [children], ill-treat them, prove incompetent, and your pay will cease, *and we shall take them away from you and do what we can for them....* (Emphasis added)"[31] Remember carefully this use of the word "incompetent."

The same year that Wells published *New Worlds For Old* also saw the publication of the third and final volume of Dr. Arthur W. Calhoun's *A Social History of The American Family: From Colonial Times to the Present.* This work would become an authoritative text for American social-service and welfare workers, as well as for educators and others who would work on behalf of the emerging custodial state.

Like Wells' Fabian socialists, Calhoun was an undisguised apostle of the unlimited secular state who preached the inevitable creation of a socialist world order. He wrote that "American history consummates the disappearance of the wider [or extended] familism and the substitution of the parentalism of society."[32]

Rebuking those who sought to restore the increasingly embattled traditional family, Calhoun explained: "The new view is that the higher and more obligatory relation is to society rather than to the family; the family goes back to the age of savagery while the state belongs to the age of civilization. The modern individual is a world citizen, served by the world, and home interests can no longer be supreme."[33]

With remarkable prescience, Calhoun adumbrated the American social revolution which has occurred during the past seven decades — including some measures which have yet to be implemented fully. He predicted "absolute sex equality so far as social regulations can go; scientific pedagogy of sex relations; a thoroughgoing eugenics enforced at the outset by legislation and by public opinion;... volitional limitation of the size of the family ... equality of opportunity for every child born in so far as social control, and subsidy where necessary, can secure such equality...." And, eventually, this socialist world society would result in "the evolution of a spiritualized family" based not on kinship but rather "on aesthetic, idealistic, spiritual values and loyalties."[34]

Fascist Assault on the Family

Like Calhoun, H.G. Wells taught that "Socialism, in fact, is the state family. The old family of the private individual must vanish before it...."[35] This idea was adapted by Mussolini — an ardent socialist who devised that variant of the collectivist state now known as fascism. The fascist dictionary compiled by Mussolini contained the following entry: "Family. *See* Fascist state."[36] Hitler's National Socialist state, which borrowed generously from both Marxist and Fascist models, also subordinated the family to the all-powerful state. As Chesterton observed:

> Hitler's way of defending the independence of the family is to make every family dependent on him and his semi-Socialist State; and to preserve the authority of parents by authoritatively telling all the parents what to do.... In other words, he appears to interfere with family life more even than the Bolshevists do; and to do it in the name of the sacredness of the family.[37]

The government of Nazi Germany created a policy called *Muter und Kind* (Mother and Child) which followed the contours of the Fabian program outlined by Wells. At the time, an analyst explained that *Muter und Kind* was intended to provide a nationwide program of "advice, instruction and help for young mothers and for children, especially those below school age.... Recuperation homes are made available for mothers after child-birth, nurseries, and kindergartens have been provided ... and a network of advisory health centres has been established all over [Germany]. In general, the aim is to diminish infant and child mortality [and] to raise the standard of health in the early years of child life ..."[38]

Eventually, Hitler's state enacted the entire program sketched out by Calhoun. However, families that became dependent on "assistance" from the National Socialist state soon found that — in harmony with Wells' program — the state stood ready to seize children from parents who were adjudged "incompetent" to carry out their state-assigned role. On June 18, 1933, Hitler declared: "If the older generation cannot get accustomed to us, we shall take their children away from them and rear them as needful for the Fatherland."[39] A similar warning came on November 6, 1933: "When an opponent declares, 'I will not come over to your side,' I calmly say, 'Your child belongs to us already ... What are you? You will pass on. Your descendants, however, now stand in the new camp. In a short time they will know nothing else but this new community."[40] On May Day 1937, Hitler stated that "This new Reich will give its youth to no one, but will itself take youth and give to youth its own education and its own upbringing."[41]

The Soviet State vs. the Family

The totalitarian notion that the state must supplant the parents as the primary custodian of a nation's children arguably was given its most thorough exposition by Soviet family theorist A.S. Makarenko. In his 1937 work *A Book for Parents*, Makarenko wrote that the Soviet family "is not a closed-in, collective body, like the bourgeois family. It is an organic part of Soviet society...."[42] In language nearly identical to Rousseau's, Makarenko declared that "parents are not without authority ... but this authority is only the reflection of social authority."[43]

Since Makarenko was an atheist it is hardly surprising that he explicitly repudiated the Biblical foundations of parental authority, stating that in the pre-socialist world "parental authority issued from the Lord's commandment. In our modern family things are different."[44] He denounced the pre-socialist father as an "odious figure" — "Master, overseer, teacher, judge and sometimes executioner," "despotic," a monarch who exploited his children.[45] He taught that society must forbid parental physical punishment and "maternal indulgence" (that is, women must be "encouraged" to leave the home.)[46]

In 1967, Makarenko's book was published in the United States as *The Collective Family: A Handbook for Russian Parents* with an introduction written by Urie Bronfenbrenner. At the time, Bronfenbrenner (a Russian expatriate) was a member of the Planning Committee for the Head Start program. According to Bronfenbrenner, the wisdom offered in Makarenko's Soviet handbook should help shape American social policy:

> *The Collective Family* also has something to say to the Western world.... Soviet leaders and educators have emphasized that effective character training requires imposing on the child challenging responsibilities for service and self-discipline not only within the family but, equally importantly, in his collective or peer group both within and outside the school.
>
> Can we really assert that analogous considerations do not apply in our own society?... The question therefore arises whether we cannot profit by taking to heart Makarenko's injunctions regarding the constructive influence of imposing communal responsibility within both family and peer group.... We too must teach morality through the imposition on children of concrete responsibilities and expectations consistent with the welfare of all....[47]

Of course, the "moral" or "character" education urged by Makarenko was intended to indoctrinate children in the socialist worldview: "Morality requires general emulation of the most perfect conduct. Our morality must already be the morality of communist society."[48] Makarenko exulted that "We are living on the summit of the greatest pass in history, our day has seen the beginning of *a new order in human relations*, a new morality, a new law, the foundation of which is the victorious idea of human solidarity (Emphasis added)."[49] "In our country he alone is a man of worth whose needs and desires are the needs and desires of a collectivist. Our family offers rich soil for the cultivation of such collectivism."[50]

Cultivating Collectivism in America

Bronfenbrenner's casual endorsement of Makarenko's socialist family philosophy demonstrates the collectivist kinship between the Soviet system and the American welfare state.

Education guru Mortimer J. Adler, a major editor of the Great Books series and a member of the Aspen Institute,[51] is among those who maintain that education for equality in a world society will require early and effective intervention by the state in the home.

In his 1991 book *Haves Without Have-Nots: Essays for the 21st Century on Democracy and Socialism*, Adler predicted that "the USA and its NATO allies [and] the USSR and its Warsaw Pact allies ... will be replaced by the USDR (a union of socialist democratic republics)" as "a penultimate stage of progress toward a truly global world federal union that will eliminate the remaining potentially threatening conflict between the have and the have-not nations."[52]

Of course, a necessary preliminary stage for the creation of a global socialist utopia will be the elimination of domestic inequality through the education/welfare system. During the early 1980s, Adler was the leader of The Paideia Group, an assemblage of educrat notables which composed a proposal for uniform national education in the interests of "equality." In *The Paideia Proposal: An Educational Manifesto*, Adler wrote:

> For the school to succeed in giving the same quality of basic education to all children, all must be prepared for it in roughly equal measure. Hence, at least one year — or better, two or three years — of preschool tutelage must be provided for those who do not get such preparation from favorable environments.... The sooner a democratic society intervenes to remedy the cultural inequality of homes and environments, the sooner it will succeed in fulfilling the democratic mandate of equal opportunity for all.[53]

These sentiments permeated the education and social services culture in the United States, encouraging the development of an intricate nexus of "family support" bureaucracies which linked the home with the school, often justified in the name of helping make children "ready to learn" by the time they enter the public school system.

In 1991, a task force of education and social service elites was summoned into existence by the Carnegie Corporation to study "the developmental needs and condition of children under age three"; that task force's findings were published in April 1994 as *Starting Points: Meeting the Needs of Our Youngest Children* (note carefully: "Our" children).* Bewailing a "'quiet crisis' of national neglect affecting this crucial age group," the Carnegie panel declared that "parenthood must be responsibly planned to prevent ... unwanted births by women of any age... A responsible parenthood is thus more often a planned parenthood."[54]

According to the Carnegie Corp., collectivist child-rearing is a necessity for a healthy upbringing: "For healthy development, infants and toddlers need close relationships with a small number of caring people, beginning with their parents and later including other adults."[55] That the "other adults" referred to here are not members of a child's extended family is demonstrated by this passage: "The Carnegie task force strongly recommended that every community in America focus on the needs of children under age three and their families by initiating a community-based strategic planning process and by experimenting with the creation of

---

* According to the 1953 report of the congressional Special Committee to Investigate Tax-Exempt Foundations, "The Impact of foundation money upon education has been very heavy, largely tending to promote uniformity in approach and method, tending to induce the educator to become an agent for social change and a protagonist for the development of our society in the direction of some form of collectivism.... Foundations have supported a conscious distortion of history, propagandized blindly for the United Nations as the hope of the world, supported that organization's agencies to an extent beyond general public acceptance, and leaned toward a generally 'leftist' approach to international problems." (As quoted in William F. Jasper, "Nationalizing U.S. Education", *The New American*, June 30, 1986, p. 49.)

The *Starting Points* report represents a continuation and an expansion of the Carnegie Corporation's campaign to create a socialist America with a UN-dominated world order.

family and child centers in all communities"[56] — in short, Hitler's *Muter und Kind* revisited.

At the same time that the *Starting Points* committee was meeting, the Committee for Economic Development (CED), an august panel of "250 business leaders and educators," published *The Unfinished Agenda: A New Vision for Child Development*. A vice chair of the committee which produced this 1991 report, Donna Shalala (CFR, TC), went on to become the Secretary of Health and Human Services in the Clinton Administration. Like *Starting Points*, the CED report urged that federal and state governments should make increased efforts to connect families to social services, convert public schools into social service agencies, and focus on the "educational and developmental needs" of all children from birth to age five.[57]

Rather than speaking candidly of "controlling" children, American political elites soothingly refer to making "investments" in children and families — hoping that distracted Americans will fail to understand that with federal *money* comes federal *control*.

The Clinton Administration's annual budget for 1995 contained dozens of pages of specifically targeted "investments" in child immunization programs, "Family Preservation and Support Funds," the Women, Infants, and Children Program, and of course, Head Start. To justify this expansion of state control over the home, the Clinton Administration cited — you guessed it! — Plato's blueprint for totalitarianism:

> As early as the fourth century B.C., the philosopher Plato stressed the importance ... of investing in children from an early age. In *The Republic*, he discusses the type of poetry youth should learn, physical exercise they should undertake and diets they should follow.... He observes "... the first step, as you know, is always what matters most, particularly when we are dealing with those who are young and tender. That is the time when they are taking shape and when *any impression we choose to make leaves a permanent mark*." [Emphasis added]

The Administration triumphantly asserts, "Several millennia later, numerous scientific studies confirm Plato's suppositions about the importance of investing in *our children*."[58] (Emphasis added)

Of course, Plato's musings have no Constitutional authority, and the United States Constitution does not permit the federal government to choose the "impression" it will make upon American children. Nevertheless, the American governing elite remains deeply committed to such totalitarian assumptions.

Licensing Parents

As the social services net has tightened around American families, American social engineers have not neglected the other half of the socialist formula: The presumption that the State may take children away from "incompetent" parents.

In 1980, self-described children's rights activist Hugh LaFollette published an essay entitled *Licensing Parents* in which he contended that since parenting is an activity which is "potentially harmful to others" it should require a state-issued license.[59] LaFollette maintained that "since some people hold unacceptable views about what is best for children ... people do not automatically have rights to rear children just because they will rear them in a way they deem appropriate."[60] Among the "unacceptable views" mentioned by LaFollette was the belief that "parents own, or at least have natural sovereignty over, their children.... This belief is abhorrent and needs to be supplanted with a more child-centered view.... to prepare children for life as adults and to protect them from maltreatment, this attitude toward children must be dislodged."[61] Obviously, the easiest way to dislodge the Biblical view of parenthood would be a licensing system which would make parenthood revocable on the state's whim.

LaFollette may have been among the first American social engineers to propose parental licensure, but the idea did not die with his essay. In 1981, Gene Stephens, an associate professor of criminal justice at the University of South Carolina predicted that "Parental care in the year 2000 may be different from today's and better, *since by then the movement to license or certify parents may be well under way* (Emphasis added)." Stephens believed that "incompetent" parents produce criminal offspring, and that the effort to fight crime will require the nationalization of parental functions — as opposed to more effective (and less despotic) alternatives, such as effective incarceration of actual offenders and unshackling local police. In fact, like Calhoun and the German National Socialists, Stephens suggested a fully-realized program of eugenics:

> In most cases, certified couples would be allowed to have their own natural children. In some instances, however, genetic scanning may find that some women and men can produce "super" babies but are not well suited to rear them. These couples will be licensed to breed, but will give up their children to other people licensed to rear them. The couple who raises the child will be especially suited to provide love and compassion and take the best possible care that the child feels wanted and needed in society. The very fact that children will feel wanted could lead to better development of their egos and, thus, of their capabilities. *Child breeding and rearing, then, may be considered too important to be left to chance....* [Wanted] children will have fewer environmental reasons to turn to crime, and controlled breeding will result in fewer biological reasons for crime [Emphasis added].[62]

In October 1994, the movement to license parents predicted by Stephens stepped out of the shadows of socialist scholarship with the publication of *Licensing Parents: Can We Prevent Child Abuse and Neglect?* by Dr. Jack C. Westman of the University of Wisconsin-Madison. Westman, a professor of psychiatry, explains that "We license drivers. We license day care. We license marriage. Now it's time to license parents. Licensing parents would convey the message that parenting is at least as important as marriage [or] driving a motor vehicle...." Dr. Westman quickly made a copy of his book available to Secretary of Health and Human Services Donna Shalala, the former Chancellor of U.W.-

Madison.[63]

Westman insists that although the act of licensing parents is "seemingly unthinkable," it is "eminently logical" and "would not compromise the right of each woman and man to conceive and each woman to give birth to a child. It would elevate parenting a child to the level of a privilege."[64] Through this Orwellian subterfuge (which is familiar to students of the communist and UN concepts of "rights"), a God-given right would be transmuted into a revocable, state-assigned "privilege."

From Westman's perspective, the secular state has first claim upon children by virtue of what might be called "biological collectivism." He writes that there is "a biological basis for the legal position that we do not own our children. The genes we give to our children are not our own. In the process of reproduction our genes are mixed with another assortment. But our genes are not really ours; they are only a part of the species' store. They have a life of their own beyond our control extending back through previous generations and into successive generations. We are only temporary hosts to our own genes and to our children."[65] In Westman's scheme, the agency to which "temporary hosts" must make an accounting is not The Almighty, but rather the almighty state.

Westman suggests that a system to assess parental competence could be operated "through the existing marriage license procedures" or "[t]he already established procedure for registering births." A parent license "would be obtained for each parent and validated for each child." Furthermore, because the damage which can be done by "incompetent" parents is so serious, Westman's proposal would act upon what amounts to a presumption of guilt: "From the legal point of view, the burden of proof would lie with parents to demonstrate evidence of minimal competence, or of their 'parental fitness' in legal terms, rather than on the state, as is now the case, to prove 'parental unfitness.'"[66]

Westman was aware that his proposal would encounter resistance from Americans inured to traditional concepts of liberty. However, he maintains that while "Licensing parents might seem like an invasion of the privacy of the family and an undue restriction of personal freedom," his proposed system "would invade privacy and restrict freedom no more than existing child abuse and neglect laws do."[67]

This is hardly reassuring to those who are acquainted with the abuses wrought by "child protection" agencies in the name of preventing child abuse. K.L. Billingsley, an investigative journalist who has documented the abuses committed by government agencies in the name of "child protection," describes the system as "corrupt, incompetent, and motivated by anti-family zealotry.... [T]heir jobs depend on the perception that child abuse is, as the National Center for the Prevention of Child Abuse puts it, 'an American Tradition.'"

No responsible observer denies that child abuse is a vicious crime and a growing problem. However, Douglas Besharov, the former director of the National Center on Child Abuse, reports that at least 60 percent of all child abuse reports are utterly baseless. By exaggerating the extent of the problem, a "crisis" has been created which screams for a drastic federal "remedy" — and Westman's parental licensure proposal is the logical continuation of previous "solutions" offered by the supervisors of the welfare state.

But the "abuses" Westman seeks to cure need not be defined in conventional terms. To create a new rationale for "civil rights" intervention on behalf of children, Westman has minted a new prejudice, "juvenile ageism," which he insists "is as virulent as racism and as pervasive as sexism, [and] the greatest barrier to recognizing the interests of children in our political processes, in child caring systems, *and in households* [Emphasis added]."[68]

A Totalitarian Proposal

Westman anticipated concerns about potential abuses produced by a parent licensing system, and has offered this singularly opaque assurance: "The possibility of such abuse of government powers is remote in the United States because of constitutional guarantees and the modus operandi of our democratic government."[69] As is the case with many who mistakenly refer to America's constitutional republic as a "democracy," Westman's "reasoning" is relentlessly majoritarian, recognizing no limitations upon the power of government to regiment the lives of individuals in the name of the perceived "common good." Typical of this perspective is Westman's statement that "the degree of harm required to evoke a sanction depends on public sentiment" — not on reason, deliberation, proportionality, or principle, but *sentiment*, the raw material of demagoguery. Westman displays no understanding of the fact that constitutional guarantees are intended to protect the rights of individuals from unjust impositions which are fueled by "public sentiment."

Asked if abuses of parental rights would increase if his proposal were implemented, Dr. Westman unbosomed himself of a genuinely Orwellian response: "These things happen because we haven't set standards for parents. If the standards were set and followed, we wouldn't have to bring in the agencies.... By setting standards for parents, we'll be putting all back on the parents."[70] In other words, parents — who are incompetent until proven otherwise — are to blame when the state violates their rights!

Like socialists throughout history, Westman has a purely functionalist view of parental rights: "[T]he integrity of society itself depends upon the competent parenting of its children. Incompetent parenting threatens the very survival of a society. Therefore, competent parenting is an essential function of society and *deserves the status of a right* [Emphasis added]."[71] In other words, a "right" consists of permission to carry out what society's supervisors decide are one's "essential functions."

These state-allocated "rights" are referred to as "moral rights." Westman maintains that:

> Because children have a moral right to competent parenting and a legal right to be protected from incompetent parenting, the logical inference is that parents have the moral right to be, and to become, competent parents whenever possible. This also implies that persons need protection from being incompetent parents.... Accordingly,

identifying incompetent parenting needs to be a high priority for our society.[72]

The concept of "parental competence" extends well beyond considerations of the physical and emotional welfare of children. Westman insists that "the overall objective of childrearing in the United States is the development of each individual's potential to function competently within our evolving, democratic society."[73] What about parents who to teach their children that their first responsibility is to honor and serve God, rather than the secular state?

The rights of those American families who entertain a "big picture" different from the one described by Westman would be particularly tenuous under a system of parental licensure. When it was pointed out to Westman that conservative Christians and Orthodox Jews do not embrace the secular "big picture," he responded: "Would they not believe in democracy? They live in a democracy which permits them to follow their traditions." Asked to define the threshold at which compulsion would be used under his proposal, Westman answered that intervention would occur "If the values [followed by a family or group] were destructive to children. The Waco, Texas situation was such a case, as is the case of the cults. It's significant that the Waco group was on the verge of being investigated for child abuse and neglect."[74] In fact, the Branch Davidian community had already been investigated and exonerated of child abuse complaints. It is significant that while millions of Americans regard the Waco tragedy to be an object lesson about the dangers of unchecked federal power, Westman (and social engineers of his ilk) regard the incident as an object lesson of the "need" for more extensive government intervention in the family.

Westman makes use of what could be called the "argument from futility" — that is, the decline of the traditional family is irreversible, and society must intervene to deal with the "crisis" created by the family's dissolution. However he concedes that "Incompetent parents" are "few in number."[75] But if the offenders are so few, why impose licensure on all parents? Why not seek the restoration of the traditional family? According to Westman, those who would recommend such a course must surrender their "obtuse freedom-based resistance to licensing parents" and asserts that "A more logical and responsible 'big picture' policy would be to focus on providing competent parenting for all children through setting expectations for parents and thereby preventing the damage to children by parental abuse and neglect."*[76]

A Crusading Judge

In the foreword to Dr. Westman's book, Judge Charles D. Gill of the Connecticut Superior Court, a co-founder of the National Task Force for Children's Constitutional Rights (NTFCCR), observes that he once considered the concept of parental licensure

---

* Similar arguments were deployed by President Clinton during the April 19, 1994 "Enough is Enough" forum on MTV. (Apparently Mr. Clinton, a supremely unlikely champion of the family, perceived no irony in his decision to lament the assault on the family during a forum sponsored by one of the guiltiest assailants.) According to Mr. Clinton, the erosion of the family has made the implementation of police state measures necessary:

> "What's happened in America today is too many people live in areas where there's no family structure, no community structure, and no work structure. And so there's a lot of irresponsibility. And so a lot of people say there's too much personal freedom. When personal freedom's being abused, you have to move to limit it.... [And so] we're going to have weapon sweeps and more things like that to try to make people safer in their communities."

It is significant that these remarks were offered in the context of President Clinton's directive to conduct warrantless "weapons sweeps" in public housing projects; these sweeps represented an abridgement of the constitutional rights of welfare recipients, thereby creating an injurious precedent regarding the liberties of all Americans. Similarly, Dr. Westman has said that parental licensure would probably begin "with people who are on public assistance" — creating another damaging precedent by targeting those who already suffer from an excess of government interference. In all of this we see the diligent application of what could be called the "Burning Reichstag Gambit." The German National Socialists stampeded the German public into a police state by screaming, "The Reichstag's on fire — suspend the Constitution!" Westman and his ilk insist that crime has become such a "crisis" that basic liberties must be curtailed, and that government derives its power from expediency, not from the consent of the governed.

to be "akin to totalitarianism." However, amid what Gill refers to as a "national emergency" of crime, delinquency, and family dysfunction, he declares that the book "changed my mind" about the virtues of a parent licensing system, and states: "This is the book that changed it. And this is the book that can change America."[77]

Judge Gill's endorsement of parental licensure is significant for at least two reasons. First, Judge Gill is a member of a UN-aligned coalition which seeks the ratification of the Convention and the creation of a "children's rights" amendment to the U.S. Constitution. Second, he is a judge who deals extensively with matters of family law, and thus is a prime example of the "competent authorities" who would be empowered to act in the "best interests of the child" if the UN "children's rights" convention were ratified.

When Judge Gill was asked by this author if he still regards the concept of parental licensure to be totalitarian, Gill replied that this question "is a tangent, because it's such a small part of the issue. To debate that aspect is to deny the seriousness of the problem." Gill admits that the parental licensure proposal "sounds as if government is prepared to be so intrusive into the private affairs of the family. But we end up putting these children into jail, and had government put its nose into family affairs earlier, maybe those children wouldn't be there."[78]

Like Westman, Gill concedes that the present "child welfare" system is frequently abusive and corrupt. Asked how abuses of parental licensing could be prevented, Gill replied, "I don't know. Government overreaching is a serious problem, and there have always been abuses, but we have to have some kind of a standard up there... I can't give all the mechanics right now." Gill suggested that once the proposal is enacted, all necessary details would emerge as part of "the struggle of our democracy." Gill compares the struggle against "incompetent parenting" to the "war on drugs," which has led to abridgements of individual liberties and even the death of law-abiding citizens in full-force drug enforcement raids. Despite these abuses, Gill states, "Nobody says, 'Hey, government's doing too much in that area,' and it would be foolish to do that."*[79]

Judge Gill is in the tradition of socialist "children's rights" advocates like Marx, Engels, and Wells. Gill believes that the family is all but beyond redemption: "I often say that children can't learn values from families that have none."[80] He told the *New York Times* that "Americans have a great hesitancy to take children away from parents, because, I think, we personalize that. We see someone taking our children away from us or taking us away from our parents. But believe me, the realities of [contemporary] America ... are such that the worse [sic] thing in the world we can do for millions of children is leave them at home with the criminals who are their parents."[81]

This concept of the family as a crime factory was made to order for yet another "expert," psychology professor David Lykken of the University of Minnesota, who in early 1995 published a book entitled *The American Crime Factory: How it Works and How to Slow it Down*, which proposed a system of parental licensing to "weed out" incompetent parents. Citing the "crisis" of violent crime as his justification, Lykken took up where H.G. Wells had left off the better part of a century before: "If you live in the projects on welfare, then you can't have a baby.... the question is, if you live in a plague area, have you a right to bring a child into

---

* Interestingly, Judge Gill's organization, the National Center for Children's Constitutional Rights, received the warm endorsement of former Education Secretary William J. Bennett, a prominent "conservative" intellectual and moralist. As the Bush Administration's "Drug Czar," Bennett wrote to Gill's organization to explain that the Bush Administration was "considering proposals to change Federal laws and regulations to make it easier for parental rights to be terminated when such action is appropriate." Granted, Bennett was referring specifically to drug-related cases. However, the ease with which a figure regarded as an intellectual champion of "conservatism" endorsed an extra-Constitutional role for the federal government in questions of parental rights is significant — and troubling. It is not difficult to imagine a scenario in which Westman's ideas would find favor with "conservative" Republicans as part of a "welfare reform" package. (William J. Bennett to Charles D. Gill and Dr. Ann Burgess, undated letter on the letterhead of the Office Of National Drug Control Policy, Executive Office of the President, copy provided by the National Task Force for Children's Constitutional Rights in possession of author.)

the plague area?" The Minneapolis *Star-Tribune* summarized Lykken's proposed penalties for "incompetent" or "unauthorized" parenting: "Under Lykken's system, if children were born to unlicensed parents, the state would intervene immediately. Licenses would be checked in hospital maternity wards. Unlicensed parents would lose their children permanently. Adoptions would be final and irreversible."

Furthermore, according to Lykken, "Repeat offenders might be required to submit to an implant of Norplant as a way to keep them from having another baby for five years."[82] Once again, the question of eugenics is implied here, as well as the possibility of using parental licensure for purposes of coercive population control — a possibility mentioned in LaFollette's original essay.[83] The linkage between parental licensure proposals and radical population control will be discussed at length in a later chapter.

Enter the UN

When proponents of parental licensure are queried about the source of the state's authority to regulate the "privilege" of parenting, they are likely to offer the following answer: The UN Convention on the Rights of the Child makes the government the ultimate supervisor of the child's welfare. LaFollette insinuated this answer in *Whose Child?*, a collection of essays by "children's rights" activists published in 1980.[84] Westman and Gill are among those who unambiguously support the UN's "children's rights" convention (and other instruments which would mandate UN intervention within the home) and who cite the UN documents as authority for state-mandated parental licensure programs.

Westman predicts that the process of licensing parents "would be the rallying call for a series of essential multilevel interventions to promote competent parenting."[85] This is because "it seems clear that the American cultural will is to promote the competent parenting of its children, as it is for the United Nations."[86] In fact, from the perspective of the UN and social engineers like Westman, there is no more dangerous place than home. Westman maintains that "The *United Nations Convention* [on the Rights of the Child] clearly declares that the state has a role in child-rearing. Because the consent of children is not required for the exercise of parental power, it is in the privacy of their homes that their civil rights are the least assured."[87]

The organization Gill co-founded, the National Task Force for Children's Constitutional Rights (NTFCCR), supports a "children's rights" amendment to the Constitution. Gill contends that the absence of such an amendment is a scandal. "Imagine the fifty-six men who wrote the Constitution giving [Americans] freedom of speech and religion and assembly, but saying, 'Well, we can't write this about freedom of speech, because someday somebody might burn a flag.' But they did put that into the Constitution, despite the problems that could result, and thank God they did. Yet we don't have that kind of statement about the rights of children."[88]

A pamphlet published by NTFCCR states that "[A children's rights] amendment is the most feasible way for America to conform its laws to the U.N. Convention on the Rights of the Child. The U.N. Convention, which mirror images many of the proposals [of the NTFCCR], requires that America comport its presently inferior laws to the higher international standard of child citizens rights within two years of ratification." The supposedly "superior" standards embraced by the NTFCCR are rooted in the socialist philosophy that rights are a gift of the state rather than an endowment from God. The organization insists that a children's rights amendment would place "the individual rights of the child citizen on par with the individual rights of adults, *which were of course all achieved by constitutional amendments.*" [Emphasis added][89]

Predictably, the constitutional amendment proposed by NTFCCR is unambiguously socialist in both its tone and substance. Section 1 of the document reads: "All citizens of the United States who are fifteen years of age or younger shall enjoy the right to live in a home that is safe and healthy; the right to adequate health care; the right to an adequate education and the right to the care of a loving family *or a substitute thereof,* which approximates as closely as possible such family [Emphasis added]."[90] To secure such "rights," state intervention in the home would of necessity increase. Furthermore, the amendment would allow the state to seize a child and place him in a family "substitute" if such actions can be justified in the name of "the best interests of the child."

In *Essay on the Status of the American Child, 2000 A.D.: Chattel or Constitutionally Protected Child Citizen?*, an article published in the Ohio Northern University Law Review in 1991, Judge Gill writes: "The [UN] Convention makes a total break from previous approaches to children's rights. Previous 'rights' were paternalistic, whereas the Convention makes the state directly responsible to the child."[91] A quotation extracted by Gill from an essay published in the periodical *American Psychologist* explained that "The child has a right to be brought up by his or her parents, but he or she also has the right to be placed in an alternative family setting should this be necessary."[92] Presumably the state would decide when it would be "necessary" to wrest a child from his parents.

By using American and UN/socialist concepts of rights interchangeably, the NTFCCR seeks to allay concerns about state intrusion in the home. For example, the group's literature dismisses concerns about "the horror stories of parents losing their children because of false charges against them": "We would argue that the same arguments might have been used against other amendments. The First Amendment, which gives us freedom of speech, might have its horror stories as well. When that amendment was considered, a detractor might have said, 'What if some fool wrongfully yells 'fire' in a crowded theater?' Or some furious protestor burns the American flag? The First Amendment survives the horror stories, as will this amendment."[93]

The problem with this analogy is that, unlike the proposed children's rights amendment, which would mandate government intervention, the First Amendment is a *limitation* of federal government power. The question is not whether the children's rights amendment would be able to survive "horror stories," but whether it would create them and subsist upon them.

UN "Enlightenment"

The efforts of Judge Gill and his group have earned the praise of the United Nations. On Earth Day in 1991, Judge Gill was invited to address the UN General Assembly. Earth Day co-chair Monica Getz proclaimed that Gill "and his group of multidisciplinary visionaries have proposed that the United States Constitution be amended to insure maximum survival for those most precious national treasures, our children. Many other countries have already done so. [Gill's] National Task Force for Children's Constitutional Rights is the first new response of this country to the enlightenment of the United Nations Convention on the Rights of the Child."[94]

Writing in the New York Law School's *Journal of Human Rights,* Gill observes that the UN "children's rights" convention "extends to children personal rights to which they, not their parents, are *entitled*" and candidly admits that the state would be called upon to administer these "rights" within the home.[95] In the essay he takes issue with child advocate Sylvia Hewlett's statement that "We should remember that the state cannot take direct responsibility for the young." Gill rejoins:

> Egads! This goes against the turning tide of child advocacy in America and indeed in the world via the United Nations Convention! National groups, with their feet in the trenches ... are demanding that the government take direct responsibility [for children] as a matter of right, the children's right. The National Committee for the Rights of the Child, Defense for Children International, the National Education Association, the American Academy of Child and Adolescent Psychiatry and the National Task Force for Children's Constitutional Rights make this point in varying degrees.[96]

Gill urges readers of his law review article — most of whom are lawyers, judges, and legal scholars — to dispense with their "analytical and objective" mind-set and "Forget about your legal training. Instead, let us engage in a little role playing. Let us pretend that you are the chairperson of a commission for the city of

Cleveland. Presume also that the stork delivers babies. Today the stork has delivered three babies and it is your task to distribute them to families. Being a conscientious and diligent person, you are about to interview applicants for the positions as parents."

Gill then describes three families, each of which suffers from some combination of drug-related problems and domestic abuse. Having limited the hypothetical "chairperson's" choices to a variety of dysfunctional homes — which apparently represents Gill's perception of the typical family — the Judge asks: "Well dear chairperson, let us start the distribution of these three babies. What is this? You hesitate? Stop looking through the eyes of these babies. This is only pretend. In the real world distribution is automatic. Who ever begets them, gets them."[97]

Through the concept of parental licensure, government authorities would be granted the God-like power — but, of course, not the divine wisdom — to "distribute babies" as they see fit. This is the logical consummation of the socialist worldview, and the ineluctable destination of UN programs and policies.

International Year of the Family

Nineteen ninety-four was proclaimed the "International Year of the Family" by the United Nations. According to the UN's official IYF program, "In the context of social change, families must also become the medium for promoting new values and behaviour consistent with the rights of individual family members, as established by various United Nations instruments."[98] The UN frets that "efforts to preserve the best of the past may be seen also as perpetrating attitudes that have, at times, worked to the detriment of society and some family members, notably women."[99] Furthermore, efforts to preserve the traditional family may lead to "negative behaviour or exploitation."

Accordingly, the organization urges families and governments to acknowledge that "government policy intervention may be needed to counter ... negative behaviour or exploitation in the family."[100] Governments are instructed to "design ... more effective policy interventions" within families.[101] This will require the construction of global "family law" networks. "IYF should facilitate global exchange of information by national legal institutes, associations and societies and encourage legal reform .... "

This would, in turn, require "the establishment of data banks, data networks, the exchange of data, and the identification of statistical trends related to families."[102] Thus the IYF culminated with the UN "Patron Cities Conference" in March 1995 in Salt Lake City, Utah — home of the conspicuously family-friendly Church of Jesus Christ of Latter-Day Saints, which endorsed the IYF.[103] According to Patron Cities conference director Michael Stewart, the creation of global data bases was to be one of the chief objectives of the Salt Lake City event.[104]

These networks will be of tremendous value to UN-approved social engineers who seek to "save" children from their "incompetent" parents. During a January 1994 session in Geneva, the UN Committee on the Rights of the Child recalled that the Convention holds that "children should not be separated from their parents, unless by competent authorities for their well-being...."[105]

Brenda Scott, an author and researcher with a specialized background in domestic abuse issues, has documented the anti-family passions which motivate many who find employment within "child protection" agencies. She categorically asserts that the creation of national and international data bases and networks of the sort envisioned by the Patron Cities program would be disastrous for families:

> There is a growing push to set up a national [child abuse] registry. This would be a horrendous weapon to place in the hands of anyone with any reason, political or personal, to destroy the life and career of someone else.[106]

The reasons cited by "child protection" workers to justify the seizure of children are often capricious or ideologically motivated. Scott reports that "The New York State Council of Family and Child Caring Agencies (CFCCA) warns that parents who resist state interference, believe in spanking, or display an 'over involve-ment in religion' are suspect" regarding child abuse.[107]

She also recounts the experience of a mother who was interro-gated by a Child Protective Services (CPS) psychiatrist regarding the parent's views on discipline. When the questions took on a distinctly religious cast, the mother protested: "I believed we had religious freedom. Why are you asking these questions?" The so-cial worker replied, "Because certain religious beliefs prejudice you against being a good parent."[108]

Scott points out that anti-religious (specifically, anti-Biblical) sentiments are rampant within the "child protection" bureaucracy in North America. This is particularly true among those "child savers" who support the movement to normalize homosexuality. She writes: "The [public] school system has been deeply involved in 're-educating' young people to a new concept of family. *Heather Has Two Mommies* and *Daddy's Roommate*, two beginning read-ers, were designed to introduce homosexual liaisons as acceptable family alternatives. Health textbooks define family as any group of people living together."[109]

The expansive tolerance of homosexual perversion is often coupled with a dogmatic suspicion (rooted in Freud's fraudulent theories) of the traditional family as a cesspool of incest and sexual exploitation. As a result, parents who seek to preserve tra-ditional standards of sexual morality often find themselves ac-cused of child abuse. States Scott, "Parents who do pull their children out of such classes are in danger of being turned in to CPS for sexual abuse. Some risk assessment guidelines actually tell teachers and social workers to be suspicious of any parent who objects to such curriculum."[110]

The UN's Embrace of Perversion

The UN has unabashedly embraced the cause of "gay rights," including *pedophile* "rights," and is committed to the redefinition of the family. On July 30, 1993, the UN delegations of 22 nations — including the United States — voted to allow the International Lesbian and Gay Association (ILGA) into the UN's Economic and

Social Council (ECOSOC) — the division of the UN which supervised the International Year of the Family. ILGA is an international umbrella group which at the time included pedophile groups such as the North American Man-Boy Love Association (NAMBLA).[111] Disclosure of this connection resulted in a public outcry, and ILGA eventually expelled its pedophile constituents and was itself eventually evicted from ECOSOC — more as a damage control measure than anything else.

The UN, through its subsidiaries and its pronouncements during the "International Year of the Family," has urged the abandonment of the traditional family model. As we will see in Chapter Five, the UN's agenda for "sustainable development" and "social development" employs the calculated subversion of the patriarchal family, and the encouragement of the concept of "families of choice" — which would essentially define any group of co-habitating people to be a "family." The March 1994 issue of *UN Chronicle* celebrated the "diversity" of families. According to the publication, "nuclear families" include "one-parent" families — a significant revision which would surprise many people. Furthermore,

> With the advances of equality between the sexes, new technologies facilitating child-bearing, and economic changes that provide women with independent sources of income, the nuclear family itself is changing. Non-traditional family types are becoming more and more common, such as cohabitation, same-gender relationships, [and] single-parent families....[112]

Pro-family advocates should take this rhetoric at least as seriously as the Lavender Lobby does. In Canada, NAMBLA activists and radical feminists were among the most energetic supporters of that country's ratification of the UN Convention on the Rights of the Child. As a Canadian newsweekly explained, "The North American Man-Boy Love Association, which advocates adult-child sexual relations,.... thought the convention could be used to support its belief that children as young as six have the right to choose to have sex."[113]

Parents around the world have reason to regret Canada's ratification of the UN "children's rights" convention. The International Tribunal for Children's Rights (ITCR), founded by Quebec provincial court judge Andree Ruffo, will be based in Montreal. The 21-member tribunal, which will prosecute violations of the convention, will include former UN Secretary-General Javier Perez de Cuellar. Judge Ruffo, a perfervid feminist and "children's rights" crusader, believes that the ITCR is necessary because "laws mean nothing if not enforced."[114] The Tribunal's mandate, at least initially, will be to encourage governments to enforce the Convention and the laws which emanate from it. One predictable result will be the spectacle of more children being taken from their parents "by competent authorities, for their own well-being."

The State as Savior?

How does one account for the inexhaustible faith in the benevolence of the state in a century which has witnessed two world wars, numerous acts of genocide, and other state-created atrocities? According to Dr. Bryce J. Christensen of the Rockford Institute, social engineers like Westman and Gill are inspired by the concept of "the state as savior":

> Many of the elites who generate these proposals regard the state as a surrogate god — infallible and limitlessly competent. Therefore, those things which are politically engineered are trusted, and those things — such as the family — which cannot be engineered cannot be trusted, at least until they are brought under political control.[115]

Dr. Christensen, a professional acquaintance of Jack Westman, reports that the concept of parental licensure is nothing new to those familiar with the literature of family law. "Some legal experts say that we ought to license parents in the interests of consistency — that is, that we already have licensing on an ad hoc, case-by case basis," Christensen reflects. Absorption of parental functions by the state is innately totalitarian, and Christensen explains that "This kind of thinking is inherent in the rhetoric we hear about children being 'America's most precious resource' — as if we had nationalized children. This is particularly a favorite theme of the Janet Reno crowd."[116]

Dr. Richard Ebeling, the Ludwig Von Mises professor of economics at Hillsdale College, points out that the relationship between the state and the family is one of permanent hostility and mutually exclusive claims upon the loyalty of the individual. Ebeling points out that Westman's concept "follows the same Rousseauist idea that was the cause of the French Revolutionary terror, that the state is the instrument of the 'common will' and that the individual gives up his rights in exchange for state-appointed 'privileges.'"[117]

After sifting through the rubble of the societies which have been ruined by such statist "benevolence," one cannot escape this conclusion: Those who esteem the family policies of Soviet Russia, Red China, and Nazi Germany will be similarly smitten with the UN's family philosophy.

CHAPTER 4

"Empowerment" or Enslavement?

There is no way of influencing men so powerfully as by means of the women. These should, therefore, be our chief study. We should insinuate ourselves into their good opinion, give them hints of emancipation from the tyranny of public opinion, and of standing up for themselves; it will be an immense relief to their enslaved minds to be freed from any one bond of restraint, and it will fire them the more, and cause them to work for us with zeal.

— Instructions found in the personal papers
of Illuminist Baron Bassus, 1787[1]

In order to build a great socialist society, it is of the utmost importance to arouse the broad masses of women to join productive activity.... Genuine equality between the sexes can only be realized in the process of socialist transformation of society as a whole.

— Mao Tse-Tung, 1955[2]

Equality and empowerment of women means more than just the right to birth control. It means power-sharing; it means better access to political leadership.... Women want redistribution in all aspects of their lives.

— Johanna Dohnal
Austrian Minister for Women's Affairs
Speech before the UN International Conference
on Population and Development
September 6, 1994[3]

After a decade of bitter and occasionally acrimonious nation-wide debate, the so-called Equal Rights Amendment (ERA) was defeated on June 30, 1982, when the deadline for ratification expired. The dream of a constitutional amendment intended to codify radical sexual egalitarianism, which had been pursued intermittently for more than 60 years, appeared to be dead. Little has been done since then to revive the ERA, and for good reason: The socialist and feminist groups which sought to write radical feminist assumptions into the Constitution are seeking to impose their vision by *circumventing* the Constitution altogether via the UN's Convention on the Eradication of All Forms of Discrimination Against Women (CEDAW).

CEDAW: A Global ERA

Speaking during a workshop at the 1995 International Development Conference in Washington, DC, Seble Dawit of ALLIANCES, a UN-linked legal activist group, urged the activists in the audience to press for Senate ratification of CEDAW. After all, explained Dawit, echoing a common constitutional misinterpretation, "In the United States, a ratified treaty becomes part and parcel of domestic law.... *What you couldn't get ten years ago with the ERA, you could shove down some people's throats with the Convention* [CEDAW]."[Emphasis added][4]

Opposition to the ERA focused upon the fact that the measure mandated, but did not define, equality of rights under law between men and women. This formulation constituted a blank check for judicial activism, inviting courts throughout the country to adopt the trendiest intellectual heresies as social policy. Opponents of the ERA — the most vocal and organized of which, it should be noted, were millions of mainstream, pro-family women — charged that adoption of the measure would result in the military conscription of women, the elevation of homosexuality to the status of a legitimate "alternative lifestyle," the passage of laws which would require religious hospitals to perform abortions in defiance of their principles, and the proliferation of subversive sex education courses throughout American public schools. Additionally, it was understood that the ERA would enshrine in law a unisex perspective which would ignore the irreducible differences between the genders.

It is sobering to realize the extent to which the ERA's objectives have been realized *without* ratification. Although there is no draft, women have been integrated into quasi-combat roles, with full combat participation in sight; homosexuality is exalted in our culture as not only legitimate, but perhaps even a superior way of life; sex education courses in many states — most notoriously Massachusetts and New Jersey — legitimize all varieties of perversion, including homosexuality. It is therefore reasonable to ask: What are the unconsummated elements of the ERA agenda which are to be "shoved down our throats" via the UN's "women's rights" convention?

The most cherished ambition of feminism is the abolition of the "patriarchal" family. In this feminism displays its kinship to the collectivist movements discussed in the previous chapter, which recognized that socialism cannot be achieved as long as the family remains the primary social organization. In her influential feminist tract *The Dialectic of Sex: The Case for Feminist Revolution*, Shulamith Firestone put the proposition plainly enough:

> Marx was onto something more profound than he knew when he observed that the family contained within itself in embryo all the antagonisms that later develop on a wide scale within the society and the state. For unless revolution uproots the basic social organization, the biological family — the vinculum [connecting link] through which the psychology of power can always be smuggled — the tapeworm of exploitation will never be annihilated. We shall need a sexual revolution much larger than — inclusive of — a socialist one to truly eradicate all class systems.[5]

CEDAW's chief purpose is to uproot the basic social organization — the biological family — by bringing family relationships decisively within the ambit of state authority. Through CEDAW, and the national laws which it will inspire, the state will be required to intervene within the home to regulate domestic affairs and broker contending claims of "rights." In the name of protecting women from domestic abuse, CEDAW will leave them vulnerable to *public* abuse inflicted upon them by the state. To understand how this dichotomy will work, consider the case of Communist China, which was selected to host the 1995 UN World Conference on Women.

Monopoly on Violence

The Communist Chinese government has signed many UN "human rights" instruments, including those specifically concerned with "women's rights"; however, China has no compunction about imposing compulsory abortion and sterilization upon women who attempt to bear "unauthorized" children and killing "unauthorized" female infants outright. The same Chinese state which commits daily acts of "gender-specific" violence against women also seeks to "protect" women from the influence of the traditional family.

Following a long and heavily publicized trial in late 1994, the Communist Chinese government jailed Jing Zhiping, a resident of the northern Heilongjiang province, after he was convicted of raping his wife. Jing's show trial was intended to illustrate the determination of the Chinese government to crack down on violence against women — that is, *private* violence against women. As the *Chicago Tribune* pointed out, the trial followed a dramatic "consciousness raising" campaign in which the government-controlled Beijing Women's Research Institute "staged a series of plays that graphically depicted violence in the household."

The communist government was anxious to continue Chairman Mao's crusade to uproot the traditional Chinese family — an objective which just happens to coincide with the UN's desires. According to a press account from Beijing, "The daily reports of women being forced into prostitution, kidnapped and sold to remote peasants, gang-raped and abused by their spouses have become an embarrassment to a government anxious to project itself for the women's conference as a modern socialist nation that respects women's rights."[6] Of course, the policies pursued by the Communist government would not end violence against women, but rather bring about a government monopoly on such violence.

The Chinese government's anti-domestic violence campaign was a direct adaptation of a larger effort which had been used by UN-supported "women's groups" in preparation for the 1995 Women's Conference. From 1991-93, UN-aligned feminist groups conducted a global "consciousness-raising" campaign called the "Global Campaign for Women's Human Rights," which collected grievances (some of them quite legitimate) from women around the world.

In June 1993, as an adjunct to the UN's World Conference on Human Rights in Vienna, and with the assistance of the United Nations Development Fund for Women (UNIFEM)[7] — the global feminist network conducted the "Global Tribunal on Violations of Women's Human Rights" — a carefully stage-managed show trial in which feminist activists offered testimony, feminist prosecutors framed the accusations, and feminist judges (including Gertrude Mongella, who would later serve as the Secretary-General of the Beijing Conference) rendered foreordained "judgements." Thirty-three women presented testimony of their experiences — some of which were genuinely atrocious — as alleged surrogates for the female population of the entire planet.

State-inflicted human rights offenses against women, such as those committed by communist China, were not addressed by the Tribunal, nor were they condemned in the Tribunal's verdict. Instead, the Tribunal decreed that an end must be put to the "obstacles to women's enjoyment of human rights that stem from the distinction between public and private, especially around violence against women" and the need for state action against "some claims to cultural and religious rights [which] impede the universality of human rights with respect to women."[8] In short, the Tribunal embraced Mussolini's totalitarian formula: "Everything within the state, nothing outside the state, nothing against the state."

This theme was woven into nearly every statement made during the Global Tribunal. The first session of the Tribunal dealt with the subject of "Human Rights Abuse In The Family." After hearing testimony, "Judge" Elizabeth Odio of the UN Commission against Torture stated:

> ... there is a "trap" from which we have not escaped. When the family is defined to be behind closed doors, we go back to the old Roman version of rights, in which rights within the family do not get publicly discussed. From the door through to the inside of the house, rights are governed by the father's rule, and we have not progressed beyond this point.
>
> What we need to do about this "trap" is to make the international community understand that men and women must work toward the elimination of the absurd discrepancies between private and public rights.

Odio insisted that the seven testimonies of domestic violence presented to the Tribunal "can be generalized to the whole world" and that "national legislations [sic] do not give answers to violence against women...."[9] In short, some variety of global intervention in the family would be necessary in order to prevent domestic violence against women.

By using expansive and contrived definitions of women's rights, the Tribunal was able to dispense with criticism of the choice of Beijing as the site of the 1995 Women's Conference. Inasmuch as no government on earth has yet succeeded in entirely destroying the patriarchal family, all governments are sinful and thus fall short of the UN's standards. This point was addressed specifically by "Judge" Gertrude Mongella in her statement before the Tribunal:

> I've been asked many times as the Secretary General of the World Conference on Women, why China? Why should we go to China? China violates human rights. Now, this morning, we've been hearing from North, South, West and East the violations of human rights.... I kept on answering — show me any nation which has not violated women's human rights and we will have the conference there.[10]

To bring about the vindication of "women's rights" as the UN understands them, the "Judges" issued a decree containing the following recommendations:

- "The establishment of an International Criminal Court for Women to protect and enforce women's human rights...";
- "The strengthening and enforcement of the *Convention on the Elimination of All Forms of Discrimination Against Women...*";
- "The integration of gender perspectives in all human rights committees established under human rights treaties to ensure the application of all human rights treaties to all forms of subordination of women";
- "The expansion of the work of the UN and its specialized agencies for preventing and redressing all forms of violations of women's rights";
- "The need to recognize that many of these violations take place in the private sphere of the family and that domestic violence is a violation of human rights" and the recognition of "all forms of supportive relationships that exist inside and outside institutionalized family arrangements" as the moral equivalent of the traditional family;
- "The adoption by the General Assembly of the United Nations of the *Draft Declaration on the Prohibition of Violence Against Women*";
- "The establishment of a Special Rapporteur with a broad mandate to investigate violations of women's human rights."[11]

Once again, all of these recommendations target the family, not the state, as the primary violator of women's rights. To italicize this point, the Tribunal sketched out a detailed strategy which includes "effective implementation and the elimination of cultural, religious and traditional stereotypes and practices which impede [the] implementation" of CEDAW; this totalitarian campaign would include "the re-interpretation of religious norms in light of the principles of human rights...."[12] Thus the crusade against patriarchy would assume contours similar to Mao's Cultural Revolution, which eventually produced the policies of the present Chinese regime.

"Homophobia" as an International Crime

Most public discussions of "gender-based" violence deal with the inexpressibly horrible crime of rape, particularly with the revolting spectacle of mass rape in warfare (as in the former Yugoslavia). However, men and women of good will should understand that when the UN and its feminist allies refer to "gender-based violence" they are referring to an ideologically dictated spectrum in which the criminal offense of rape is morally interchangeable with the effort to preserve the traditional male-headed household: Both are supposedly manifestations of the patriarchal suppression of women.

The Global Tribunal denounced "forced conformity to dominant heterosexual norms" as an offense against "indivisible and universal" women's rights. One prosecutor told the Tribunal that "enforced heterosexuality is used to control women of all sexual orientations" and that lesbians are particularly victimized because they "pose the most visible and profound challenge to this coercion and are therefore often explicitly and legally persecuted by their families...."[13] In other words, "homophobic" actions or teachings by parents could conceivably be construed as criminal by UN authorities.

The supposed need to eradicate "homophobia" and bring about radical sexual "emancipation" for women has shown up elsewhere in UN publications. In 1993, *Development*, the journal of the Society for International Development (SID) — a UN-linked transnational organization which receives funding through AID, the World Bank, the IMF, UNICEF, UNFPA, and the UNDP — published a special issue dealing with "The Family, Women's Rights and Community Responsibilities." This was done in anticipation of the UN's International Year of the Family in 1994.

Among the family "experts" donating expertise to the SID was Jim Hyde, the general manager of the Victorian AIDS Council/Gay Men's Health Centre in Melbourne, Australia. Hyde urged the UN-aligned "development community" to promote the concept of "families of choice" — "Single parents, usually women, people who live in group or commune arrangements, male/male or female/female couples who may or may not be homosexual" — as a new family model.[14] He denounced "homophobia" (which, in defiance of the rules of English construction, is said to consist of "prejudice against homosexuals") as "a denial of the rights of empowerment and community development."[15]

In the same issue of *Development*, editor of the publication and SID Programme Officer Wendy Harcourt stridently attacked the traditional family as an impediment to the "sexual fulfillment" of women and suggested that there is a "right" to such fulfillment that the UN should enforce.

Lamented Harcourt:

> [In the family] The need or right for women to make their own sexual choices is often unacknowledged or flatly denied; certainly it is usually outside the definitions of social and cultural norms. It is the family which usually instructs the young girl of what she can expect from marriage, and determines the suitable marriage partner. And it is only in the family that the woman can express her sexuality. If a woman steps outside of the family domain as an unmarried mother, lesbian or as a prostitute ... she and her family are stigmatized.... If we continue to ignore sexuality, dismissing it as a western feminist concept which has no place in discussions on the family and development or as a subject too sensitive to discuss, we fail to take up an important path for change.[16]

Women as "Agents of Change"

The idea of using women as "change agents" within the home plays a prominent role in the UN's agenda for "sustainable development" and "global human security." The next chapter will deal with ways in which the UN uses promises of "empowerment" to beguile women into population control programs. Here we will consider the UN's strategy for subverting the home in the name of "social development" or "social integration."

In March 1995, the UN convened the World Summit on Social Development in Copenhagen, Denmark. Among the commitments contained in the Copenhagen Declaration, which was signed by heads of state or their designates at that event, is the following declaration: "We commit ourselves to achieving full equity and equality between women and men and to recognizing and enhancing the participation of women in social progress and development." To achieve this commitment, the document directed national governments to "Promote changes in attitudes, policies and practices in order to eliminate all obstacles to full gender equity and equality" and to ratify CEDAW without reservations.[17] In short, the UN's agenda to "empower" women would require all national governments to embark on expansive and intensive campaigns of social engineering and attitude control.

Coordinating the UN's efforts to "empower" women is UNIFEM, whose director, Noeleen Heyzer of Singapore, states that "I would like to see UNIFEM as a household word."[18] Heyzer explains that the organization seeks to create a "holistic view" of the UN's "social development" agenda: "It is necessary to understand as one interrelated whole the issues of sustainable development, human rights, population, society and women that respectively constitute the topics of debate at Rio, Vienna, Cairo, Copenhagen, and Beijing." According to Heyzer, UNIFEM will play a crucial role in defining "where we, as a human race, should go from here."[19]

Toward the Chinese Model?

Once again, it is of no small importance to note that the capital of communist China was selected as the venue for the 1995 Women's Conference — a symbolic indication of the direction in which UNIFEM would take the world's women. At the 1995 International Development Conference, several workshops were held in preparation for the Beijing Conference, yet none of the panelists saw fit to criticize China's policies or even to take notice of the apparent irony embodied in the selection of Beijing.

At the IDC, a summary was made available of the regional "Platforms for Action" which were to be submitted to the UN at the Beijing conference. The collated platforms were divided into five subject headings, which in turn were divided into "Critical

Areas of Concern" and "Strategic Objectives." Under the heading "Insufficient Promotion and Protection of Women's Rights as Human Rights," the document listed "female feticide and infanticide" to be among the "Critical Areas of Concern" in the Asia/Pacific region (which includes Red China), along with various types of private neglect and violence.

However, the "Strategic Objectives" suggested as remedies were limited to the following: "Undertake community education to raise awareness about violence; develop comprehensive crisis response to violence against women; increase number of women police officers with special training" — all of which can be done, and have been done — in communist China without protecting individual women from the state's brutal misogyny.[20] Once again, this schematic for regional implementation of the UN's vision of "women's rights" would increase the power of the state and offer no protection against abuses committed by government.

At the Copenhagen Summit, great emphasis was placed upon the supposed need for numerical equity in gender representation in government policy-making and -implementing bodies. Once again, this is a distraction: The crucial issue is not the gender of governing elites, but rather the policies enacted by those elites. Apparently, the elitists at the UN believe that women who are oppressed derive some consolation in a sense of gender solidarity with their oppressors. In this, the example of China suggests itself yet again.

According to Ying Chi An, a Chinese expatriate who offered her first-person account of life under the Chinese population control program in Steven Mosher's book *A Mother's Ordeal*,[21] the regime delegates the "dirty work" of enforcing its mandatory one-child policy to the Chinese Women's Federation, which is an adjunct to the ruling Communist Party. When the one-child policy first went into effect, notes Chi An,

> The Women's Federation officials were relentless. They kept detailed notebooks on the fertility histories, monthly cycles, and means of contraception (if any) of all the young women under their

control. From this information they prepared lists of names — those to be sterilized under the new regulations, those to be fitted with IUDs, those to be X-rayed to see if previously fitted IUDs remained in place. And they served as escorts — one might almost call them guards — for the women on their lists, bringing them one by one to the commune clinics. Often they came into the operating room to witness the procedure. No slipups were tolerated.[22]

These "empowered" women were thus the key to the abominable Chinese population control system, which — as we will see in the next chapter — has received the plaudits of the UN.[23] The preference for male children, and the associated growth of the practice of female infanticide, is an ironic — but entirely predictable — consequence of that policy. Rural Chinese families prefer male children, as they are stronger and better equipped for agricultural labor; in addition, traditional Chinese culture — which has not been entirely eradicated — places great value on a male heir.

According to *New York Times* reporter Philip Shenon, "the preference for boys has meant that millions of Chinese girls have not survived to adulthood because of poor nutrition, inadequate medical care, desertion, and even murder at the hands of parents." This, in turn, has created other demographic dislocations. The 1990 Chinese State Statistical Bureau reported that 205 million Chinese over age 15 are single; of that number there is a ratio of three men for every two women. Furthermore, among single Chinese over 30, men outnumber women nearly ten to one.

Many of the private acts of violence against women which the Chinese government is now punishing with such assiduity — rape, prostitution, sexual abduction — have been created, in significant measure, by the government's own population control policies. According to a professor at the People's University in Beijing, "city women have been abducted by bounty hunters who deliver them to rural farmers desperate for brides."[24] Such have been the results of China's UN-endorsed and UN-funded social policies.

102

"Change Agents" or Moral Agents?

Like every variant of collectivism, the UN's concept of "women's rights" promises collective "empowerment" but results in individual oppression. By focusing upon women as a means to a political end, rather than regarding them as individuals blessed with God-given rights, the UN has encouraged, abetted, and subsidized some of the most horrific crimes ever committed against women. The world body's "empowerment" agenda would mandate increased state entanglement within the home, as well as propaganda campaigns intended to "cure" individuals of their religious, cultural, and social values.

True freedom does not come about as a result of being conscripted as a "change agent," but rather through a recognition of one's status as a moral agent before God. Men who see themselves as morally accountable before God do not abuse women. As one perceptive analyst wrote over two centuries ago, in reaction to the "emancipation" of women under the French Revolution, respect for women "is a refinement of manners which sprang from Christianity"; deprive women of the protection afforded by Christian conventions "and they become the drudges of man's indolence, or the pampered playthings of his idle hours, subject to his caprices, and slaves to his mean passions"[25] — conditions which can be seen wherever "empowerment" has been achieved.

CHAPTER 5

A Covenant With Death: Population Control in the Brave New World Order

We have made a covenant with death, and with hell we are at agreement.... We have made lies our refuge, and under falsehood we have hid ourselves
— Isaiah 28:15

[T]hough it is quite true that any radical eugenic policy will be for many years politically and psychologically impossible, it will be important for Unesco to see that the eugenic problem is examined with the greatest care, and that the public mind is informed of the issues at stake so that much that now is unthinkable may at least become thinkable.
— UNESCO Director-general Julian Huxley, 1947[1]

How can we reduce reproduction? Persuasion must be tried first.... Mild coercion may soon be accepted — for example, tax rewards for reproductive nonproliferation. But in the long run a purely voluntary system selects for its own failure: noncooperators outbreed cooperators. So what restraints shall we employ? A policeman under every bed? Jail sentences? Compulsory abortion? Infanticide?... Memories of Nazi Germany rise and obscure our vision.
— Population control advocate Garrett Hardin, 1970[2]

"Population stabilization" was identified as the chief objective of the "Programme of Action of the United Nations International

Conference on Population and Development" (ICPD), which was approved by representatives of more than 180 countries on September 13, 1994 in Cairo, Egypt. Timothy Wirth (CFR), the Under Secretary of State for Global Affairs and leader of the U.S. delegation to Cairo, exulted that "The world will never be the same after Cairo." The document outlines a 20-year plan to "stabilize" the world's human population at a cost of no less than $17 billion. Although the delegations of 19 Catholic and Muslim nations expressed reservations concerning the program's approach to abortion, pre-marital and extra-marital sex, and other moral issues, not a single contingent rebelled against the document's premise, which was that the growth of the human population must be restrained through the imposition of global controls.

According to the Cairo program's preamble, "All members of and groups in society have the right, and indeed the responsibility, to play an active part in efforts to reach [population control] goals."[3] This fascinating concept of "rights" is also found in Chapter II of the document, which states that the implementation of the Cairo program "is the sovereign right of each country...."[4] In other words, individuals and nations enjoy the "right" to comply with the UN's directives regarding population control, economic redistribution, and social reconstruction.

A fascinating glimpse into the mind-set behind this document was provided by Counselor Wirth. When Wirth was asked, "What's the difference between 'population control' and 'population stabilization?'" Wirth replied, "Nobody likes to be 'controlled'" — in other words, it is only a semantic distinction. Asked further, "What comes after education? What if education doesn't 'take'?" Wirth replied: "Education will 'take,' unless there are a lot of people going around trying to kill this document."[5] By this reasoning, those who resist the radical "reforms" embodied in the Cairo plan have only two choices: They may either conform to the Cairo agenda, or be blamed for the coercive measures which would be enacted after "education," "empowerment," and "sustainable development" fail. This is a formula for no-fault coercion.

"Sustainable Development": Coercion in Disguise

The preferred buzzword in UN environmental and population circles is "sustainable development." As is the case with so many other collectivist catch-phrases, "sustainable development" is uttered with sacramental reverence by social engineers who steadfastly refuse to explain or define the expression. Put simply, the phrase means this: Economic and social development supervised by an elite which enjoys privileged insight regarding the needs of a "sustainable" future. In short, socialism.

China's population control program offers a model of sustainable development in action. In 1979, 13 years before the world's heads of state endorsed "sustainable development" in principle at the UN "Earth Summit" in Rio de Janeiro, a Chinese communist party official offered the following explanation of the regime's agenda for sustainable population growth:

> Having children is not a question that we can afford to let each family, each household, decide for itself. It is a question that should be decided at the national level. China is a socialist country. This means that the interests of the individual must be subordinated to the interests of the state. Where there is a conflict between the interests of the state in reducing population and the interests of the individual in having children, it must be resolved in favor of the state. *Socialism should make it possible to regulate the reproduction of human beings so that population growth keeps in step with the growth of material production* [Emphasis added].[6]

This commissar candidly confronted the question which Mr. Wirth so artlessly ducked in Cairo: What happens if people fail or refuse to behave in a "sustainable" fashion? If government has the right and the privilege to determine a "sustainable" population target, the state must of necessity possess the power to compel acceptance of the target.

In previous chapters we have examined the assumptions of the UN, its allies among this nation's political elite, and its ideological progenitors regarding families, children, and women. We have seen that the UN, in keeping with socialist tradition, regards the family as a rival to be conquered; it considers itself to be the custodian of the world's children; and it regards women to be political "change agents" to be co-opted, rather than moral agents whose rights should be protected. All of these assumptions are at play in the question of population control.

Agitating on Behalf of the "Unthinkable"

When Julian Huxley, the first UNESCO director-general, urged the world's "intellectual community" to begin proselytizing on behalf of "unthinkable" eugenics proposals in 1947, the world was still absorbing the horrors of the Second World War. It is, in a way, a tribute to the resilient perversity of the collectivist idea that by 1970, population control advocates like Garrett Hardin could insist that memories of National Socialist atrocities could "obscure," rather than clarify, our understanding of the evils of collectivism.

Hardin understood, furthermore, that the first obstacle to be overcome on the path to global population control was the sanctity and sovereignty of the family:

> The "right" to breed implies *ownership* of children. This concept is no longer tenable. Society pays an ever larger share of the cost of raising and educating children. The idea of ownership is surely affected by the thrust of the saying that "He who pays the piper calls the tune."... If parenthood is a right, population control is impossible.[7]

From the collectivist perspective Hardin represents, people are merely resources to be managed by political elites who seek to bring about a "sustainable" global society.

In keeping with Huxley's commission to explore the "unthinkable," the Club of Rome published a study entitled *The Limits to Growth* (1972) which declared that "joint long-term planning will be necessary on a scale and scope without precedent" in order to "redirect society toward goals of equilibrium rather than growth."[8] This could be considered an early draft of the neo-Marxist concept of "sustainable development."

Of course, to bring about that sustainable — that is, socialist — world society, government will have to dictate the size of the human population. This is because socialism always entails government allocation of diminishing resources: The greater the intrusion by government, the more scarce the available resources become. Thus the logic of the environmentalist/population control mindset offers a foolproof rationale for socialism: It is always the people who cause scarcities and hardship, never the governing elite. Imposition begets imposition, until government control is complete.

Apologists for "sustainable" socialism are always reluctant to use specific figures when the discussion turns to optimum global population, as they know that such discussions engender opposition. However, in early 1994 Cornell professor David Pimentel informed the American Association for the Advancement of Science that the total world population should be no more than 2 billion, rather than the current 5.6 billion — in short, that roughly two-thirds of the human population is excess baggage. Pimentel's conclusions were given a respectful treatment in a *Los Angeles Times* op-ed column by Donella H. Meadows, who had been the lead author of the Club of Rome's *The Limits to Growth study*.[9]

Other globalist luminaries have been even more candid about the misanthropic logic behind population control. In a fashion worthy of Huxley's admonition that UNESCO and its allies help prepare the public mind to accept the "unthinkable," Jacques Cousteau, who was "one of the most venerated attractions at the Rio Summit,"[10] according to William F. Jasper (who attended the event), offered the following thoughts in the November 1991 *UNESCO Courier:*

> The damage people cause to the planet is a function of demographics — it is equal to the degree of development. One America burdens the earth much more than twenty Bangladeshes....
>
> *This is a terrible thing to say. In order to stabilize world popula-*

tion, we must eliminate 350,000 people per day. It is a horrible thing to say, but it's just as bad not to say it. [Emphasis added].[11]

Enslaving Through "Empowerment"

As Garrett Hardin intimates, a necessary prelude to *coercion* is *subversion* — specifically, a calculated effort to undermine the traditional, patriarchal family. Thus, the most important subsidiary theme of the Cairo population control conference was the "empowerment of women," which will require nothing less than the reconfiguration of all private and public institutions in conformity with feminist demands. This can be partially achieved through targeted anti-family subsidies, as Norwegian Prime Minister Gro Harlem Brundtland, the vice president of the Socialist International, explains: "Traditional religious and cultural obstacles [to population control] can be overcome by economic and social development, with the focus on enhancement of human resources."[12] By promising women financial and social "autonomy," they and their children can be pried from the home and made dependent upon the state.

The Cairo Conference's *Programme of Action* states, "The power relations that impeded women's attainment of healthy and fulfilling lives operate at many levels of society, from the most personal to the highly public."[13] From this it logically follows that government intervention at all levels — particularly within the family — is necessary in order to achieve "empowerment" for women. This concept was expounded upon during the Cairo Conference by Johanna Dohnal, Austria's Minister for Women's Affairs, who declared that "Equality and empowerment of women means [sic] more than just the right to birth control. It means power-sharing; it means better access to political leadership; it means economic self-reliance of women. *Women want redistribution in all aspects of their lives.*"[14] [Emphasis added]

To bring about this comprehensive "redistribution," the Cairo Programme instructs governments to undertake "national campaigns to foster women's awareness of the full range of their legal rights, including their rights within the family"; it directs

"Leaders at all levels of society" to "speak out and act forcefully against patterns of gender discrimination within the family"; it decrees that "The equal participation of women and men in all areas of family and household responsibilities, including family planning, child-rearing and housework, should be promoted and encouraged by Governments."[15]

The true intention behind these promises of "empowerment" was discerned by at least one left-wing writer. Helen Simons, a British socialist author, noted that as a result of Cairo, "the bureaucrats at the UN undoubtedly look back on the proceedings with a satisfied smile. After decades of failure, the UN has finally pushed the issue of population control center stage by repackaging it in a blurry concern for the rights of women."[16]

The Cairo program also seeks to subvert the family through redefinition. The document states that "While various forms of the family exist in different social, cultural, legal and political systems, the family is the basic unit of society and as such is entitled to receive comprehensive protection and support." Lest this be taken as a casual endorsement of the conventional family, the program elaborates that the conditions of modern life have wrought "considerable change in family composition and structure" and that "Traditional notions of gender-based division of parental and domestic functions ... do not reflect current realities and aspirations...."[17]

Although these elements of the Cairo program may strike the casual observer as innovative assaults on the traditional home, they are merely familiar themes from the population strategy which the UN and its allies have pursued for decades. A review of that strategy will help supply the answer to the question Tim Wirth ducked in Cairo: What comes after "education" if "education" fails?

Taking Refuge in Lies

Although contemporary population control advocates are less inclined to ventilate their thoughts about the "unthinkable" in public, they displayed no such reticence at the birth of the mod-

ern environmental movement. However, this candor about totalitarian controls took refuge in lies about the "dangers" presented
by unregulated population growth. Paul Ehrlich's 1968 book *The
Population Bomb* made use of speculative "science" to project a
dismal, dystopian world future unless drastic measures were undertaken to curb population growth. The tract presented three
scenarios which included famine, pestilence, and nuclear war
which would decimate human societies by the mid-1980s.[18]

In a 1970 book entitled *Population, Resources, Environment*,
which he co-wrote with his wife Anne, Paul Ehrlich predicted that
the environmental effects of "overpopulation" might include cata-
strophic *global cooling*, which would be a result of "increases in
the albedo [atmospheric reflection] caused by dust, other particu-
late pollution.... This increase in reflectivity has more than coun-
terbalanced the increased greenhouse effect from the CO_2
[produced by burning fossil fuels]." [Emphasis added][19] He also
predicted that the thickening of the polar ice caps could result in
"a global tidal wave that could wipe out a substantial portion of
mankind...."[20]

Of course, all of these dire predictions were made before the
"global warming" theory came into vogue. Despite the fact that
none of the dire warnings presented in *The Population Bomb*
were vindicated, Ehrlich published a follow-up volume in 1990
entitled *The Population Explosion*. In the later volume, the unrepentant false prophet of eco-apocalypse insisted that the effects
of the population "explosion" could be felt in "*Global warming*,
acid rain, depletion of the ozone layer," and other fraudulent environmental "catastrophes" [Emphasis added].[21] Like many of his
ilk, Ehrlich was not above blatant self-contradiction in his effort
to persuade the masses that radical population control is necessary to prevent global catastrophe.

In *Population, Resources, Environment*, Ehrlich did not retreat
from the implications of the population controllers' assumptions.
He allowed that "Family planning programs can provide the
means of contraception, and through their activities and educational campaigns can spread awareness of the idea of birth con-

trol among the people." However, he acknowledged that the time would come when it would be "necessary" to move beyond "education": "These [educational] programs should be expanded throughout the undeveloped world as rapidly as possible, *but other measures should be instituted immediately as well.* Additional programs beyond family planning will unquestionably be required in order to halt the population explosion."[22]

Ehrlich contended that compulsory birth control measures are humane: "Compulsory control of family size is an unpalatable idea to many, but the alternatives may be much more horrifying."[23] Furthermore, he insisted that uniform coercion is more equitable than the use of social and economic incentives: "Some coercive measures are less repressive or discriminatory, in fact, than some of the socioeconomic measures that have been proposed."[24] But he remarked that "No form of population control, even the most coercive and repressive, will succeed for long unless individuals understand the need for it and accept the idea that humanity must limit its numbers.... How can we convince a poor Pakistani villager or a middle-class American that the number of children his wife bears is of crucial importance not just to himself and his family but also to his society?"[25]

Essentially, the campaign to change attitudes about population control would be two-fold: It would seek to terrify people into believing that "unplanned" parenthood was hastening human extinction, and it would simultaneously seek to seduce people into abandoning the traditional family in favor of "alternative lifestyles." Underwriting both of these tactics was the assumption that the government is the ultimate custodian of questions of childbirth and family life, as well as the threat of coercion should people refuse to accept that assumption.

Anti-Child Blueprint

In framing his recommendations, Ehrlich drew upon a blueprint set forth in an essay published by population control advocate Kingsley Davis in a 1967 *Science* magazine essay. Davis wrote that "the conditions that cause births to be wanted or unwanted are beyond the control of family planning ... the social structure and economy must be changed before a deliberate reduction in the birthrate can be achieved."[26] According to Davis, "Changes basic enough to affect motivation for having children would be changes in the structure of the family, in the position of women and in the sexual mores." He suggested that governments could offer subsidies for voluntary sterilization and abortion, impose a "child tax," and manipulate the tax structure to discourage marriage (creating the so-called "marriage penalty").[27]

Davis also recommended that "women could be required to work outside the home, or compelled by circumstances to do so."[28] Other leaders of the international population cartel seized upon Davis' suggestions and embellished them. In 1969, Planned Parenthood Vice President Frederick Jaffe, working with concepts nearly identical to those presented by Davis, composed a memorandum for Bernard Berelson, who was then president of the Rockefeller-founded Population Council. The objective of the Jaffe memorandum was to bring about radical reductions in human fertility.

The Jaffe memorandum, which was published in the October 1970 issue of *Family Planning Perspectives*, divided possible "fertility control" options into four categories: "Social Constraints," "Economic Deterrents/Incentives," "Social Controls," and "Housing Policies." The category of "Social Constraints" included the "Compulsory education of children," the encouragement of "increased homosexuality," the restructuring of the family by altering the "image of the ideal family" and encouraging women to work outside the home, and — if all else failed — the placement of "fertility control agents in [the] water supply."[29] The "Fertility control" options referred to as "Social Controls" were even more draconian. They included "Compulsory abortion of out-of-wedlock pregnancies," "Compulsory sterilization of all who have two children except for a few who would be allowed three," the implementation of policies intended to "Confine childbearing to only a limited number of adults," and the issuance of "Stock certificate-type permits for children."[30]

The Jaffe memorandum was prepared for Population Council President Berelson, who cannibalized elements of the Jaffe memo as the basis of a 1969 speech bearing the portentous title "Beyond Family Planning." Berelson focused on what he considered to be "responsibly suggested" means — both voluntary and involuntary — of reducing human fertility. Among the options discussed by Berelson was the sterilization of all females through the administration of time-capsule contraceptives, which sterility could be reversed only with the government's approval. Mandatory sterilization of all men who had fathered three or more children and the possible infiltration of chemical sterilants into water supplies were also among the "responsibly suggested" possibilities touched upon by Berelson.

To justify such despotic means, Berelson struck a pose of forward-looking humanitarianism: "[W]hat weight should be given to the opportunities of the next generation as against the ignorance, the prejudices, or the preferences of the present one?"[31]

Lures for the Inattentive

In 1970, Ehrlich approvingly wrote, "The development of a sterilizing capsule that can be implanted under the skin and removed when pregnancy is desired opens another possibility for coercive control."[32] That birth control method now exists under the name "Norplant" — a set of capsules implanted in a woman's shoulder which can provide temporary, and supposedly reversible, sterility. Norplant advertisements depict smiling, "empowered" women, apparently oblivious to the "possibility of coercive control" referred to by Ehrlich, blissfully brandishing their scars and boasting of the freedom which the product provides. The distribution of Norplant could be considered a preliminary phase in the scheme described above.

During the Cairo Conference, several feminist groups conducted an event entitled "Crimes Against Women Related to Population Policies." Among the accounts presented at that hearing was the testimony of Marie Souza de Farias of Brazil, who had been lured into accepting Norplant. Her "doctors" had assured her that she "would always be ready for sex." However, implantation of the contraceptive caused dizziness, hemorrhage, and heart problems; belated removal of the device led to hepatitis and early menopause. The Brazilian woman stated that "I believe that Norplant acceptance in the USA is due to misguided information provided by those who coordinate the tests around the world."[33] The objective is to accustom women to thinking that Norplant offers liberation, rather than a prelude to coercion.

According to Ehrlich, "a government might require only implantation of the capsule, leaving its removal to the individual's discretion but requiring reimplantation after childbirth."[34] Under such a policy, government apologists could insist that "choice" would still be preserved; only "unplanned" births would be prevented. However, this would merely be an intermediate phase. Ehrlich pointed out that a Norplant-style option would be a logical coefficient to a system of parental licensure:

> The capsule could be implanted at puberty and might be removable, with official permission, for a limited number of births. Various approaches to administering this system have been offered, including one by economist Kenneth Boulding of the University of Colorado.* His proposal is to issue to each woman at marriage a marketable license that would entitle her to a given number of children. Under such a system the number could be two if the society desired to reduce the population size slowly. To maintain a steady size, perhaps one out of three couples might be allowed to have a

---

* Boulding, a British expatriate and former economic adviser to the League of Nations who later became a visiting scholar with the radical/globalist Russell Sage Foundation, is a leading exponent of the idea of a "holistic" world community. In his foreword to the *Gaia Atlas of Future Worlds* (1990), Boulding blames the very existence of *Homo sapiens* for the "major environmental crisis" in which we supposedly find ourselves. He also condemns Genesis for its description of man's God-given dominion over the earth and insists that mankind must love "not only the ecosystem which exists at the moment, but the whole evolutionary process which created it and will go on creating other systems." Presumably, that "evolutionary process" would include coercive population control policies administered by omniscient evolutionists such as Mr. Boulding.

third child if they purchased special tickets from the government or from other women, who, having purchased them, decided not to have a child or found they had a greater need for the money. Another idea is that permission to have a third child might be granted to a limited number of couples by lottery. This system would allow governments to regulate more or less exactly the number of births over a given period of time.[35]

Population Triage

The social triage mentality — which would dictate that the state selectively portion out liberties — was examined at length in *The Case for Compulsory Birth Control*, a 1971 book by Edgar R. Chasteen which was vetted with numerous population control luminaries, including Margaret Mead, Garrett Hardin, Paul Ehrlich, Kingsley Davis, and Planned Parenthood officials. Chasteen's book reviews the options presented by Davis — the encouragement of "alternative lifestyles," subversion of the traditional family, etc. [36]

In addition, Chasteen observed, "It has been proposed that the birth rate could be lowered by making citizens more politically insecure. If we all were subject to arrest and imprisonment, with no rights of appeal; if our homes were invaded by state authorities in the night; if we were deprived of free speech; if insecurity and uncertainty were our constant companions, then the birth rate would certainly fall."[37] Although Chasteen professed opposition to the creation of such a garrison state, he insisted that "our only real alternative is between direct and compulsory control of population size and the indirect and inhuman policies just described...."[38] In other words, our alternatives run the gamut — from "voluntary" submission to state control to "involuntary" submission to state control.

Chasteen recognized that in order for compulsory population control to work, it is necessary to convince the public that

... parenthood [is] a privilege extended by society, rather than a right inherent in the individual. Accordingly, society has both the right and the duty to limit population when either its physical existence or its quality of life is threatened.... *There are no rights if there is no society. There is no society if there is no government. It is possible to have government without rights but impossible to have rights without government.* [Emphasis added]"[39]

It is difficult to read this passage without hearing the swish of the guillotine blade or sniffing a whiff of Zyklon-B.

Chasteen's book endorsed the notion of "reversible" sterilization — which he referred to as "Reversible Fertility Immunization," as if fertility were a disease to be controlled. The book contained model legislation for "a parenthood ban which [would apply] uniformly to all people" and would include a marketable license to have children.[40] As preliminary steps toward such a system, Chasteen recommended the national legalization and distribution of contraceptives and the de-criminalization of abortion — steps which have, of course, already been taken. A "license" to have children may be the next step, given the public crusade of Dr. Jack Westman and other "children's rights" advocates.

As was the case with the Nazi eugenics program, Chasteen recommended that the program be swaddled in euphemism: "In order to generate the necessary public and political support, the program should be given a name other than compulsory birth control. The use of another word, though it would not change the intent or the operation of the program, would certainly increase its attractiveness." Chasteen pointed out that such subterfuge is commonly practiced by government: "The Social Security Administration labels the monthly deductions from wages which it compels as FICA — Federal Income Contributory Act — thus giving the program an appearance of voluntarism which, in fact, does not exist. Various Congressional Committees in 1969 and 1970 considered introducing legislation for a compulsory health care plan to cover all Americans. In their deliberations, these politically sophisticated individuals described their proposals as 'universal,' emphasizing the program's coverage, rather than 'compulsory,' which would focus public attention on methods of enforcement."[41]

This last observation is particularly provocative in light of the Clinton Administration's defeated attempt to create a compulsory federal health care rationing plan in the name of "health security."

Of course, one final solution to the problem of population growth would involve involuntary sterilization of the entire population. Ehrlich suggested "adding a sterilant to drinking water or staple foods", with the government in charge of rationing the antidote — although he generously conceded that this proposal "would pose some very difficult political and social questions, to say nothing of the technical problems."[42] One specific proposal of this type was presented by physiologist Melvin Ketchel of the Tufts University School of Medicine, who suggested the development of a sterilant which could be dispensed in adjustable amounts to achieve calibrated reductions in fertility rates.

The advantage of this plan, from Ehrlich's perspective, is that it would provide governments with complete control over human reproduction: "In this way, fertility could be adjusted from time to time to meet a society's changing needs, and there would be no need to provide an antidote." He suggested that mass sterilization of this type could be used in developing countries "at least until development and educational levels reached a point where people could be affected by small-family propaganda...."[44] Chasteen, incredibly, dismissed this proposal because "other life forms would also suffer a reduction in fertility."[45] The misanthropy of environmentalists is matched only by their solicitude for the rest of the "biosphere."

The Idea Reborn

The radical proposals entertained by Ehrlich and his comrades have proven to be imperishable. Some of them were revisited in the 1990 *Gaia Atlas of Future Worlds*, which was composed by Dr. Norman Myers, an advisor to the World Bank, the World Resources Institute, and various UN agencies. Myers maintains that humanity enjoys no special status in nature, being merely "an equal part of a community of species."[46] From a Gaian perspective, humanity's fecundity is sinfully undemocratic and must be radically restrained. Myers asserts, "One of the most radical changes ahead for the North [the developed, industrial world] is that population planning will become as essential as it already is in the [pre-industrial] South." He suggests that the populations of industrial nations such as Britain, Russia, and America would eventually have to be reduced by nearly one-half.

By way of policy suggestions, Myers revisits Ehrlich's proposal of a reproduction license:

> Government population-control policies using strong economic and social incentives have been effective in China and Singapore.... Additionally, in China strong social pressure has been brought to bear to practise [sic] vigorous birth control. Is it too far-fetched to imagine that one day people might be issued with a warrant entitling them to have a single child — a type of green stamp? This warrant might even carry commercial value, allowing individuals to decide not to have children at all and to sell their entitlements to others wanting larger families.[47]

The concept of fusing a system of parental licensure with government-inflicted "reversible" sterility has by no means disappeared. Just before the Cairo population control conference, Sir Roy Calne, a noted organ transplant surgeon and professor of surgery at Cambridge University, published a book entitled *Too Many People* which recommended a universal system of parental licensure.

Despite his admission that "My credentials to write on these matters are thin," Sir Calne has presented a population control proposal which mimics the system currently employed by communist China (where, incidentally, he had recently completed a lecture tour). Individuals would have to pass a parenting skills test and receive a state-issued "reproduction license" before being allowed to have children. A "minimum childbearing age" of 25 would be established and a strict two-child quota. Parents who violate any of these guidelines would confront severe financial penalties and possibly other state-imposed sanctions. Calne has also recommended the development of an anti-fertility virus which would be administered to women world wide as a vaccine.[48]

Calne's ideas were met with something less than unqualified approval from the British public. Robert Whelan of the London branch of the Committee on Population and the Economy, who is recognized as one of the world's leading researchers on population issues, observes that the concept of licensing parents "is a hardy perennial for the population control crowd, particularly the extremists. It's always coming up." Whelan points out that for most of Great Britain's readership, Sir Calne's book "really summoned up an image of all the horrors associated with the fascist system, particularly the idea that the whole population needs to be guided by the all-seeing and benevolent state."[49]

Nevertheless, Calne's recommendations have been endorsed by prominent British elites. According to the *Sunday Times* of London, "An Oxford theology professor has read the book and endorsed it."[50] Rev. Terry Waite, an Anglican priest who gained notoriety as a Middle East hostage negotiator and humanitarian during the 1980s, wrote the forward to Calne's book. The *Manchester Guardian* warmly endorsed Calne's recommendations, stating that "If we don't sacrifice some freedoms we may be left with none. That a great British surgeon whose humanitarian and liberal credentials are unassailable should be forcing himself to accept this is what makes *Too Many People* so absorbing — and so alarming."

America's Future?

In 1969, Alan Guttmacher, a longtime president of Planned Parenthood, stated that "Each country will have to decide its own form of coercion, determining when and how it should be employed."[51] The 1970s were a decade in which coercive birth control policies were carried out with a vengeance, most notoriously in India and China.

The International Planned Parenthood Federation (IPPF),

whose members held nearly all of the key positions at the Cairo Conference, was founded in India in 1952. Other elements of the anti-natalist lobby singled out India for special attention. The first major UN "technical assistance" program for population control was conducted in India.[52] In the late 1960s, John Lewis, head of the Indian Affairs office of the U.S. Agency for International Development (AID), promised that he would "press [population] funds on the Indian government whether it wants them or not."[53]

As a result of this concentrated anti-natalist focus on India, mass sterilization campaigns sprang up across the country. To "encourage" Indians to undergo sterilization, the central government tied the provision of public amenities such as paved roads and new wells to acceptance of sterilization — thereby creating a powerful incentive for collective coercion. Business enterprises in the thoroughly socialist Indian economy were "encouraged" to dock the paychecks of holdouts. Undisguised force led to thousands of involuntary sterilizations. [54]

In 1975, Indira Gandhi proclaimed a state of emergency and suspended the few liberties usually enjoyed by Indians. By the time the decree was lifted in 1977, 6.5 million Indian men had been vasectomized. In 1976, at the height of the compulsory sterilization campaign, India received a visit from World Bank president Robert McNamara (CFR), who applauded the government's "political will and determination" to carry out population control.[55]

China's "one-child" policy, which involves compulsory abortion and sterilization, as well as infanticide, has been generously underwritten by the UN Population Fund, the World Bank, the International Planned Parenthood Federation (IPPF), and globalist concerns like the Ford Foundation and the various Rockefeller foundations. In 1985, the U.S. government withdrew funding from the United Nations Fund for Population Activities (UNFPA) and the IPPF because of their unapologetic support for the Chinese program; those organizations remained committed to China despite the loss of their primary source of funding — the U.S. government.

Robert Whelan observes:

Far from shunning the Chinese, the international population community has welcomed China.... In 1983, when coercion in the Chinese program was at an all time high, a UN committee, with Rafael Salas, Executive Director of the UNFPA as an advisor, gave one of the first two UN population awards to Qian Xinzhong, the Minister-in Charge of the State Family Planning Commission (SFPC) of China. When presenting the award UN Secretary-General Perez de Cuellar expressed "deep appreciation" for the way in which the Chinese had "marshalled the resources necessary to implement population policies on a massive scale." In the same year IPPF welcomed the Chinese Family Planning Association into full membership.

The Western support — both financial and moral — has been fully exploited by the Chinese government. The State Family Planning Commission was able to announce, in connection with the UN Award, that 'This shows that the UN and the countries of the world approve of the achievements we have made.'"[56]

Among the unabashed supporters of the "progress" wrought by Communist China's population policies is Sharon L. Camp (CFR), the Senior Vice President of Population Action International (PAI, formerly the Population Crisis Committee), a Rockefeller-funded anti-natal lobby. Writing in the Autumn 1993 issue of *Conscience*, a journal for apostate pro-abortion Catholics, Camp approvingly noted that "China's total fertility rate now may be as low as 1.9 children per couple, a rate below replacement-level fertility. This achievement is the result of an essentially compulsory government birth control program...."[57] During the Cairo Conference, PAI declared that a four-fold increase in government expenditures for population "stabilization" would be necessary to achieve the goals of the Cairo Conference's *Programme of Action* — the largest portion of the cost to be borne by the United States, of course.[58]

Although none of the major population control advocates deny that China's policies are brutal and misogynistic, there is no serious criticism of the program: The Chinese, after all, have literally pioneered "sustainable development." In January 1989 a news organ of the Chinese government explained, "We should justly and forcefully say that we must punish those who have turned a deaf ear to dissuasion from having additional children ... and that suitable coercion should be implemented in China's family planning." In April of the same year, an Agriculture Ministry official explained, "From the perspective of future generations ... temporary coercion is actually a philanthropic and wise policy."[59] There is nothing here that cannot be justified in the name of "sustainable development" — and that has not been said by Western (including American) population controllers in their more unguarded moments.

Since the Clinton Administration restored U.S. funding to the UNFPA and the IPPF, the financial aid spigots have once again been thrown open for China's coercive program, with one tactical refinement: Such funds are often targeted for "education" or "empowerment" programs for women. Thus, among the Ford Foundation's 1994 population-oriented grants to China were donations to such entities as the "China Women's Health Network" ($122,000), and the "International Women's College in China" ($102,000).[60] In a gesture of singular cynicism, Ford also gave the Chinese Academy of Social Sciences a $120,000 grant "to promote the legal protection of women's rights" — "rights" which, as we have seen, are defined entirely by the state's objectives.[61] The crowning hypocrisy came when the UN selected Beijing as the site of its 1995 Women's Conference.

But the Chinese route to "sustainable development" represents merely one possible option. Rwanda's tragedy illustrates another possible avenue to "sustainability." During the Cairo Conference, Patric Mazimuka, the Rwandan Minister for Youth and Cooperation, held a press conference in which he described his government's plans for "post-genocide population management." Although Rwanda has lost more than 1.5 million souls — one-fifth of its population — to fratricidal warfare, Mazimuka insisted that "the government will have to try to keep the family on track because we cannot afford a big population."[62]

Mazimuka's statements provoked no controversy at the Cairo Conference, as they were perfectly harmonious with the premises contained in the Cairo *Programme of Action* — namely, that people are a "resource" to be managed by global supervisors in the interests of "sustainable development," and that the family is an administrative unit of the global mega-state. Those who wish to understand what "sustainable development" portends should imagine a Rwanda-esque tragedy on a global scale.

The Cairo Conference offered yet another "sustainability scenario" during a question-and-answer session involving Vice President Al Gore. A man who identified himself as a member of the United Nations Association from Pasadena, California made reference to the then-impending UN occupation of Haiti: "Why can't the United Nations send huge hospital ships to Haiti to deliver good medicine to an impoverished people.... Giving good medicine establishes confidence in the doctors, which could then get an agreement to have small families, to accept contraceptives, sterilization, and abortion."

Gore's reply avoided a direct response to the proposition of population control-by-extortion. However, his interlocutor persisted: "What about hospital ships that can deliver family planning?" After a brief discussion with AID Director J. Brian Atwood (CFR), Gore delivered the following answer:

> The UN force that has been authorized to re-establish stability and support the re-establishment of the legitimate government of Haiti has been supplemented by a highly developed plan to assist that nation in a sustainable economic recovery. There was a [foreign aid] Donor's conference this last week in Paris. There has been a great deal of highly sophisticated work that has given attention to a broad range of problems that need to be addressed in Haiti.... There will be an effort by the world community, by the international community, to address a broad range of problems in Haiti and help them get back on their feet."[63]

It is worth noting that Gore did not reject the suggestion that "humanitarian" aid be used as blackmail leverage on behalf of population control objectives, seeking instead to bury the matter beneath a layer of diplomatic persiflage. As Atwood could have confirmed to the Vice President, the approach which was insistently described in the question posed to Gore *had been the Clinton Administration's policy toward Haiti for more than a year*.

Left-wing journalist Alexander Cockburn obtained a copy of a June 1993 internal AID memo discussing population control policies in Haiti. In a column published while the Cairo Conference was in session, Cockburn reported that the AID memo "states policy 'targets' for Haiti baldly: to obtain 200,000 new 'acceptors' of contraception, a 'social-marketing component' target of '6,000 cycles of pills/month' and the establishment of 23 facilities to provide sterilizations — soothingly referred to as 'voluntary surgical contraception,' a goal that has been exceeded."

A Brooklyn-based Haitian woman's organization had documented the effects of the AID-supported, UN-aligned policy in Haiti:

> Local clinics offered food and money to encourage sterilization. "Acceptors" were promised that vasectomies were not only reversible, but would help prevent AIDS. Women were offered clothing in exchange for agreeing to use Norplant.... which led to a host of problems including constant bleeding, headaches, dizziness, nausea, radical weight loss, depression, and fatigue. Demands that the Norplant be taken out were obstructed.

Remarked Cockburn, "Such brute realities of population control are rarely mentioned in the United States, where reports from the UN population control conference in Cairo have depicted a clash between libertarian respect for individual choice and the medieval tyranny of the Catholic or Muslim clergy." Of course, this was a carefully constructed false dichotomy. As Cockburn pointed out, there was nothing "libertarian" about the "empowerment" agenda devised in Cairo: "Cut through all the reassuring lingo about 'empowering women' and consider the realities of U.S.

population policy today in Haiti.... [T]he fundamental goal of the American government is to keep the natives from breeding."[64]

Americans would do well to ponder the fact that "keep[ing] the natives from breeding" is not merely the goal of the American government in *foreign* affairs, but in *domestic* affairs as well. The U.S. delegation to the Cairo Conference repeatedly assured reporters and delegates that the Cairo program, like the "Agenda 21" program which was produced at the Rio "Earth Summit" in 1992, will guide American domestic policy. A government which would subsidize coercion in China and India, and underwrite bribery, extortion, and thinly disguised coercion in Haiti, would not scruple to use the same tactics against Americans.

In Cairo, U.S. delegation leader Timothy Wirth was quoted by witnesses as saying that "The population community is moving away from coercion." When asked to confirm this report, Wirth offered the clarification that the "population movement is moving away from targets and numbers. When you use targets and numbers, there's a temptation to establish quotas; people become worried about meeting their quotas, and that's the wrong way to go about doing it."[65] As Cockburn's report demonstrates, Wirth was seeking refuge in yet another lie: Targets and quotas were being pursued in Haiti as a result of AID policy.

Furthermore, somebody forgot to inform Sharon Camp of Population Action International that targets and quotas were passe. As of late 1993, Camp still endorsed government-established "targets, numbers, and quotas," and implicitly endorsed the option of coercion:

> [T]he world's governments and multilateral agencies need to commit themselves to *demographic targets* against which progress toward early population stabilization can be measured.... Governments have the right to be concerned about the demographic consequences of individual reproductive behavior. They have the responsibility to pursue democratically arrived at *demographic goals* through public education campaigns, expanded access to safe and reliable birth control, and other development interventions

> known to influence fertility directly.... *Can voluntary family plan-*
> *ning programs by themselves reduce fertility fast enough to achieve*
> *population stabilization at 9 billion people? Not by themselves* [em-
> phasis added].[66]

Was Camp simply "out of the loop"? This is almost impossible
to believe, given the intimacy of PAI's relationship with the Administration and the UN. Wirth spoke at a PAI news conference
in Cairo in which he endorsed the group's proposal for a four-fold
spending increase on population control programs.

Population Control or Democide?

The practice of democide — or, as it's more commonly called,
mass murder — has been a consistent feature of totalitarian societies since the French Revolution. What we refer to as "population control" is simply a democidal agenda made palatable by a
garnish of humanitarian rhetoric. But the premises contained
within the concept of "sustainable development" lead ineluctably
to mass murder.

The leading figures in the French Revolutionary terror candidly
discussed the supposed need for radical *depopulation* of France,
in order to bring about a more tractable and governable population. As we will see in Chapter Eight, one result of this vision was
the near annihilation of the Vendée, a province which was populated with "refractory," or fundamentalist, Catholics.

French investigator Courtois commented on papers seized at
the house of Maximilien Robespierre, summarizing that "These
men, in order to bring us to the happiness of Sparta wished to
annihilate twelve or fifteen millions of the French people...."[67]
Gracchus Babeuf, the illuminist who created a hard-core communist cell within the Paris Commune, composed an essay entitled
"Sur le Système de la Dépopulation," which set out quite candidly
the premises — and the results — of what is now referred to as
"sustainable development." Babeuf's essay was essentially a review of Robespierre's writings on the subject. According to
Babeuf, Robespierre concluded that "*depopulation was indispens-*

able, because the calculation had been made that the French population was in excess of the resources of the soil and of the requirements of useful industry...."[68]

Under the rule of Josef Stalin, the Soviet regime systematically depopulated the Ukraine through an artificially-induced famine during the 1930s; an estimated 20 to 30 million "kulaks" (or peasant farmers) were liquidated in what ex-Soviet historians Mikhail Heller and Aleksandr M. Nekrich refer to as "the first socialist genocide."[69] What distinguished the slaughter in the Ukraine from previous acts of systematic murder, according to Heller and Nekrich, was the fact that "it was directed against an indigenous population by a government of the same nationality, and in time of peace."

Furthermore, "There is no question that the Soviet city people knew about the massacre in the countryside... Stalin spoke openly about the 'liquidation of the kulaks as a class,'" and all his lieutenants echoed him. At the railroad stations, city dwellers could see the thousands of women and children who had fled from the villages and were dying of hunger. Kulaks, 'dekulakized persons,' and 'kulak henchmen' died alike. They were not considered human. Society spat them out, just as the 'disenfranchised persons' and 'has-beens' were after October 1917, just as the Jews were in Nazi Germany."[70]

As we have seen, it is Communist China which serves as the showpiece of "sustainable development." Mao's agricultural "reform" followed the contours of the initiatives of Robespierre and Stalin. Mao's government targeted the "landlord" class — who were actually poor peasant farmers, as landlords of the conventional sense have not existed in China for centuries — for liquidation. As Chinese expatriate Valentin Chu observed,

> The real purpose of Mao's land reform was political rather than economic. China had virtually no proletariat, and with Mao basing his revolutionary theory on the peasants, he had to use the landlords as a sin-offering. Many peasants who owned as little as two or three acres of land, which they tilled themselves, were included in

the estimated 5 million "landlords" liquidated.[71]

Of course, the destruction of China's agricultural economy created a famine, which required even more draconian controls by government over the allocation of resources; eventually this politically-induced famine, like its Soviet counterpart, consumed an estimated 20 to 30 million lives[72] — another bloody harvest for "sustainable development."

A Covenant with Death

Because it sets forth the supposed necessity of radical controls over human fertility, the Cairo population program is a covenant with death. Because of the UN's acceptance of inhumane premises, governments around the world have been led — and sometimes compelled — to embrace the "unthinkable" as a necessary approach to the "crisis" of population. But there is no problem created by human fecundity that cannot be overcome through the emancipation of human ingenuity from the suffocating grip of state regulation. The problem, simply put, is a surplus population of ruling elites; the solution is not the liquidation of the elites, but rather their eviction from power.

As Dr. Kajid Katme, a Muslim pro-life activist, declared at the Cairo Conference, "God is the only population controller."[73] Paul Ehrlich conceded that even the most oppressive population control program cannot prevail without the complicity of its victims. Furthermore, those who presume to usurp God's role will have to reckon with He whose role it is. As Isaiah said of the corrupt political leadership whose earlier covenant of death he assailed, "[Y]our covenant with death shall be disannulled, and your agreement with hell shall not stand; when the overflowing scourge shall pass through, then ye shall be trodden down by it."

CHAPTER 6

Multiculturalism and the UN Assault on American Nationhood

The sentiment in my [classroom] is that they don't like Christians and they don't like white people, because they saw what has been done in the name of Christianity and what the white people did to the Indians and the Africans.
— American fifth-grade teacher Lee Ellis
Explaining multicultural education to a reporter[1]

We just need to give students all the facts.... We can't do this if we're going to start by setting ourselves up as a superior nation.
— Gail Burry, President of the Florida
Education Association (an NEA affiliate)[2]

In December 1994, the UN proclaimed the beginning of the "International Decade of Indigenous Peoples," an observance which is supposedly dedicated to winning recognition of the rights and cultures of the world's "first peoples." This event marked the UN's official entry into the turbulent subject of "multiculturalism" — a doctrine of collective guilt and collective virtue which holds that the "victim" groups — particularly "indigenous peoples" — must be given enhanced standing in history and cultural observances.

In current American parlance, the enforcement arm of the multiculturalist movement is called "political correctness," and Americans find themselves amused and sometimes outraged by the antics of the P.C. compassion gestapo. However, the multiculturalist movement is much more than merely a passing fancy of the foolish. In order for a "global culture" to prevail, distinctive national cultures must be extinguished. The multicultural crusade is designed to discredit the labors of America's founders and subvert the institutions they crafted. Furthermore, it is intended to provide an interface whereby America will come under UN-directed international scrutiny.

Re-writing "Incorrect" History

Those who think that "political correctness" is a harmless, home-grown variety of political idiocy should think again. Mikhail Gorbachev's *Global Security Programme*, a blueprint for "empowering" the UN, includes a proposal for the creation of a "Transnational Network of Citizen Action Groups" which will "fill the 'blank pages of history' and revise incorrect or tendentious versions of the history of intergroup relationships." The document also recommends that political leaders seek to "express contrition for the infliction of past hurts on a victimized group" — presumably, an exemption would be granted in the case of Gorbachev's persecution of Christians, Jews, Moslems, and indigenous peoples in the former Soviet Empire.

If such gestures of contrition aren't made voluntarily, the UN and its allies might get insistent:

> [W]here leaders can not be found to demonstrate such courage, commissions might be established to document moral culpability in past violence and aggressions. A transnational network of citizens' action groups devoted to healing and building community ... could be established to share knowledge and resources for this work.[3]

Of course, such projects in "conflict resolution" would benefit from the direction of a UN-based "Commission for the Prevention and Resolution of Conflicts," a group of 10-15 "eminent persons" which would work in collaboration with the UN Secretary-General. Although it is by no means certain that Gorbachev's proposal will be adopted by the UN, the recommendations contained therein regarding a UN-aligned "citizens' network" are already being implemented. Following a game plan derived from UNESCO's *Toward International Understanding* series, multiculturalists in the classroom seek to destroy the "nationalistic" attitudes of schoolchildren, molding them into "world citizens" who have no organic relationship to America's history and institutions.

The publication of the federally funded National Standards for World History, which were withdrawn following an outburst of public indignation, represented an attempt to create a brave new multiculturalist world. It is entirely probable that some version of the rejected standards will be produced again. The National Standards for World History were an outgrowth of the 1989 Education Summit in Charlottesville, during which President George Bush and a group of American governors endorsed the creation of national history standards. With funding from the National Endowment for the Humanities the project soon became a public works project for Marxists, globalists, and other malcontent revisionists — with predictable results.

Rather than requiring students to study the essentials of American constitutionalism, the standards present classroom exercises dealing with such arcana as the following:

• Among Maya, Inca and Aztec societies, which seemed the most positive and which seemed the most negative for women?

• Research the attitude of six major Mughal emperors from Babur to Aurangzeb on an issue such as how to treat minorities, religious beliefs, military expansion, or architecture and literary accomplishments.

• Analyze the basis of social relationships in India and the social and legal position of women during the Gupta era.

• Use an evaluation form to rate the treatment and opportunities open to women in 17th and 18th century China. Rate such items as footbinding, female subordination, patriarchy, a flourishing women's culture, and literature.

• Read the report of John of Plano Carpini, the 13th century papal emissary, on the Mongol threat and analyze his social and cultural biases about the Mongols.

• Research the career of Abd al-Quadir, the Moroccan resistance leader of the 1920s.[4]

Gary Nash, co-director of the National Standards project, explained that "we're trying to let children out of the prison of facts" and gleefully predicted that with advent of the new standards classrooms would soon be "jumping with mock trials and staged debates"[5] — a situation not unfamiliar to those who remember the Chinese Cultural Revolution, which was also designed to emancipate youth from "the prison of facts."

These refinements in the art of indoctrination were matched with developments on the cultural front. In 1994, the city government of San Jose, California — a city named after the foster father of Jesus — erected a statue of the Aztec deity Quetzalcoatl on the Plaza de Cesar Chavez. The same city government decided that the new multicultural ethic required the discontinuation of the city's nativity scene, which was deemed "offensive" to non-Christians. A federal judge granted permission to display the nativity scene on the condition that it be recognized as a "cultural," rather than a religious, symbol — thereby making the Biblical Savior equal in status to a pagan Aztec idol.[6]

But San Jose was already behind the multiculturalist curve. Some Americans had already learned that the ultimate triumph of the multiculturalist worldview will require that patriotism itself be redefined as a crime.

Criminalizing Patriotism

Indeed, as the case of Lake County, Florida, illustrates, in some American jurisdictions educators are effectively forbidden to extol the superiority of America's cultural heritage. In early 1994, a divided Lake County school board approved curriculum guidelines that required instructors to recognize that America's traditional civic, social, and economic concepts and institutions are superior to other foreign and historic cultures. This measure was produced by concerns over a 1991 state statute which created a state task force on multicultural education. The statute's preamble stated that "to live, learn, and work in a pluralistic world every person needs to build an awareness of his or her own cultural and ethnic heritage, develop an understanding, respect, and appreciate [sic] for the history, culture, and contributions of other groups, and *eliminate personal and national ethnocentrism* so that he or she understands that a specific culture is not intrinsically superior or inferior to another...." (Emphasis added)[7]

This declaration, which is obviously derivative of UNESCO's "world understanding" approach, is a mandate for attitude reconstruction. State legislator Tom Feeney explains that the statute was the work of "the educrats — state and federal bureaucrats, radical unions, and social engineers. They have sought to rewrite the social studies and history courses."[8] The Lake County policy simply sought to insure that America's distinctive institutions — republican government, free-market economics, and Biblical morality — would not be sacrificed on the multiculturalist altar.

Nothing in the policy could be construed as an attempt to denigrate any individual because of his racial, ethnic, or religious background. Lake County school board chairman Pat Hart points out that "During our school board hearings, Americans of all racial backgrounds expressed support for this revision. One of our statements came from a man from Turkey who came to America with about $20.00 in his pocket. He's now teaching programs in adult literacy, contributing to the community. It's not the color of the skin that matters, but the values that you embrace, that makes you an American."[9]

But the subversion of America's distinctive values is the chief aim of multiculturalism. Accordingly, the educrat nexus described by Rep. Fenney promptly went to battle against the Lake County policy; the grievance industry and the Establishment media conscripted the familiar artless canards about prejudice and displaced hostility that have been part of the pro-UN rhetorical arsenal since the 1950s. The Florida Education Association (FEA) filed a lawsuit contending that the Lake County policy violated both state and federal law.

In large measure because of the furor created by the "America First" curriculum — which had literally become a global controversy, thanks to the Establishment media cartel — supporters of the proposed policy were voted out of office in a primary election in October 1994. Pat Hart explained that "We have endured over two years of constant anti-Christian bashing by the liberal media, truckloads of teachers union money and efforts by administrators and teachers against us."[10] In this fashion, the "tolerance" industry thus prevented an outbreak of virulent patriotism in Florida.

Vilifying Columbus

There is no greater villain for multiculturalists than Christopher Columbus, who introduced Western Christian civilization to the Americas. The Colombian Quincentennial in 1992 was greeted by multiculturalists as an opportunity to vilify Columbus and the civilization he represented.

Preparations for the anti-Columbus campaign began in 1990, when the 35,000-member American Library Association (ALA) condemned the forthcoming 500th anniversary celebration. According to the ALA, events after 1492 "begin a legacy of European piracy, brutality, slave trading, murder, disease, conquest, and ethnocide."[11] In 1991, the National Education Association weighed in against the Admiral of the Ocean Seas, urging its members at a national conference to promote the new multiculturalist party line that Columbus was a mass murderer and criminal. *NEA Today* predicted, "Never again will Christopher Columbus sit on a pedestal in United States history."[12] Lending its dubious moral weight to the hate campaign, the National Council of Churches in 1991 issued a condemnation of Columbus's voyages, claiming, "For [Indians], Christopher Columbus's invasion marked the beginning of slavery and eventual genocide."[13]

In order to guarantee that the inmates of America's public education system were force-fed the new party line, the National Council of Education activists produced a 97-page guide entitled *Rethinking Columbus*. The chapter titles in this booklet display a Mao-like gift for ideological pedagogy: "We Have No Reason to Celebrate an Invasion"; "Why I Am Not Thankful for Thanksgiving"; "Helping Children Critique Columbus Books"; "Once Upon a Genocide"; "Struggles Unite Native Peoples"; "Maps: Taking

Europe off Center Stage."14

The tenor of the anti-Columbus indoctrination campaign can be appreciated by the following excerpt from a fourth-grade spelling test which was given in Chapel Hill, North Carolina in "honor" of Columbus Day, 1992:

> They [the Indians] were called *SAVAGE*, and because they were all killed in a short period of time by disease and slavery, their *HISTORY* has almost been forgotten.
>
> Many Native American peoples say that the early Europeans committed cultural *GENOCIDE* when they killed all of the people in a tribe or removed people from their homelands and forced them to live in unfamiliar regions with tribes whose ways were very different from their own.
>
> The people of the small village of Miwetok awoke late at night to soaring flames. The whole village was destroyed in a fiery *HOLOCAUST* and the people were trembling in terror, left cold, hungry, and homeless.
>
> The early Spanish *CONQUISTADORS CONQUERED* lands which were already occupied, and proceeded to *ANNIHILATE* and *SUBJUGATE* the native peoples, forcing them into slavery, or taking over their homelands.
>
> Sometimes the early colonists called the Native American people *HEATHENS* because their religion was unfamiliar to them, being neither Christian, nor Jew, nor Moslem.
>
> Often, one group will spread false rumors and *PROPAGANDA* about another, trying to sway the public to their own point of view.15

This "spelling test," which seeks to indoctrinate and radicalize, bears a filial resemblance to similar exercises found in the reading and spelling primers used in literacy campaigns in communist Cuba and Sandinista-era Nicaragua. Derived from the "conscientization" or "liberation education" pedagogy of Brazilian Marxist Paulo Freire, the Cuban/Nicaraguan literacy campaigns selected words which were deemed "relevant to the pupil's social and political reality" — that is, as that "reality" was approved by

the government.[16] Bill Bigelow, an Oregon teacher who coordinated the 1991-92 "Rethinking Colombus" project for the left-wing
Network of Educators on Central America, has acknowledged the
influence of Freire's Marxist pedagogy on the anti-Columbus hate
campaign.[17]

As Richard Bernstein points out in his book *Dictatorship of Virtue: Multiculturalism and America's Future*,* the anti-Columbus
crusade is remarkably uncontaminated by reliable scholarship:

> [The] challenge to Christopher Columbus ... is based on no new
> knowledge, no new information about Columbus himself or about
> his voyages or even what happened as a consequence of them. Noth-
> ing has been brought to light, no details of Columbus's biography,
> no new archeological findings, no discovery of previously unknown
> manuscripts, no uncovering of original diaries, journals, letters, or
> contemporary accounts.[18]

During the celebration of Columbus Day in 1892, Americans of
all ethnic backgrounds proudly and gratefully acknowledged the
noble Admiral as an exemplar of Western Christian virtues. One
hundred years later, things were — not to put too fine a point on
the question — rather different.

The 1992 Columbus Day parade in Denver was cancelled in response to threats of violence from a multiculturalist mob. Colorado was the first state to make Columbus Day an official holiday,
a fact not lost on Russell Means, the veteran "Indian Rights" activist who had presided over the anti-Columbus riot. "It's a clear-
cut victory. This is where Columbus Day began. We stopped it
here, and the rest of the country has to follow suit."[19] In the
People's Republic of Berkeley, California, a gaggle of leftists in-

---

* Interestingly, Bernstein, a reporter for the *New York Times*, covered the subject
of multiculturalism for approximately five years before publishing his book,
which is larded with telling examples of the totalitarian nature and radical objectives of the movement. However, the *Times* apparently never deemed any of
these stories "fit to print"; thus, Bernstein — an unrepentant liberal — found it
necessary to publish his reportage in the form of a book.

augurated "Indigenous Peoples' Day" as an official replacement for Columbus Day. A sign observed at the Berkeley Event summarized the message of multiculturalism: "U.S. Out of North America."[20]

Of course, the United States cannot physically leave North America, and Americans of European ancestry are not expected to repatriate themselves to their ancestral homelands overseas. However, the literal destruction of the United States can be achieved just as effectively by invalidating the history and culture which created the distinctive institutions which define this nation. This is what multiculturalism seeks to accomplish, and the ritualistic execration of Columbus has been a key element in this campaign of destruction.

The Tree of Hate

Richard Bernstein points out that because of the anti-Columbus campaign, "multiculturalism has already succeeded in making several basic changes in the nature of public discourse":

> First is the elimination from acceptable discourse of any claim of superiority or even special status for Europe, or any definition of the United States as derived primarily from European civilization.
>
> Second is *the attack on the very notion of the individual and the concomitant paramount status accorded group identification.* Columbus in the quincentennial became the prototype of the white race.
>
> Third ... *[m]ulticulturalism here is the indictment of one group and the exculpation of all the others.* The attack on Columbus was a tactic ... in the furtherance of the cult of the victim, in which society is viewed as an arena of oppression exercised by the white majority over everybody else [Emphasis added]."[21]

Multiculturalism is therefore a form of racial collectivism, and as such is kindred to the ideology which animated Hitler's National Socialist regime. This is not to say that multiculturalists seek to cast Euro-Americans into crematoria; rather, they will be satisfied with wreaking similar atrocities upon America's institutions of liberty. Nor should it be thought that multiculturalism is a recent innovation in ideological perversity; rather, it is a descendant of a long-lived libel against the Americas which was diligently propagated by the same cluster of illuminist intellectuals which inspired the French Revolution.

The Black Legend

Historian Philip Wayne Powell points out that Spain's political adversaries — particularly English, Dutch, French, Italian and German government and commercial elites — had an interest in the destruction of Spain's reputation, and the embryonic printing and publishing industry offered a ready means of defamation. Lurid tales of Spanish brutality blackened broadsides and pamphlets. Many of the atrocity stories were invented *ex nihilo*, or were grotesquely exaggerated accounts devoid of nuance and balance. Religious hostilities combined with economic rivalries to promote the idea that Spain was uniquely cruel, venal, and superstitious. This resulted in what many historians refer to as the "Black Legend" of Spanish depravity.

Interestingly, the first significant anti-Spanish propagandist was a Spaniard, just as the most venomous anti-American multiculturalists today are pampered, well-fed American intellectuals of European descent. Bartolomé De Las Casas, a Spanish monk, was a fundamentally decent man who, like most Spanish clerics in the New World, was obsessed with a noble cause: humane treatment of the Indians. Las Casas was an energetic polemicist whose zeal far outstripped his devotion to the truth. Powell wryly remarks that "With his pen, Las Casas destroyed more Indians than his countrymen could possibly have killed."[22] Although the Black Legend was a creation of political, commercial, and sectarian rivalries, it proved to be quite compatible with the secular dogma of the Enlightenment.

By the late 17th century, the Spanish Empire was in a steep decline. Where Spain had once been hated because of its power, it was now scorned because of its relative debility, and it found itself targeted for a different reason. As Powell explains, "Spain ... [was] a Colossus of Roman Catholicism in an age that took as one of its intellectual guidelines a disdainful skepticism of revealed and hierarchical religion in general and of the Roman [Catholic] version in particular."[23] The anti-Spanish and anti-American propaganda themes favored by the French secularists and other illumines, according to Powell, were "rehashed Las Casas, with an Enlightenment twist...."[24]

In the 1700s, the *illumines* seized upon the Black Legend and appropriated it in their crusade to destroy Christian society. Its critique of the Spanish colonization of the Americans was a natural compliment to Rousseau's doctrine of the "noble savage." Secularists like Rousseau maintained that the Christian colonization of the Americas was a sin against the natural equality of the continent's indigenous inhabitants. Voltaire, who believed that "man is not born wicked" and that he is made evil by the "horrors of human society," played a significant role in the propagation of the secularized Black Legend within Spain's governing elite.

Pedro Pablo Abarca de Bolea, the tenth Count of Aranda, was a Spanish general who became the power behind the Spanish throne in the mid-1700s. Through shared membership in a masonic lodge, Count Aranda became a close friend of Voltaire; this helped catalyze the Count's implacable hatred of all religion, particularly Catholicism. Historian George Hills recounts that "With Voltaire Aranda appreciated that an international Church was too difficult to destroy all at once by frontal attack." Accordingly, Aranda's first target was the Jesuit order, which presided over the education of thousands of students in Spain and elsewhere. According to Hills, "Without this learned body of several thousand men, who somehow always reconciled the findings of new scientific research with Christianity, the field would be clear for the new French philosophy."[25]

Led by Aranda, the Secularists expelled the Jesuits from Spain in 1767, and the military brutally suppressed popular protests on behalf of the Catholic order; this was done by King Charles III at Abarca's urging.[26] Church property was seized by the government; relatively autonomous communities were bought under direct government control. Education fell into disrepair. Where the Jesuit colleges had been open to all people of sufficient diligence and ability, the secular colleges were reserved to a small elite.[27]

Powell refers to the Black Legend as the "Tree of Hate." Spanish elites, following the inspiration of the French *illumines*, eagerly sought refuge under that tree: By 1778, many of the highest officials in Spain were devout disciples of the Encyclopedists, including the King. Count Aranda, Voltaire's pupil and secret society comrade, was a personal advisor to Charles III. According to historian Will Durant, "Under his [Aranda's] guidance Charles joined the ranks of those 'enlightened despots' to whom the *philosophes* were looking as their likeliest aides in the spread of education, liberty, and reason."[28]

But just as a diseased tree cannot bear wholesome fruit, the reign of a despot — even an "illuminated" one — cannot produce education, liberty, and reason. As a consequence of the illuminist influence upon Spain's ruling elites, the nation underwent over a century and a half of civil strife, cultural anarchy and a chronic crisis of government legitimacy. With its Christian traditions under constant siege, Spain lost its political virility and civic discipline. Now, centuries after the process began, Spain is an unassuming province of the European superstate.

The Unwanted Legacy

The Black Legend became a legacy of the European civilization in the Americas. In the middle and late 1700s, the *illumines* turned their rhetorical fire upon the English colonies which later became the United States. Among the most vicious of these enemies of America's Christian civilization could be found the radicalized clergy — atheists in clerical garb who precisely prefigure contemporary Marxist "Liberation Theologians."[29] A typical premature multiculturalist was the Abbe Corneille de Pauw, who condemned the European colonization of the Americas as "the greatest of all misfortunes to befall mankind."[30]

It is beyond serious dispute that the most influential exponent of the "enlightened" Black Legend was the Abbe Guillaume Raynal, who composed a ten-volume work entitled *A Philosophical and Political History of the Settlements and Trade of the Europeans in the East and West Indies*. According to Durant, many of the *illumines* considered Raynal's history to be the most important work produced by the Enlightenment — an anti-Christian weapon more potent than Diderot's Encyclopedia or the writings of Rousseau or Voltaire.[31] Historian Leo Gershoy states that among the Illuminist "humanitarians" who congregated in pre-Revolutionary France, "the Abbe Raynal's many-sided diatribe against intolerance ... was their bible."[32] At last — here was the definitive indictment of Christian ignorance, bigotry, and greed!

In the closing pages of his sprawling, rambling harangue, Raynal put the question plainly:

> Let us stop here, and consider ourselves as existing at the time when America and India were unknown. Let me suppose that I address myself to the most cruel of the Europeans in the following terms: There exist regions which will furnish thee with rich metals, agreeable clothing, and delicious food; but read this history [i.e., the assembled fictions that composed the Black Legend] and behold at what price the discovery is promised to thee. Dost thou wish or not that it should be made? Is it to be imagined that there exists a being infernal enough to answer this question in the affirmative? Let it be remembered, that there will not be a single instant in futurity when my question will not have the same force.[33]

In 1792, the 300th anniversary of Columbus' voyage, France was tearing itself to pieces in pursuit of "liberty, equality and fraternity." Raynal, whose labors had helped prepare the way for the guillotine, sponsored an essay contest at the Academy of Lyons. Contestants were offered a prize of 1,200 francs for the best treatment of this question: "Was the discovery of America a blessing or a curse to mankind? If it was a blessing, by what means are we to conserve and enhance its benefits? If it was a curse, by what means are we to repair the damage?" Of course, Raynal was hardly a fair-minded critic, having already published his anti-American tract, and — with the economy typical of leftist self-promotion — Raynal won his own contest.

Of America Raynal wrote, "How many calamities, which cannot be compensated, have not attended the conquest of these regions?" He did not deny that the discovery and colonization of the Americans had enriched Europe, "But before these enjoyments were obtained, were we less healthy, less robust, less intelligent, or less happy? Are these frivolous advantages, so cruelly obtained, so unequally distributed, and so obstinately disputed, worth one drop of that blood which has been spilt, and which will still be spilt for them?" Raynal spared no rhetorical exertion in his abuse of Americans, referring to them as "A new species of anomalous savages [who] traverse so many countries and who in the end belong in none. [They have] harassed the globe and stained it with blood."[34] None of this is unfamiliar to those who have even a cursory acquaintance with multiculturalism, or any other strain of 20th-century Anti-Americanism.

In another foreshadowing of modern multiculturalism, Raynal's scholarship, however politically correct, was empirically impoverished. The Durants, devout disciples of the Enlightenment, are dismissive of Raynal's "history": "Careless in its facts, it mistook legends for history, neglected dates, gave no references to authorities, confused its materials, and engaged ... in oratorical effusions and emotional appeals hardly becoming a work of history."[35]

Raynal's Descendants

It should surprise no one that there is a direct correspondence between the anti-Christian secularists of Raynal's era and the contemporary multiculturalist movement.

One unmistakable intellectual descendant of Raynal is Kirkpatrick Sale, a leftist historian and a founder of the New York Green Party and a faculty member at New Age University. Sale could be considered the doctrinal leader of the anti-Columbus movement: His 1990 book *The Conquest of Paradise: Christopher Columbus and the Colombian Legacy* is a multiculturalist primer. Like Raynal, whom he quotes as an historical authority, Sale contends that the European discovery of the New World was an unmitigated disaster for the entire planet.

Sale is palpably contemptuous of the Christian Europe that produced Columbus: "Why should one suppose that a culture like Europe's, steeped as it was in the ardor of wealth, the habit of violence, and the pride of intolerance ... would be able to come upon new societies in a fertile world, innocent and defenseless, and not displace and subdue, if necessary destroy, them?"[36]

Columbus, Cortez, and other Christian explorers believed that they took salvation to the New World. Sale maintains that the Indian cultures of pre-Columbian America offered salvation to Europe: "The salvation there, had the Europeans known where and how to look for it, was obviously in the integrative tribal ways, the nurturant communitarian values, the rich interplay with nature that made up the Indian cultures." Sale refers to this as the "biological outlook on life," in which

> Culture [is] not human-centered but comes from the sense of being at one with nature, biocentric, ecocentric, and where there was myth but no history, circular rather than linear time, renewal and restoration but not progress ... an interpenetration into earth and its life-forms that superseded an identification with self or species.[37]

The world view Sale adopts from the pre-Columbian American cultures is one in which there is no concept of the individual, hence no individual rights, and man is but another "life-form" sharing the planet with animals and insects. Furthermore, there is no history, but only official myths; this arrangement is quite attractive to multiculturalist fantasy-peddlers.

Sale believes that the "biological outlook" should have prevailed 500 years ago, and that it must be adopted now:

> It was salvation then, it might possibly be salvation now. Certainly there is no other.... There is only one way to live in America, and there can be only one way, and that is as Americans — the origi-

nal Americans — for that is what the earth of America demands. We have tried for five centuries to resist that simple truth. We resist it further only at the risk of the imperilment — worse, the likely destruction — of the earth.[38]

Although it is tempting to believe that such notions cling to the margins of the political elite, "respectable" intellectual figures have labored to grant these views unearned legitimacy. No better example of this can be found than the efforts of Kennedy Court Historian Arthur Schlesinger Jr. (CFR), who has traced the pedigree of the anti-Columbus campaign and debunked many of its assertions — yet has concluded that "If we are compelled to give this anniversary a balance sheet" the negative costs of the conquest "weigh heavily against Columbus and even more against those who followed him."

According to Schlesinger, "No one can doubt the arrogance and brutality of the European invaders, their callous and destructive ways, the human and ecological devastation they left in their trail." By contrast, according to Schlesinger, "Obviously one also wishes that the Europeans had understood as much about preserving the balance of nature as the Amerindians did, or as our ecologists do today."[39] It is impossible to find a better example of Establishment double-speak: Schlesinger laments the "excesses" of the radicals even as he urges us to adopt their basic assumptions. In short, scholars like Schlesinger are serving a function analogous to that performed in 18th-century Spain by Count Abarca: They make radical assumptions palatable to governing elites and "educated" opinion, thereby setting the stage for social revolution.

Taking AIM

The disruption of the 1992 Columbus Day celebration in Denver was a triumph for AIM, the so-called American Indian Movement. As we have seen, former AIM leader Russell Means presided over the mob which shut down the Denver Columbus Day parade, and Means insists that the suppression of Columbus Day festivities in Colorado represents a binding precedent for the nation. But this is merely one superficial manifestation of AIM's long-term strategy, which is intended to bring about permanent UN intervention in American affairs — and the destruction of America as it presently exists.

AIM is most notorious for its 1973 occupation of Wounded Knee, South Dakota. The 71-day standoff between AIM and federal law enforcement officials came at the end of a lengthy terrorist campaign in which AIM occupied the Washington, DC office of the Bureau of Indian Affairs and committed various acts of mayhem and violence in Custer, South Dakota. Despite the group's demonstrated penchant for violence and the illegality of its seizure of Wounded Knee, federal officials took great pains to minimize bloodshed — a fastidiousness which was not displayed, incidentally, when the FBI and ATF attacked the relatively tranquil eccentrics who belonged to the Branch Davidian congregation in Waco.

The restraint shown by federal law enforcement officials at Wounded Knee was not the first example of federal solicitude toward AIM. Between the group's founding in 1968 and the seizure of Wounded Knee five years later, the group received more than $400,000 in federal funding, the largest portion of which was channelled through the now-defunct Office of Economic Opportunity. Another $284,000 was given to AIM by various national church organizations.[40] Approximately half of the 258 AIM members and fellow travellers who occupied Wounded Knee had been employees of various government funded social welfare programs.[41] The group's association with the federal government, appropriately, gave it a taste for plunder: AIM's 1972 "Trail of Broken Treaties Campaign" — essentially a combination roadshow/rampage through the midwest — netted several hundred thousand dollars through blatant extortion.

Summoning the UN

In 1974, AIM convened its first international treaty convention in Aberdeen, South Dakota; that meeting was attended by representatives of many foreign countries.[42] Recalled Doug Durham, an FBI informant who spent two years undercover with AIM, "The idea was to get all the treaty issues [involving Indian tribes] taken out of the hands of the United States, and put them either before the World Court, or the United Nations."[43] The "treaty conference" produced a "Declaration of Continuing Independence of the First National Indian Treaty Council" which read, in part:

> We recognize that there is only one color of Mankind in the world who are [sic] not represented in the United Nations. And that is the indigenous Redman of the Western Hemisphere. We recognize this lack of representation in the United Nations comes from the genocidal policies of the colonial power of the United States.
>
> The International Indian Treaty Council established by this conference is directed to make application to the United Nations for recognition and membership of the sovereign Native Nations. We pledge our support to any similar application by any aboriginal people.[44]

The document condemned "the continuing refusal by the United States of America to sign the United Nations 1948 treaty on genocide." That refusal ended in 1988, when President Ronald Reagan quietly signed the UN Genocide Convention — thus opening an avenue for direct relations between the UN and American Indian "nations."

The 1974 international treaty convention gave birth to an "International Treaty Office" (ITO) located on UN Plaza in New York City. Jimmy Durham (no relation to Doug Durham), a marxist activist with ties to Fidel Castro, headed the ITO; his wife Ann Gael was a liaison with the New York Native American Solidarity Committee. Among the projects initiated by Durham and Gael was a petition drive with the announced intention of "asking the UN to take note ... that the Native American issue is not an 'internal problem' of the USA."[45]

Arguably, Jimmy Durham deserves credit for composing the modern multiculturalist catechism. In 1974, Durham published a seminal essay entitled "American Indian Culture: Traditional-

148

ism and Spiritualism in a Revolutionary Struggle." According to Durham, "Marx used our societies as examples of what he meant by communism." Like Raynal, Rousseau, and Sale, Durham insisted that Western Christian civilization destroyed the primitive communal harmony between the Indians and nature: [The] wars against Indians were not only to take over land but also to squash the threatening example of Indian communism....Our societies were and are communistic societies."[46]

Although Durham assailed what he called "white progressives" for their "political missionary-ism," he insisted that the Indians had to ally themselves with white leftists and their sponsors. Despite the "eurocentric" tendencies he discerned in Marx, Durham declared: "We do need Marxism-Leninism as a method and system for knowing the human world as it is today and for knowing how to most effectively fight our oppressor. We do need to join forces with world Marxism-Leninism, because that is the liberation movement for the world."[47]

One crucial refinement to Marxism/Leninism offered by Durham was the addition of a "spiritual" component: "Our 'Spiritualism' is a controversial issue right now. Marx said that religion is the opium of the people. We agree that for Europe and Asia religion is a drug that exploits people for the State. That is why we have fought Christianity so totally. But we say that our religion is a force of liberation."[48] This proposition was endorsed exactly 20 years later in a speech by Mikhail Gorbachev before the Environmental Media Association in Hollywood. Referring to the supposed need to create a new global religious ethic, Gorbachev — who remains a committed Marxist — declared: "The time has come for mankind to adopt the wise philosophy of Native Americans: 'We do not inherit this planet from our fathers, we borrow it from our children.'"[49]

Maurice Strong, the Canadian oil mogul who served as secretary-general of the UN "Earth Summit" in Rio and Gorbachev's collaborator in the composition of an authoritative "Earth Charter," struck a similar pose in the foreword to the *Gaia Atlas of First Peoples: A Future for the Indigenous World*:

As this turbulent century closes, we must alter radically our ways of life, patterns of consumption, systems of values, even the manner in which we organize our societies, if we are to ensure survival of the Earth, and ourselves.... [W]e will need to look to the world's more than 250 million indigenous peoples. They are the guardians of the extensive and fragile ecosystems that are vital to the wellbeing of the planet.[50]

Published in 1990 — the year when the entire international Marxist/Socialist network suddenly "discovered" environmentalism — the *Gaia Atlas* contains a world roster of 73 "Indigenous Organizations" (including AIM), most of which are affiliated with the World Indigenous Peoples Council (WIPC), a UN-aligned network.[51] Almost all of these groups play a role similar to that of AIM: They are used to create a groundswell of grievance which will serve as a pretext for UN intervention in the name of "human rights." Twenty years after AIM first sought UN interference in America's domestic affairs, the world body began to oblige.

UN Meddling in America

On September 19, 1994, the State Department presented its first report to the UN Human Rights Committee regarding compliance with the International Covenant on Civil and Political Rights. In his press briefing that day, John Shattuck, the Administration's Assistant Secretary of State for Democracy, Human Rights, and Labor, cited the "virtual destruction of many Native American civilizations" as a debit in the U.S. human rights record — a matter, it should be noted, in which contemporary Americans bear no guilt.[52]

In 1994, AIM and allied groups organized a nation wide tour by Miguel Alfonzo Martinez, a Cuban official who was appointed as a UN Special Rapporteur on Human Rights in 1989. (Martinez's human rights credentials now include service as a spokesman for the Cuban government's Foreign Ministry.) Martinez conducted hearings with Indian activists in California, Washington, New Mexico, Minnesota, South Dakota, and New York.[53] According to Bill Simmons, the Treaty Study Coordinator for the Indian Treaty Council (the offshoot of Durham's Indian Treaty Organization), Martinez's U.S. tour was a fulfillment of AIM's long-term objectives: This is "[t]he same organization that started the work in 1974; this is a continuation of that effort. I look at this as beginning with the 1960s and 1970s Indian Movement. What really put it into focus was the occupation of Wounded Knee."[54]

Through its links to the WIPC, AIM and the ITC have obtained remarkable influence. Several AIM-aligned activists were sent to Chiapas, Mexico in early 1994 to work as "observers" or "mediators" between the Marxist *Zapatista* rebels and the government.*[55] Andrea Carmen, ITC's executive director, has lent similar "service" during visits to Ecuador, Nicaragua, and Panama, and ITC activist Tony Ibarra was sent to Rwanda as a UN observer.[56] The ITC board also includes Nobel Peace Prize Laureate Rigoberta Menchu,[57] a Guatemalan Marxist whose autobiography, *I, Rigoberta Menchu*, is prominent in the multiculturalist canon.

---

* During the 21st World Conference of the Society for International Development in Mexico City in 1994, a remarkable thing happened. As the Closing Plenary session on "Building Partnerships and Collaboration Towards Global Transformation" commenced, a representative of the *Zapatistas*, the Marxist rebels from the southern Mexican state of Chiapas, was given recognition to speak as an authentic representative of "the indigenous peoples" of Mexico. David C. Korten of The People-Centered Development Forum, a socialist-oriented UN-recognized NGO, recounts: "When the speaker from Chiapas finished, the vast majority of those present in the conference hall of the Sheraton Maria Isabel Hotel rose to their feet in applause."

Of course, there is nothing indigenous about the Zapatista rebellion in Mexico; it is simply the most recent example of "liberation theology" — Marxism engrafted onto a framework of nominal Christianity. However, Korten correctly pointed out that the Chiapas uprising, and SID's enthusiastic endorsement of it, represents a convergence of two forces: "Globalization from above" by the transnational money elite, and "globalization from below" undertaken by "indigenous" rebellions. In short, it is an application of the time-honored communist "scissors strategy." (David C. Korten, "Sustainable Societies and Global Governance: The People-Centered Concensus [sic], The People-Centered Development Forum, October 4, 1994.)

Menchu's revolutionary activities have included murder and lesbianism, and she maintains that the world's indigenous peoples are in a state of war with all ruling elites. Well — would you believe — *almost* all ruling elites? Like Jim Durham and other AIM leaders, Menchu's militancy evaporates when it encounters Marxist oppression of indigenous peoples. As Richard Grenier explains in a profile of Menchu:

> To put it simply, Rigoberta Menchu — who in Nicaragua championed Daniel Ortega's Sandinistas against the country's Indian rebels — is a Marxist-Leninist groupie first and an Indian second....
>
> The Sandinistas murdered scores of Nicaraguan Indians, displaced 70,000 of them in areas controlled by the Contras, and burned countless Indian villages to the ground. And what was Rigoberta Menchu's response to this large-scale repression of Indian peoples? Why, she was a total and fervent defender of Sandinista orthodoxy, going among the Nicaraguan Indians, arrogantly lecturing them on why they should be perfectly happy to accept deportation from their Indian villages.[58]

The actions of Menchu and Durham's efforts to reconcile Marxism with Indian spirituality illustrate that the Indian/Indigenous People's "rights" movement is not about freedom, but about collectivism. This is readily admitted by ITC leaders. Tony Gonzales declares that Martinez's U.S. tour was an effort to secure the "collective rights of Native Americans." [59] Andrea Carmen expatiates upon this concept at some length: "Human rights are considered individual rights, which is good, but we focus on group rights, like the right to development, which is really crucial to indigenous peoples worldwide. We talk about relationships of responsibility, rather than rights. This whole concept of rights, I think, is sort of a Western, European concept." Furthermore, according to Carmen, "The 'human rights' designation separates the human from the non-human world."[60]

Which brings us back to the "biological worldview" touted by Kirkpatrick Sale and Maurice Strong. The *Gaia Atlas* offers this tidy summation of that worldview from "Indigenous Rights" activist John Trudell:

> We must go beyond the arrogance of human rights. We must go beyond the ignorance of civil rights. We must step into the reality of natural rights because all the natural world has a right to existence. We are only a small part of it. There can be no trade-off.[61]

Because the UN-aligned "Indigenous Rights" movement is meant to serve the advancement of this "biological collectivism," the movement promotes a collectivist caricature of Indian history, and every effort is made to keep the neo-Rousseauist "Noble Savage" innocent of the taint of individualism. Of course, this is a racist stereotype of a particularly obnoxious variety: It is intended not only to suppress the individuality of Indians, but also to advance the suppression of non-Indian people in the name of "sustainable development."

Professor Terry Anderson of Montana State University, who — unlike Strong, Sale, and other dilettante multiculturalists — has made the study of Indian cultures both his vocation and avocation, points out, "Contrary to popular belief, Indians used varying degrees of private ownership for many assets including household goods, horses, land, and hunting and trapping territories. Prior to the arrival of Europeans, Indians understood the importance of individual rights to property and enforced those rights through formal and informal institutions."[62] There is a kernel of truth to the indictment of Western Civilization posed by multiculturalists: It is the State — specifically, the quasi-socialist reservation system — which has abetted the destruction of Indian communities and folkways. Yet AIM and its globalist allies seek to promote socialist "solutions" and make American Indians wards of a *global* reservation.

Exalting Pagan Collectivism

In cobbling together their caricature of the "history" of pre-Colombian America, multiculturalists ignore the individualist Indian societies and direct much of their devotion instead to the hemisphere's most tyrannical, theocratic despotisms: The Inca and Aztec empires. Why is this so? One possible answer is this: The Aztecs embodied the "Biological Outlook" which is supposedly the key to planetary salvation.

If, as the "Biological Outlook" dictates, man enjoys no special status in nature, cannibalism is a matter of moral indifference. Devouring a human being would be no more offensive than eating an eggplant — both are merely kindred "life-forms." Cannibalism was a fact of life under the Aztec ruling elite, a fact that was accepted without question. When Montezuma dispatched a messenger to Cortez to learn if the Conquistador was the deity Quetzalcoatl, he issued the following instructions: "If, by chance, he does not like the food which you have given him, and if he is desirous of eating human flesh, and would like to eat you allow yourself to be eaten. I assure you that I will look after your wife, relations, and children...."[63] (Of course, for multiculturalists the pertinent lesson of this episode is that the Aztec welfare state was more generous than ours.)

Multiculturalists describe slavery as an evil imported to America from Europe. However, nearly every American Indian tribe practiced some form of slavery. The Aztecs used slave labor to build their spectacular cities; they also used slaves as sacrificial livestock. "Citizenship" itself under the Inca and Aztec regimes was tantamount to slavery. People were property that could be casually disposed of, at any time and in any quantity chosen by their rulers.

In 1487 a warlord named Tlacaelel, who had long been the power behind the Aztec throne, organized a temple dedication in Tenochtitlan in honor of Huitzilopochtli, the hummingbird-god. For four days and nights sacrificial victims were paraded four abreast up the temple steps and slaughtered.[64] Estimates of the final death toll run as high as 136,000 people.[65] From our perspective, one that is distorted by the genocidal accomplishments of Hitler and Lenin's disciples, a death toll in the "merely" tens of thousands is not particularly impressive. But Aztec ritual sacrifice was not the tidy, impersonal affair that modern killing has become. Each priest had to restrain his victim by main force while plunging an obsidian dagger into his breast.

The Incas, whose rulers were less bloodthirsty than the Aztec elite, are looked upon favorably by multiculturalists because of their sophisticated irrigation system and food distribution network. But the Inca system of government, as Peruvian novelist Mario Vargas Llosa instructs us, involved a "vertical ... totalitarian structure". The Inca society was "a beehive — laborious, efficient, stoic."[66]

As the following chapters will illustrate, these glimpses of the totalitarian theocracies adored by multiculturalists may prefigure the emerging global state — a socialist despotism founded upon a pagan worldview. Under a fully-realized new world order, all of the earth's inhabitants would know the suffering of being consigned to an Indian reservation — forever.

Chapter 7

One World Under Gaia

We have now a new spirituality, what has been called the New Age movement.... This is now beginning to influence concepts of politics and community in ecology.... This is the Gaia [Mother Earth] politique ... planetary culture.

— William Irwin Thompson
founder of the Lindisfarne Association[1]

I believe the appropriate symbol of the Cosmic Christ ... is that of Jesus as Mother Earth crucified yet rising daily.... [T]he symbol of which I speak holds the capacity to launch a global spirituality of untold dimensions appropriate to the third millennium.

— Globalist theologian Matthew Fox[2]

Each person must learn to think like Earth, to act like Earth, to be Earth....

— Gerald Barney, founder and executive director of the Millennium Institute[3]

Jean-Jacques Rousseau, the prophet of the French Revolution, insisted, "No state has ever been established without a religious basis."[4] This was true of the murderous Revolutionary French regime, which (as the next chapter will illustrate) was based on Rousseau's "civil religion," and it was also true of the American constitutional republic, which was rooted in principles of individual liberty and accountability revealed by the God of Sinai. The word "culture" is derived from *cultus*, or adoration — i.e., worship. Every culture is rooted in religious assumptions. As the previous chapter documented, the UN is seeking to extinguish

America's traditional Western, Biblical culture in the interest of promoting a "Biological outlook." But that worldview is just one part of a larger religious view which guides and inspires the UN and its allies.

Promoting "Understanding"

According to Robert Muller, a former UN Assistant Secretary-General, "If Christ came back to earth, his first visit would be to the United Nations to see if his dream of human oneness and brotherhood had come true."[5] Muller has suggested that the UN itself symbolizes "the body of Christ" and that people world wide should "display the UN flag in all houses of worship."[6]

For Muller, world government is both an inevitable political development and an indispensable step toward spiritual fulfillment:

> I have come to believe firmly today that our future, peace, justice, and fulfillment, happiness and harmony on this planet will not depend on world government but on divine or cosmic government.... [M]y great personal dream is to get a tremendous alliance between all major religions and the U.N.[7]

A foreshadowing of this proposed global religious alliance is the world body's "Temple of Understanding," which was constructed on 50 acres by the Potomac River in Washington, DC. Although some of the $5 million devoted to the construction of the Temple and the establishment of its "Non-Profit, Tax-exempt Corporation for Educational Purposes" came in the form of small individual donations, sponsors of the project included many of the usual suspects, such as John D. Rockefeller IV (CFR), socialist leader Norman Thomas, and Robert S. McNamara (CFR).[8]

The design of the Temple building is suggestive of the worldview which inspired its construction. A pamphlet published by the Temple's corporation prior to the building's completion explains its architectural symbolism: "Radiating from [the] central hall will extend six wings, each to represent one of the six religions of the world which are international in scope: Hinduism, Judaism, Buddhism, Confucianism, Christianity and Islam." The intended effect is that of "a sun with six radiating rays." The central hall is capped by a glass dome shaped like a cut diamond; this dome remains constantly illuminated at night "in order to indicate, symbolically, that even while the world sleeps, the light of understanding continues to shine."[9] The priesthood which helped create and operate the Temple of Understanding is the United Lodge of Theosophists of New York, through the tax-exempt Lucis Trust.[10]

The Lucis Trust has also maintained the Meditation room at the UN headquarters (which is depicted on the cover of this book). Designed in 1952 by the late Dag Hammarskjold, the room is bereft of any conventional religious symbols, containing instead "a rectangular six-ton block of iron ore lit by a single shaft of light and a muted abstract painting at the far end of the small room, similarly illuminated."[11] The significance of the meditation room is explained by Theosophist authors Eunice and Felix Layton, who connect the room's symbolism with "the story of the descent of the divine into every human life, its apparent death and burial in the material world and its inevitable final triumphant resurrection."[12]

Of course, the UN's concept of the "divine" represents a radical departure from the views of most Americans. Mohammed Ramadan, president of the UN's Society for Enlightenment and Transformation, has opened the UN's headquarters to all varieties of "spiritual sages" — mystics, "channelers," UFO enthusiasts, and the like. He explains: "As 'international civil servants,' we often feel our colleagues are here by divine appointment to serve the world through the United Nations.... Our society's role is to further this divine service by serving the servers, teaching them and inspiring them, whether here in the headquarters or in the field."[13]

Ramadan and his comrades take their ministry quite seriously, according to the *Boston Globe*: "From a small, basement headquarters at the United Nations, Ramadan and other spiritual seekers have established several metaphysical associations with the intention of radiating karmic energy into the upper reaches of UN headquarters, where Secretary General Boutros Boutros-Ghali and other eminent diplomats work."[14] But Boutros-Ghali and his comrades are not the only ones who are spreading the happy tidings of what Robert Muller describes as "cosmic government."

Havel's Globalist Oration

On July 4, 1994, visitors to Philadelphia's Independence Hall received an unexpected primer in "cosmic government" by Czech President Vaclav Havel, who was on hand to receive the Independence medal. Speaking in the shadow of a building in which America's Founders had declared their "firm reliance on the protection of Divine Providence" in their effort to obtain American independence, Havel urged Americans to surrender themselves into the embrace of a syncretistic global faith.

According to Havel,

Today, many things indicate that we are going through a transitional period, when it seems that something is on the way out and something else is painfully being born.... The artificial world order of the past decades has collapsed, and a new, more just order has not yet emerged. The central political task of the final years of this century, then, is the creation of a new model of coexistence among the various cultures, peoples, races, and religious spheres within a single interconnected civilization.[15]

This "single interconnected civilization," according to Havel, must be founded upon a concept of human rights "anchored in a different place, and in a different way, than has been the case so far."[16] Havel finds the rudiments of this worldview in "postmodern science," beginning with the "Anthropic Cosmological Principle" — the idea that mankind is not "just an accidental anomaly ... we are mysteriously connected to the entire universe, we are mirrored in it, just as the entire evolution of universe is mirrored in us." To whom or to what does mankind owe thanks for this felicitous state of affairs? Eschewing the Biblical tradition, which most Americans would consult for an answer, Havel chose instead to cite the "Gaia Hypothesis," the concept that "the organic and inorganic portions of the Earth's surface form a single system, a kind of mega-organism, a living planet — Gaia — named after an ancient goddess who is recognizable as an archetype of the Earth Mother in perhaps all religions." Furthermore, in a fashion peculiar to "post-modern science," this "hypothesis" serves double duty as a religious dogma: "According to the Gaia Hypothesis, we are parts of a greater whole. Our destiny is not dependent merely on what we do for ourselves, but also on what we do for Gaia as a whole. If we endanger her, she will dispense with us in the interests of a higher value — that is, life itself."[17]

Quoting an anonymous philosopher who once said, "Only a God can save us now," Havel declared: "Yes, the only real hope of people today is probably a renewal of our certainty that we are rooted in the Earth and, at the same time, the cosmos.... We are not here alone nor for ourselves alone, but that we are an integral part of higher, mysterious entities against whom it is not advisable to blaspheme."

Who are "The Masters"?

Who are these "higher, mysterious entities" referred to by Havel, whom we fail to propitiate at our peril? This question was never treated in any of the scores of articles which were written about Havel's speech. One clue to their identity may be found in the fact that a significant portion of Havel's speech was reprinted in *Share International*, a journal produced by the Non-Governmental Organization of the same name in association with the UN's Department of Public Information. *Share International*'s chief editor is Benjamin Creme, a British theosophist who claims to speak on behalf of "Lord Maitreya."

According to Monte Leach, the United States editor for *Share International*, Maitreya is the most exalted member of the "Spiritual Hierarchy" of the "Ascended Masters," who intervene in human affairs periodically in order to assist mankind's evolution. Creme announced in 1982 that Maitreya, whom he designated "the Christ," is presently on earth and appearing occasionally to minister among men. Furthermore, according to Leach, "Now, for the first time in thousands of years, the Masters are returning to work openly among humanity. Not since the Atlantean era in pre-history has such a thing happened. In a way, it's unprecedented. They usually work through disciples, like Buddha. But now they're among us and ready to help our world take its next step."[18]

The New World Religion

At or near the top of the "Master's" agenda for humanity, according to South African theosophist Aart Jurriaanse, is the creation of "the One Church and the New World Religion." Writing in the December 1994 issue of *Share International*, Jurriaanse explains:

> This great objective of eventually gathering all peoples of the world into the one great Universal Church, is the task of Masters Koot Hoomi and Morya, assisted by the Master Jesus [as Creme and his followers understand him].... It is out of the present religious turbulence that the New World Church is eventually going to evolve. These great changes must inevitably take time, but will come sooner than is generally expected.[19]

It was through Helena Petrovna Blavatsky, a 19th-century Russian occultist, that Koot Hoomi and Morya expressed their will. Leach explains that "Blavatsky was the first in recent times to talk about the Masters, and that was the first phase of the modern teaching. The second phase came with Alice Bailey, who expanded the teaching. The third phase began just a little over a decade ago" [20] with Benjamin Creme's annunciation of Maitreya's advent. To understand the pedigree of the UN's New World Religion, it is useful to review the works of Blavatsky, who is universally acclaimed as the "mother of the New Age."

The provenance of the term "theosophy" is uncertain. Hermetic brotherhoods of the 18th century, including those associated with the Illuminati, incorporated theosophist concepts in their canons, along with other mystical and cabalistic tenets.[21] According to Blavatsky, the "Masters" led her to Tibet where she underwent "certain initiations" which introduced her into the secrets of the "ancient wisdom."[22] In 1874, Blavatsky travelled to the United States to spread her message of "enlightenment." A year later she founded the Theosophical Society, which was intended "to collect and diffuse a knowledge of the laws which govern the universe."[23] Blavatsky claimed to be a spiritual tuning fork that vibrated along the same wavelength as the hidden "Masters" of the occult Brotherhood. Two years after founding the Theosophical Society, Blavatsky published her magnum opus: *Isis Unveiled*, a farrago of mysticism and poorly parsed pseudo-science which consumed more than 1,200 pages. According to Col. Henry Steel Olcott, a disciple of Blavatsky, *Isis Unveiled* was written under the spiritual guidance of "several Initiates or Adepts of the Occult Brotherhood, one or two of whom are known to some extent, the others practically unknown." While Blavatsky dutifully scribbled away, recalls Olcott, "one or another of these Initiates temporarily overshadowed her outer form and used it."[24] For instance, Blavatsky herself told an acquaintance: "I am writing *Isis*; not writing, rather copying out and drawing that which *She personally* is showing me."[25]

Photographs of Blavatsky demonstrate irrefutably that she was not an ancient Egyptian goddess, and the product of her pen proves just as conclusively that she was neither a scientist nor a theologian. However indigestible Blavatsky's scribblings may be to friends of the English language, they have proven to be irresistible to occult-minded intellectuals and spiritual pilgrims. It was Blavatsky who pioneered, over a century ago, the tenets of the "post-modern science" which so enchanted Havel. Furthermore, in anticipation of the "Gaia Hypothesis," Blavatsky described the Earth as a *"living* organism."[26]

Like Havel, Blavatsky issued stern warnings about "blasphemy" — and presented a rather remarkable definition of that dire offense: "To accept the Bible as a 'revelation' and nail belief to a literal translation, is worse than absurdity — it is a blasphemy against the Divine majesty of the 'Unseen.'"[27] She also dismissed the Biblical God as "an idol [and] a fiction...."[28] One entire chapter of her work is devoted to "Christian crimes and Heathen Virtues" — an apt summation of the approach favored in "multiculturalist" history. Indeed, subverting Christianity appeared to be her chief preoccupation: "The present volumes have been written to small purpose if they have not shown ... that Jesus, the Christ-God, is a myth...."[29]

It was Blavatsky's mission to destroy the Biblical worldview in order to clear the way for the restoration of a different spiritual order: *"[T]he religion of the ancients is the religion of the future."*[30] One illustration of that ancient religion was offered by the Biblical story of the Tower of Babel. Blavatsky fondly wrote that Babel's builders "were astrologers and adepts of the primitive Wisdom-Religion, or ... what we term the Secret Doctrine."[31] Her desire to invert the Biblical message led her to rehabilitate Cain: "Cain is a murderer, but he is also the creator of nations, and an inventor" — and thus, apparently, a worthy exemplar for those who seek the "Secret Doctrine."[32]

But who, exactly, are those "higher, mysterious entities" — those whom Theosophists describe as the "Masters, Adepts, or Mahatmas ... The Elder Brethren, the Brotherhood of the Masters of Wisdom, the Occult Brotherhood, the Universal Mystic Brotherhood"? [33] According to Theosophist doctrine, these are individuals "who have evolved spiritually well beyond the ordinary human level" and "are concerned about struggling humanity and in subtle ways guide the evolution of the planet and of individuals."[34] So subtle is the Brotherhood's supervision, according to Theosophist doctrine, that "like the ideal ruler described in the Tao Teh Ching, they lead without anyone knowing it, so that people say, 'we did it ourselves.'"[35]

It was these "entities" who allegedly guided Blavatsky's hand as she wrote, and fueled her lust to invert the Bible's message. It was therefore the Occult Brotherhood who prompted Blavatsky to write that "The Great Serpent of the Garden of Eden and the 'Lord God' are identical."[36] This appalling blasphemy was given more extensive treatment in Blavatsky's 1888 work *The Secret Doctrine*, in which she stated (in an apparent self-contradiction) that Lucifer "is higher and older than Jehovah."[37] In that work, Blavatsky divulged the identity of the Occult Brotherhood — those whom Col. Olcott designated "the 'Brothers,' 'Adepts,' 'Sages,' 'Masters,' as they have been variously called."[38] She stated that the "Lords of Wisdom" are "Satan and his Host."[39]

For those who hadn't the appetite to plow through the recondite pages of Blavatsky's works in pursuit of this tidbit, she offered a more accessible token of her religious convictions. On September 15, 1887, Blavatsky unveiled a monthly journal called *Lucifer*, "A Theosophical Magazine, designed to 'bring to light the hidden things of darkness.'"[40] Under the leadership of Annie Besant, the Fabian Socialist who became the president of the Theosophical Society, the journal's name was changed to *The Theosophist*. However, the publication remained linked to the Lucifer Press, which later changed its name to the Lucis Trust — the entity which helped create the UN's "Temple of Understanding" and Meditation room.[41]

"Universal Brotherhood"

More than any other movement or group, Blavatsky's Society is responsible for the movement toward syncretism and the dissemination of Eastern mysticism in the United States. Joscelyn Godwin of Colgate University points out that "it had always been the intention of the Theosophical Society to overcome the barriers between religions and peoples, indeed 'to form a nucleus of the Universal Brotherhood of Humanity, without distinction of race, creed, sex, caste or color.'"[42] Blavatsky herself stated that her desire was "to gather the oldest of the tenets together and to make of them one harmonious and unbroken whole." She insisted,

> The teachings, however fragmentary and incomplete ... belong neither to the Hindu, the Zoroastrian, the Chaldean nor the Egyp-

tian religion, neither to Buddhism, Islam, Judaism nor Christianity exclusively. *The Secret Doctrine* is the essence of all these. Sprung from it in their origins, *the various religious schemes are now made to merge back into their original element....* [Emphasis added][43]

Blavatsky would probably recognize the UN's Temple of Understanding as the architectural embodiment of these aspirations.

Because Blavatsky's concept of "brotherhood" is both pantheistic and Luciferian, she "despised every form of institutional Christianity."[44] Professor Godwin observes that while Blavatsky and her followers took "the terrifying step of renouncing, even blaspheming, [their] own religious tradition," they proselytized on behalf of Eastern mysticism:

> [Blavatsky's] Society, its members, and its offshoots became the main vehicle for Buddhist and Hindu philosophies to enter the Western consciousness, not merely as an academic study but as something worth embracing. In so doing, they paved the way for ... the oriental gurus who have taken up residence in the West. They introduced into the vernacular such concepts as karma and reincarnation, meditation, and the spiritual path. Together with the Western occult tradition, the Theosophists have provided almost all the underpinnings of the 'New Age' movement....[45]

Of course, Blavatsky's political influence has been quite substantial as well. In his recent work, *The Theosophical Enlightenment*, Professor Godwin points out that Blavatsky's theosophy was a product of the union of 18th-century Enlightenment rationalism — typified by the works of Voltaire and Diderot — and the "practical occultism" of many individuals and groups, including Adam Weishaupt's Bavarian Illuminati.[46] Godwin observes that "The Theosophical Society ... holds a crucial position as the place where all these currents temporarily united, before diverging again."[47] In 1970, leftist author Kurt Vonnegut (who is an original co-endorser of Planetary Citizens, a New Age group which enjoys "consultative status" at the UN[48]) offered this tribute to Blavatsky: "At a minimum, Madame Blavatsky brought America wisdom from the East which it very much needed, which it still very much needs.... She was a citizen of the world."[49]

The Occult Gateway

For some, the New Age movement has become the cultural wallpaper of our time: At best decorative, at worst tacky, but in any case unobtrusive. For others it is valuable chiefly as a source for facile comedy. However, the Luciferian emphasis of Blavatsky's writings — which are, in essence, the founding canon of the New Age religion — should obviously be troubling to those who profess a Biblical faith. Furthermore, when "International Civil Servants" and world leaders like Vaclav Havel preach renunciation of nationalism and submission to "higher, mysterious entities" as political imperatives, even those who are otherwise untroubled by blasphemy should take notice. The New Age movement provides globally minded political leaders with a political theodicy — a doctrine which can rationalize the mysterious workings of the omnipotent world government and comfort those who would be oppressed and impoverished by the omnipotent global state.

This is not to say that Blavatsky's intellectual offspring intend to allow subjects of a world government to retain the sovereignty of their conscience. Any residual ambiguity in this regard can be relieved by consulting the works of David Spangler, who was co-director of Scotland's occult Findhorn Community, an early endorser of Planetary Citizens, and is presently a faculty member of the Lindisfarne Institute, a Rockefeller-funded New Age "think-tank" with offices in Manhattan's Cathedral of St. John the Divine.[50]

Spangler describes the "four levels at which the New Age can be explored."[51] First, there is "a superficial level, usually in a commercial setting. A quick perusal of *New Age* magazine [on whose masthead Spangler's name used to appear] or *East West Journal*, both of which have national distribution, or of any of the many smaller new age-oriented publications will demonstrate this application: one can acquire new age shoes, wear new age clothes, use new age toothpaste, shop at new age businesses, and eat at new age restaurants where new age music is played softly in the background." Or, for that matter, children can be exposed to New Age themes through cartoons, popular music, and other supposedly "benign" forms of entertainment.

Spangler continues: "The second level is what I call the 'new age as glamour.' This is the context in which individuals and groups are living out their own fantasies of adventure and power, usually of an occult or millenarian form." At this level, the proselytes envelop themselves in "a private world of ego fulfillment" through such things as science-fiction fantasies. Some may find themselves succeptible to the New Age concepts which suffuse the Star Trek subculture, or George Lucas's Star Wars trilogy.[52]

The third level, states Spangler, is "the new age as an image of change. Here the distinguishing characteristic is the idea of transformation itself, usually expressed as a paradigm shift. This image of the new age is the one most popularly presented to the public, in books such as Willis Harman's *An Incomplete Guide to the Future*, Marilyn Ferguson's *The Aquarian Conspiracy*, and physicist Fritjof Capra's *The Turning Point*. It is the level discussed in many international and regional conferences, debated by futurists and social theorists, and explored in government projects such as the Global 2000 report to President Jimmy Carter."

But the political, social, and economic alterations discussed — and, to an extent, implemented — at level three are merely a prologue to level four, which Spangler defines as "fundamentally a spiritual event, the birth of a new consciousness, a new awareness and experience of life." Spangler specifies that a definitive example of the fourth level of the new age was offered by the Luciferian Theosophical Society.[53]

Spangler presented a sampling of the spiritual "truths" to be gained at the fourth level in his book *Reflections On the Christ*. According to Spangler:

[T]he path to the Christ comes from Lucifer.... He stands no longer as the tester or the tempter but as the great initiator, the one who hands the soul over to the Christ and from the Christ on into even greater realms.... Lucifer works within each of us to bring us to wholeness, and as we move into a new age, which is the age of man's wholeness, each of us in some way is brought to that point which I term the Luciferic initation, the particular doorway through which the individual must pass if he is to come fully into the presence of his light and his wholeness.... Lucifer comes to give us the final gift of wholeness. If we accept it then he is free and we are free. *That is the Luciferic initiation. It is one that many people now, and in the days ahead, will be facing, for it is an initiation into the New Age.* [Emphasis added][54]

Accordingly, the challenge for Luciferians is to find some way to guide the world's peoples carefully into a new age "Luciferic initiation." Spangler suggests that this might be accomplished by appropriating the sacred name of Christ as a symbol for the New Age gospel of Luciferian universalism:

The need of our time is to allow the image of the Christ to grow in our minds to become truly holistic and not a symbol of a particular group of people or of a particular ideology. We may need to drop the name itself because of its historical and cultural connotations, or we may need to invest a new, more universal, more holistic meaning into that name, one that is truly planetary and inclusive of all life-forms and manifestations on our world. In short, the Christ needs to be our doorway into a state of dynamic beingness and relationship in which we become planetary, universal, in our outlook and behaviour.[55]

One of the main vehicles through which religious individuals are being led to adopt Spangler's "planetary" outlook is the global environmentalist movement, which seeks to redirect the devotion of worshippers from the Creator to the Creation.

The Gospel of Gaia

In 1990, as though an unseen hand had thrown a switch, nearly every segment of the "social justice industry" suddenly redirected its energies away from supporting Marxist insurgencies in the Third World to laboring on behalf of "Gaia." The "class struggle" was suddenly redefined as a global quest for "sustainable development"; this led to the creation of what has come to be known as "Watermelon environmentalism" — green on the outside, red within. This sudden doctrinal shift was noted and assimilated by the globalist movement's religious auxiliary.

Seeking to "empower" congregations to "think globally and act locally" for Earth Day 1990, The Greenhouse Crisis Foundation and the Eco-Justice Working Group of the National Council of Churches published *101 Ways To Help Save The Earth*, a liturgical guide which presented "Fifty-two Weeks of Congregational Activities to Save the Earth." The program was purged of every remnant of the Christian calendar, making Earth Day the central observance. Although Christmas and Easter were cast away, congregations were encouraged to take note of such new "holidays" as "World Environment Day" (the anniversary of the founding of the United Nations Environment Program) and the UN-designated "Environmental Sabbath" in June.

Some secular "holidays," safely free from the taint of Biblical religion, are retained in order to be infused with an ecologically correct meaning. In the "reformed" calendar, Mother's Day becomes Gaia Day, as worshippers are instructed to "Include images of the Earth as 'mother' in your celebrations of Mother's Day." The Fourth of July is recast as a day to celebrate "freedom from pollution." Thanksgiving, an observance with an inescapable Biblical pedigree, is retained but carefully coopted: Congregations are admonished to "Give thanks for the gift of food from the environment and for those who produce it." Those still acquainted with the historic origins of Thanksgiving will notice a crucial omission in this formulation.[56]

Although some might contend that this program is intended to supplement Christian worship, the unmistakable truth is that the revised eco-calendar is designed to supplant the Christian calendar: One cannot "supplement" the Biblical worldview with assumptions derived from a directly contradictory worldview.

Gaia's adepts are continuing to spread the "good news" of pagan globalism. In 1991, HarperSanFrancisco books, a publishing house which wages a jihad against the Christian faith, published a collection entitled *Earth Prayers From Around the World: 365 Prayers, Poems, and Invocations for Honoring the Earth.* The volume contains a daily liturgical calendar which describes the various high holy days of environmentalism and prescribes the proper "earth prayer" for each occasion. The editors of the collection explain, in terms familiar to students of Blavatsky, that "the prayers in this book remind us of [the] universal marriage of matter and spirit.... They make it clear that we humans are not here simply as transients waiting for a ticket to somewhere else. The Earth itself *is* Christos, *is* Buddha, *is* Allah, *is* Gaia."[57]

The book's contents are a Babylonian hodgepodge of Biblical quotations, literary excerpts, New Age affirmations, shamanistic chants, and pagan invocations composed by the likes of theosophist/Fabian socialist Annie Besant, Ho Chi Minh, black communist author W.E.B. DuBois, and Nicaraguan communist leader Ernesto Cardenal. The collection also includes the prayer written for the UN's Environmental Sabbath program.[58]

Of course, Gaia's book of common prayer will be of little use without a congregation. On October 4, 1993, representatives from 75 "mainline" religious denominations met with Vice President Al Gore to create the "National Religious Partnership for the Environment" (NRPE). On that occasion Gore predicted, "This new partnership is going to have a ripple effect throughout the religious community, the scientific community, and throughout this country and in other countries as well."[59]

The Partnership is a coalition of four component groups: the National Council of Churches, the U.S. Catholic Conference, the Evangelic Environmental Network, and the Consultation on the Environment and Jewish Life. It also has what is described as a "consultative relationship" with the Union of Concerned Scientists and such scientists as Stephen Jay Gould, Carl Sagan, and E.O. Wilson. A statement issued by the Partnership's leaders announced, "Ancient faith communities are hereby resolving to in-

171

tegrate a new world historical challenge throughout all dimensions of religious life.... This is not only a contribution to global justice and sustainability but *an affirmation of what it must mean from now on to be truly and fully religious* (emphasis added)."[60] According to Paul Gorman, the NRPE's executive director, the group "represents the full and formal entry of the religious community into environmental work."[61]

Gorman has stated that his organization represents 53,000 congregations encompassing more than 100 million "heartland, mainstream, religious Americans."[62] However, the Partnership was not summoned into existence to satisfy the eco-passions of religious Americans, nor is it accountable to them. Rather, it received its "mandate" and funding from the same nexus of tax-exempt foundations that has enriched the coffers of Establishment environmental organizations since the late 1960s. Between October 1992 and June 1993, the Partnership received more than $3.5 million from foundations.[63] Furthermore, the mainstream Christians and Jews supposedly represented by the Partnership may find it peculiar that the organization's office is located at the Cathedral of St. John the Divine, which also houses the globalist "Temple of Understanding" and the office of the Lindisfarne Association, a Luciferian group.[64]

In his speech at the Partnership's inauguration, Gore declared: "This will trigger the beginning of grass roots activities in tens of thousands of congregations throughout this nation focusing on the environment and environmental justice."[65] This centrally-directed "grass roots" effort produced some interesting results:

• The Christ the Good Shepherd Eastern Orthodox Church in St. Louis held an Epiphany service, entitled "The Great Blessing of the Waters," on the banks of the Mississippi. The congregation's children threw an old Ethiopian cloth into the river in a gesture which supposedly symbolized "the guardianship of the world and sanctification of the water."

• The Temple Emmanuel in Lowell, Massachusetts, a Reformed Jewish congregation, has conducted a bar/bat Mitzvah for its solar-powered light. Furthermore, "At each equinox and solstice, the turning of the season is liturgically marked by services such as the autumn 'Yaacov's Lantern' ... and the winter 'Snow Service."

• St. Leonard's Roman Catholic Church in Louisville, Kentucky has held a "Garbage Mass" in which "all sorts of litter — bottles, cans, plastics — [are placed] around the church sanctuary." The ritual included a symbolic clearing of the sanctuary.

• Perhaps the most environmentally committed congregation is the St. John the Evangelist Roman Catholic Church in Colombia, Maryland. Tom McCarthy, Co-Chair of the congregation's Environmental Committee, reports: "St. John the Evangelist's Roman Catholic Church has a special liturgy for Earth Day Sunday in which every aspect of the worship is environmentally oriented.... Parishioners carrying an Earth Flag banner and potted plants lead the procession into the worship space.... A resource table displays environmentally sound household products."[66]

By Earth Day 1994, the NRPE's fabricated "grass roots" effort was depicted by the mainstream press as a fully realized "eco-spiritual movement" which was spawning "environmental ministries for young clerics."[67]

The "eco-spiritual" movement has no more devoted disciple than Mr. Gore, who spoke at the NRPE's inauguration. Gore's 1992 book *Earth In The Balance: Ecology and the Human Spirit* was reminiscent of Blavatsky's works: Gore's tome offered politically ambitious mysticism wrapped in patently fallacious pseudoscience. A follower of New Age shamans like John Bradshaw, Gore insists that Western industrial civilization is "dysfunctional" and that those who resist radical environmental prescriptions are "in denial." Therapeutic language like this is a direct assault on individual autonomy: After all, mentally infirm individuals cannot be trusted to exercise their rights.

In a chapter devoted to "Environmentalism of the Spirit," Gore follows Blavatsky's template, exalting pagan religious systems (Native American spiritualism, Hinduism, Ba'hai, goddess worship) while indicting the Judeo-Christian theology of human dominion over the earth for the environmental "crisis." Wonders

173

Gore: "When giving us dominion over the Earth, did God choose an appropriate technology?"[68] Attributing the origin of the belief in a single God to the Egyptian "heretic-king" Akenaton, Gore writes that monotheism was once useful because it was "a profoundly empowering idea."[69] However, according to Gore, "empowerment" must now be obtained by consulting "the wisdom distilled by all faiths." "This panreligious perspective may prove especially important where our global civilization's responsibility for the earth is concerned."[70]

Gore's neo-theosophist religious ideas service his political vision, which demands a New Common Purpose: "We must all become partners in a bold effort to change the very foundation of our civilization."[71] According to Gore, "we must make the rescue of the environment the central organizing principle for civilization."[72] This is a formula for totalitarianism on a global scale.[73]

The "Earth Charter"

The task of writing a globalist environmental catechism has fallen upon former Soviet dictator Mikhail Gorbachev and Canadian oil mogul Maurice Strong, who served as chairman of the 1992 UN Conference on the Environment and Development (the "Earth Summit") in Rio. They were commissioned by the UN to compose an "Earth Charter," an authoritative set of ethical guidelines for regulating human interactions with the natural environment. Strong is something of an enthusiast of the occult, having cooperated with the new age Aspen Institute and the Lindisfarne Association to create the Baca Grande spiritual center in Colorado's San Luis Valley.[74] There is reason to suspect that Gorbachev has been communing with the "Masters" as well.

Mikhail Gorbachev's devotion to the cause of environmentally correct religion began while he was still the dictator of the Soviet Union. Significantly, Gorby got religion at about the same time that Russia's intelligentsia re-discovered theosophy. Nineteen ninety-one, the centennial of Blavatsky's death, was designated the "International Year of Blavatsky" by the state-controlled Moscow press.[75] This fulfilled a prediction made over half a century ago by a Russian Theosophist named Nicholas Roerich, who founded a group called "Peace Through Culture" which disseminated Theosophist ideals among the Russian intelligentsia.*

In 1939, Roerich prophesied that "[t]here will come a time when [Blavatsky's] name will resound all over Russia, with dignity and respect...."[76] Mikhail and Raisa Gorbachev have played a role in keeping Roerich's memory alive, and may have thereby helped to foster the resurrection of Theosophy as an intellectual force in Russia. In 1990, Roerich's son met with Mikhail Gorbachev and persuaded the Soviet dictator to lend him a government airplane to retrieve some of his father's artwork, which the older Roerich's disciples believe contain cryptic symbols of "world awareness."[77] In that same year, Raisa Gorbachev inaugurated the "Roerich Fund."[78]

Thus it may be considered unsurprising that in recent years Gorbachev has been occupied with eco-religious pursuits. He organized the "Global Forum of Spiritual and Parliamentary Leaders for Human Survival," which brought over 1,000 political and religious leaders to Moscow.[79] That meeting led to the creation of the Green Cross/Green Crescent organization, through which Gorbachev evangelizes on behalf of Gaia. It was through his work with Green Cross/Green Crescent that Gorbachev was ordained to help compose the "Earth Charter," which is to be unveiled dur-

---

* Nor was his influence limited to Russia: Roerich was a close friend of Henry Wallace, a committed Marxist who served as FDR's Agriculture Secretary and later as his Vice President. Wallace, an enthusiast of the occult, according to John T. Flynn's *The Roosevelt Myth*, is credited with the suggestion that the U.S. dollar bill be emblazoned with the all-seeing eye, an occultic symbol; according to a recent scholarly biography of Blavatsky, it was Roerich who suggested the adoption of the all-seeing eye to Wallace. During a White House ceremony in 1935, Wallace hailed the Russian theosophist as "a great versatile genius" and "one of the greatest figures and true leaders of contemporary culture."

In letters sent to Blavatsky's Russian disciple, Wallace addressed Roerich as "My dear Guru." Those who doubt that theosophy is a threat to America's political institutions may wish to reflect upon the fact that had FDR retained Wallace as his running mate in 1944, America would have had a theosophist in the Oval Office in 1945.

ing the UN's 50th Anniversary in October 1995.

Gorbachev offered a preview of the Earth Charter during his October 17, 1994 address to the Environmental Media Association in Beverly Hills. Before a swooning crowd of Hollywood cognoscenti (vulgar practitioners of the conspicuous consumption which has supposedly wrought such hardships for mother Gaia), Gorbachev — a committed Marxist-Leninist who still seeks the destruction of religion [80] — declared, "At a time when the religious foundations of our culture are wearing thin, new value systems are needed more than ever before."[81] Feeling the unfamiliar intoxication of piety, the atheistic socialist declared: "There must be a kind of ten commandments for the environment, *something that no one would be allowed to violate*." [Emphasis added][82] It is worth noting that the Author of the original Ten Commandments did not see fit to enforce them through prior restraint.

Pantheism and Misanthropy

True to its kinship with theosophy — and, by derivation, illuminism — modern environmentalism is a doctrine of pantheism, the idea that nature, or literally everything, is divine, and that true transcendence will occur when all humanity achieves unity with nature under the direction of an enlightened master. Furthermore, environmentalism is aggressively misanthropic. Dr. Michael S. Coffman, a free market environmental consultant, points out that "if nature is god, nature itself must be sacred and 'all knowing.' Thus, nature knows best. If nature knows best, then anything that man does must be less than best." Regarding the "Biological outlook" championed by Kirkpatrick Sale and other radical Greens, Coffman observes:

> [I]f everything is equal, then everything has equal, intrinsic value. Hence, mankind must change from looking at the world from a 'man-centered' point of view ... to looking at it from a 'life-centered' perspective.... If everything is equal because it is equally god, then man has no more value than a tree, rock, water, mouse, mosquito, rattlesnake, or bubonic plague virus.[83]

As we have seen, the "biological" or "biocentric" worldview sustained the bloodthirsty Meso-American empires of the Aztecs and Incas, whose rulers looked upon human sacrifice with utter indifference.

Radical Greens have not yet ascended to Aztec-esque heights of misanthropy yet, although the zeal with which some population control advocates promote abortion is suggestive of a desire to duplicate the accomplishments of Huitzilopochtli's priesthood. The anti-human element of eco-pantheism is visible on occasion. Take, for instance, the case of the man-eating California mountain lions.

In 1990, California voters approved Proposition 117, a measure which outlawed the sport hunting of mountain lions. The state's Green lobby gulled a distracted public into believing that the typical cougar — a feral, carnivorous beast — was simply a tabby with a hyperactive thyroid. Eco-pagans, who are eager to preserve the sanctity of nature's inscrutable mysteries, are frequently ignorant regarding the natural dislocations which occur in the train of "pro-environment" actions; in the case of the ban on cougar hunting, those dislocations had literally murderous consequences.

The ban followed a decade of growth in the cougar population. The state Fish and Game Department had suggested a resumption of the cougar hunt (which had been "temporarily" banned in 1972) in order to reduce the danger to both livestock and human beings. The 1990 ban exacerbated the problems, and the human casualty count began to grow. In September 1993, a cougar attacked a ten-year-old girl near Los Angeles; two tearful park rangers reluctantly dispatched the crazed predator. The tears, by the way, were shed on behalf of the cougar, not the traumatized youngster.[84]

Other attacks resulted in physical injury to human beings. Finally, in April 1994, a woman named Barbara Schoener was attacked by an 82-pound female cougar. After the cat crushed Schoener's skull, it dragged the hapless jogger 300 feet and devoured her face and most of her internal organs. The cat was tracked down and killed by Fish and Game officials — much to

177

the outrage of the state's Green lobby. One eco-adept complained in a letter to the *Sacramento Bee*:

> We should take into account that this noble creature may well have been venting centuries of mountain-lion anger against the humans who have driven it from its land, destroyed its home, ruthlessly hunted it down, and, as the final indignity, debased it to an advertising device to sell cars.[85]

When mobs rioted in South-Central L.A., multiculturalists explained that they were releasing pent-up anger over oppression; when cougars attack, kill, and devour people, multi-speciesists explain that the animals are undergoing a similar catharsis of injustice.

According to Wayne Pacelle, a vice president of the Humane Society, those who were outraged by the killing of Barbara Schoener are guilty of using harmful stereotypes:

> The HSUS [Humane Society] accepts that individual animals judged to be a threat to people should be removed. But the injurious act of one animal should not provide a license to wreak vengeance on other members of an animal population. We are encroaching on their habitat, and we must respect that they should have a place to live as well.[86]

In other words, man enjoys no privileged status in nature and should not seek to exalt himself above other species — except, of course, for the enlightened few who are to instruct the rest of us. Presumably, from the Humane Society's point of view, relations between human and animal species should be conducted on the basis of strict equality, and the due process "rights" of animals should be treated with a fastidiousness worthy of the Warren Court.

There are those who go even further still. "Progressive" theologian Matthew Fox, an ardent practitioner of Blavatsky-style syncretism who longs for a UN-administered socialist millennium,

178

has suggested that mankind — except, perhaps, the enlightened residue to which he belongs — should be exiled from the planet, for Gaia's sake:

> It has been suggested that we call a United Species Conference — a conference far more representative than the United Nations is — and put this one question to the ten million representatives (one for each species): "Should the human species be allowed to continue on this planet?" The vote would most likely be 9,999,999 to 1 that we humans, with our dualistic hatred of earth,... be banished to some distant place in the galaxy so that Mother Earth could resume her birthing of beauty, amazement, colors, and health.[87]

Similar views were expressed by World Bank/UN adviser Norman Myers in the *Gaia Atlas of Future Worlds*. Citing the misnamed "Gaia Hypothesis," Myers states that there is a "super-interdependency that permeates all aspects all of our lives, and intimately ties in with Gaia" — whether we believe in the earth goddess or not:

> The 30 million species on Earth, with all their diverse communities, make up a system where each can make its voice heard — but only to the extent that one does not shout down the others. This contrasts with humankind's attitude to its fellow species, a highly undemocratic response.[88]

To become an authentically adult human being, proclaims Myers, it is necessary to become a citizen "of the globe and of Gaia": "[T]here is no longer any 'we' and 'they.' For the first time, and for all time, there is only 'us' — all of us humans, together with all our fellow species and other members of the Gaian community."[89]

Once again, these demented sentiments are in harmony with the UN's stated designs and ambitions. At the Rio Earth Summit in 1992, the event which produced the tree-slaughtering, 700-page *Agenda 21* blueprint for global eco-totalitarianism began with the recitation of the Declaration of the Sacred Earth. Maurice Strong invoked that declaration as he declared:

> The changes in behavior and direction called for here must be rooted in our deepest spiritual, moral, and ethical values.... The crisis transcends all national, religious, cultural, social, political, and economic boundaries.... The responsibility of each human being today is to choose between the force of darkness and the force of light.... We must therefore transform our attitudes and values, and adopt a renewed respect for the superior laws of Divine Nature.[90]

Who is to represent the "force of light" in a world benighted by the supposed obscurantism of Biblical religion? Obviously, it would be the "enlightened" adepts of Blavatsky's tradition, who will teach the toiling masses the gospel of Gaia and dictate laws which we "would [not] be allowed to violate." As the next chapter will demonstrate, the mechanism to enforce such laws is already under construction.

A 21st-Century Heaven?

Were Blavatsky not enduring the eternal recompense of her mortal actions, the achievements of her disciples would give her a well-earned sense of satisfaction. As momentum toward the creation of a New World Religion accelerates, a prophecy contained in Blavatsky's *The Key to Theosophy* work may be coming true: "[I]f the Theosophical Society survives and lives true to its mission, to its original impulses through the next hundred years ... earth will be a heaven in the twenty-first century in comparison with what it is now!"[91]

For those who observe the monotheistic faiths which Blavatsky so detested — the prospect of living in Theosophical "heaven" is anything but delightful.

CHAPTER 8

The Coming Persecution of the Faithful?

[A]n internationally famous, highly influential author on sustainable development told me bluntly, "Religion must die. It is the fundamental cause of virtually all social, economic, and ecological problems and much of the violence in the world."
— Gerald Barney, director of the Millennium Institute and former director of the Rockefeller Brothers Fund [1]

Any form of ... church conservatism is to be rejected.... To put it bluntly: No regressive or repressive religion — whether Christian, Islamic, Jewish or of whatever provenance — has a long-term future.
— Globalist theologian Hans Küng [2]

We will all be changed by this global discussion. In time, individuals will change their outlook. Societies will change their mores. Religions will interpret their beliefs differently....
— AID chairman J. Brian Atwood, speaking to the UN population control conference in Cairo [3]

There is a tacit, yet emphatic, "Or Else!" hanging from Atwood's pronouncement. What will happen to those individuals, societies, and religions which refuse to bring their mores and beliefs into conformity with the UN's desires? With the fate of the planet literally in the balance — as Al Gore and other eco-puritans would insist — will the UN and its masters abide principled disagreement and tolerate respectful dissent? Will peaceful secession be permitted to those nations or cultures which choose to opt out of

181

the new world order?

One partial answer to these questions can be found in the statement of Sir Shridath Ramphal quoted at the beginning of the first chapter: Nobody will be able to leave the "global neighborhood" because "there are no sanctuaries left — there's no place to run to." This will present insuperable obstacles to those whose cultural and religious values are of paramount importance to them. Neighborhoods, after all, have historically been defined by shared values, and those who reside within them have historically enjoyed the option to relocate to more congenial surroundings if one's present neighborhood is unsuitable. But the UN and the elites which support and control it are seeking to circumscribe this option by bringing all social functions — including religion — within the UN's jurisdiction.

A "UN of Religions"?

Almost all of the proposals to "restructure" the United Nations during the body's 50th anniversary envision some form of UN ministry of religion. Harold Stassen (CFR), who was among the signers of the UN Charter in San Francisco, has composed a working paper for UN reform which suggests the creation of "a Worldwide Conference of Religions" as a formal appendage to the UN.[4] A more detailed treatment of this idea appeared in the September/October 1994 issue of *The Futurist*. In an essay entitled "Temples of Tomorrow: Toward a United Religions Organization," Richard Kirby of the World Network of Religious Futurists and the late Earl D.C. Brewer wrote that "Religions are now headed toward what may eventually form a United Religions Organization (URO), structured in much the same way as the United Nations and sharing the same goals." Once the URO is created, they predict, it will be given the task of creating a "New Covenant" for the planet: "The URO ... will discern the nature of that covenant, and with it the *responsibilities*, rather than the *rights*, of planetary citizenship." [Emphasis added] In other words, these paid prophets of the new world order would be called upon to help keep restive religionists in line.[5]

The "Global Ethic"

Hans Küng, a globalist theologian who resides in Switzerland, may be considered the author of the first draft of the UN's "New Covenant." At a 1991 UNESCO conference in Paris, Küng and ecumenical author Leonard Swindler proposed the creation of a document which would serve as the religious equivalent of the Universal Declaration of Human Rights — a document which would define "the fundamental attitude toward good and evil, and the basic principles to carry that attitude into action." Küng also suggested "A world-wide dialogue, a global dialogue,... which will lead to the building of a consensus on a Global Ethos."[6]

Thoughtfully, by that time, Küng had already composed the first draft of the "Global Ethos" in his 1991 book *Global Responsibility: In Search of a New World Ethic*. In the spirit of the eco-pantheistic "biological worldview," Küng insists that religious conviction in the new world order must include "action in global responsibility for the whole of the biosphere.... [T]his includes a self-imposed limitation by human beings on their freedom in the present for the sake of their survival in the future" — particularly with respect to population growth.[7]

Like nearly every apologist for a global leviathan state, Küng repeatedly invokes the concept of "pluralism." However, he leaves little doubt that the practice of "pluralism" would be aggressively monolithic: "If ethics is to function for the wellbeing [sic] of all, it must be indivisible. The undivided world increasingly needs an undivided ethic. Postmodern men and women need common values, goals, ideals, visions. But the great question in dispute is: does not all this presuppose a religious faith?"[8]

Not surprisingly, Küng answers his own question: "What we need is an ecumenical world order!"[9] Once this conclusion had been reached, Küng's co-author Leonard Swindler pointed out, an event would have to be held to devise a binding Global Ethos. Stated Swindler: "The question is who will fund it and who will appoint its scholars."[10] This question was answered in 1993 at the second Parliament of the World's Religions in Chicago.

Spiritual "Swap-Meet"

Referred to derisively as a "spiritual swap-meet" by one commentator,[11] the 1993 Parliament of World Religions was in some ways a homage to the first such event, which took place as an adjunct to the Colombian Exposition of 1893. According to *The Quest*, a quarterly journal published by the Theosophical Society, the 1993 Parliament has facilitated a "Theosophical Revival," in part because the event "reminded religious scholars that the Theosophical Society had been a major participant in the first Parliament a hundred years before...."[12]

The 1893 Parliament meeting marked the beginning of the "interfaith movement."[13] In his opening address, Dr. John Henry Barrows, the chairman of the parliament, struck a note which resonated with Madame Blavatsky's desire to bring all religions into "one harmonious whole" and make them "merge back into their original element":

> Religion, like the white light of Heaven, has been broken into many colored fragments by the prisms of men. One of the objects of the Parliament of Religions has been to change the many-colored radiance back into the white light of heavenly truth.[14]

The Theosophical Society was represented at the 1893 event by Annie Besant, who went on to become president of the society in 1905. Both of the Theosophical Society's objectives — the drive for religious syncretism and the propagation of eastern mysticism — were served by the 1893 parliament. The event signalled the introduction into America of eastern religions such as Hinduism, which was represented by Swami Vivikenanda, a fellow traveller of Madame Blavatsky's society. Vivikenanda, a minor figure in the event, urged religious assimilation as a means of promoting "tolerance" and condemned "fundamentalism" as the source of the world's enduring misery.[15]

The 1893 Parliament's official transcript records that Vivikenanda's impact upon most of the assembled religious leaders was negligible.[16] However, a small but influential number of the delegates took the Swami's message to heart and devoted themselves to preaching assimilation and modernism to their congregations.[17] Over the decades a multiculturalist myth has flourished, in which Vivikenanda is portrayed as a gentle, learned advocate of tolerance whose eloquence utterly captivated the parliament.

In the late 1980s, a small group of Vivikenanda's followers in Illinois and Wisconsin began preparations for an event to commemorate the 100th anniversary of the Swami's address.[18] The leader of this group was a small, bespectacled man named Daniel Gomez-Ibanez, who is a trustee of the Millennium Institute, an Arlington, Virginia group that describes itself as "A non-profit organization promoting long-term integrated global thinking."[19] On January 25, 1993, Gomez-Ibanez joined a colorful collection of religious leaders around the "Peace Altar" at the UN's Temple of Understanding to inaugurate the "Year of Inter-religious Cooperation and Understanding."[20]

Joining Gomez-Ibanez at the Institute is Gerald Barney, who wrote the *Global 2000* report for the Carter Administration. (It should be recalled that Luciferian disciple David Spangler cited the *Global 2000* report as an example of "level three" of the New Age — an attempt at a political "paradigm shift.") Barney is also the former director of the national program for the Rockefeller Brothers Fund and was editor of the Fund's report *The Unfinished Agenda*.[21] He has since compiled and published a document entitled *Global 2000 Revisited: What Shall We Do?*, which served as the primary text for the 1993 Religious Parliament. Barney also delivered the keynote address to the gathering.

As we have seen, the term "sustainable development" is currently in vogue among globalists and environmentalists; "sustainability" is measured by an individual's or an institution's willingness to submit to the authority of a global government. Barney's message to the leaders at the Religious Parliament contained an oblique ultimatum: Make your religious traditions "sustainable" — or else. It is here that we find the answer to the question implied in J. Brian Atwood's statement in Cairo: What will happen to religions which refuse to conform to the UN's "sustainability" dictates?

Barney recalled that "an internationally famous, highly influential author on sustainable development told me bluntly, 'Religion must die. It is the fundamental cause of virtually all social, economic, and ecological problems and much of the violence in the world.'" Another prominent environmental authority told Barney that Christianity was "a menace to the future of the Earth." The second unnamed "authority" told Barney, "You have done some very important work, but just think of how much more you could have done if your parents had not exposed you to the pernicious influence of Christianity!"22

According to Barney, Christianity is not a "sustainable" faith "as it is understood and practiced now." Furthermore, he condemned religious "exceptionalism," which is essentially the monotheistic belief in a universal, omniscient God. What is required of the world's religious leaders, asserted Barney, is a "reinterpretation and even [a] rejection of ancient traditions and assumptions" and an effort to synthesize "a 'sustainable' faith tradition on earth ... a faith such that if everyone adopted and followed it, we would be assured a sustainable, just and humane future for Earth and her people."23 Presuming to speak on behalf of "not just all humans, but on behalf of the whole community of life," Barney made this demand of the assembled religious leaders: "Would you devote the next seven years of your lives to helping all six billion of us humans to learn from each other and from the earth how to live sustainably, justly, and humanely on the earth in the next millennium?"

Barney urged the religious leaders to create a "community of earth's faith traditions" that would organize a planet-wide spiritual "celebration of earth's entry into a new era" in the year 2000: "[Would you] bring every person, every community, and every country to the celebration with appropriate gifts?" The only appropriate "gift" a person can bring to the eco-Nativity, according to Barney, is a promise to serve Gaia with all one's soul:

> Over the next five years all five billion of us humans must prepare to die to 20th century ways of thinking and being.... Every per-

son must learn to think like Earth, to act like Earth, to be Earth....
As soon as we humans learn to think like Earth, we together will
see a new future for Earth. Then we can die in peace, all five billion
of us, to our old ways of thinking. We can cross the waters together.
And we can celebrate earth's safe arrival in a new era in a way that
will be remembered forever.[24]

If Barney's ambition is realized, at the dawn of the year 2000
all humans everywhere will be forced to bend the knee to Gaia.

The appendix to the *Global 2000 Revisited* report contains a
proposal that reads like an aberrant fantasy: it is an invitation
for heads of state and religious leaders to convene in Thingvellir,
Iceland on January 1, 2000. There, in a tent surrounding a stone
altar, the gathered leaders are to present hand-written covenants
pledging loyalty to Gaia and the world state that will govern in
her name.[25] This would compose what Barney calls "a ritual
death to and giving up of the old 20th century and its ways of
being and thinking...."[26]

What is the fascination with Thingvellir, Iceland? Barney
makes mention of the "Thingvellir Oath" of mutual support and
protection, which he believes all summit participants (and presumably everybody else in the church of Gaia) should take.[27] According to tradition, the entire nation of Iceland converted to
Christianity at the beginning of the second millennium.[28] The
ritual described by Barney would amount to a reversal of this con-
version — not only for Iceland, but for Christians around the
world. It may also be significant that the pagan religion of
Wotanism, which stressed man's supposed subordination to the
natural order, was the ancient religion of Iceland.*

The Religious Parliament was intended to produce a "consen-

* Wotanism influenced the development of proto-Nazi *volkisch* movements in
early 20th-century Germany. According to Nicholas Goodrick-Clarke's book *The
Occultic Roots of Nazism*, Wotanism "described the universe in terms of a cease-
less process of transformation through 'birth,' 'being,' 'death' and 'rebirth.'... Man
was an integral part of the unified cosmos and thus obliged to follow a single
ethical precept: to live in accordance with Nature."

sus" on behalf of a "single ethical precept," and the event ended with the signing of the "Declaration of a Global Ethic" which had been composed by Küng.[29] According to Parliament chairman David Ramage, the Global Ethic Document, which was signed by almost every religious representative present in Chicago, was composed in order to "establish an alternative framework for religion *to which people would be held accountable* (emphasis added)."[30]

The "Declaration of a Global Ethic" presumes to dictate "an irrevocable, unconditional norm for all areas of life, for families and communities, for races, nations and religions."[31] Significantly, the word *God* is not found anywhere in the Global Ethic document; this omission was necessary to placate the representatives of "non-theistic" belief systems (such as Buddhism, Taoism, and various humanist philosophies) who attended the Parliament. The acceptance of the "Global Ethic," according to the document, is the *sine qua non* of becoming "authentically human."[32] Students of 20th-century totalitarian movements are quite familiar with the common fate of those found to be less than "authentically" human.

Apparently, "authentic" humans have little use for individual rights. The document asserts that individual freedom cannot be allowed except in the context of "global responsibility": "Self-determination and self-realization are thoroughly legitimate so long as they are not separated from human self-responsibility and global responsibility, that is ... responsibility for fellow humans and for the planet Earth."[33] Apparently, we will be free to do as we are told to do by a global government. Property rights are also defined away: "no one has the right to use her or his possessions without concern for the needs of society and Earth."[34] Schoolchildren are to be taught that freedom to own property is limited by the needs of the "common good" of the global community.[35]

Among the Global Ethic's "Irrevocable Directives" is a "Commitment to a culture of tolerance" which suggests that religious leaders who preach "intolerance" (however the offense may be defined) should be punished by the loss of their congregations:

"When [representatives of religion] stir up prejudice, hatred, and enmity towards those of different belief, or even incite or legitimate religious wars, they deserve the condemnation of humankind and the loss of their adherents."[36] While no sane and sensible person encourages or sustains prejudice, sane and sensible people should rebel at the thought of an entity capable of imposing the sanctions implied by this passage.

Stalking "Fundamentalists"

Ecumenicist religious leaders have wasted no time in the effort to define "authentic" religious belief. In February 1994, 500 Christian and Jewish clergymen from 90 countries gathered in Jerusalem for the "Religious Leadership in Secular Society" conference. The topic of "religious fundamentalism" was featured prominently at this conference — a somewhat understandable choice in light of the bloodshed which has tragically resulted from contending claims upon a city revered by the three great monotheistic religions.[37] However, the conference sought to indict "fundamentalism" as a global menace. The consensus at the Jerusalem meeting was summarized by *Washington Times* reporter Larry Witham: "Extremist religion is on the rise globally in reaction to secularism, demanding that conventional Judaism, Christianity and Islam provide a better alternative...."[38]

According to Monsignor Michael Sabbah, the Roman Catholic patriarch of Jerusalem, "authentic religious leadership has to deal with religious extremism." This note was taken up by Archbishop of Canterbury George Carey, who urged leaders of the three monotheistic religions to weed out the extremes from their respective faiths. Carey suggested that an enhanced interfaith movement — perhaps akin to that which created the Parliament of World Religions — could lead to "moderating, whenever possible, unstable and *pathological* faith expressions" [Emphasis added]; his preferred illustration of such "pathological" faith was Waco's Branch Davidian sect, which perished as a result of an unprovoked federal blitzkrieg.

Although Carey respectfully cited the example of the Jewish

freedom fighters who died at Masada rather than submit to Roman Rule and the early Christian martyrs, he disclosed a rather different estimate of the Davidians: "What made the Davidians dangerous ... was not that they believed deeply, but that what they believed was enslaving."[39] Apart from theological matters which will be adjudicated in the eternities, it has never been shown that the beliefs of the Davidians presented a danger to anyone, nor has Carey or anybody else vindicated the wisdom of an armed government raid which "liberated" that small sect from the travails of mortality. The experience of the Branch Davidians is of some relevance to those who wish to know how "inauthentic" religious groups will fare under the new world religion.

Americans who are concerned about religious freedom remain astounded and horrified by the federal government's infamous assault upon the Branch Davidian congregation in Waco, Texas — an operation which led to the deaths of approximately 80 American civilians, including 17 children. It is not necessary for our purposes to review the familiar — but still shocking — account of this atrocity, which has been capably chronicled elsewhere.[40] For our purposes, it is important to note the extent to which the American public — which has the unparalleled benefit of a constitutional tradition of religious liberty — passively accepted a federal government assault upon an entire religious denomination.

During the Waco siege, the opinion cartel dutifully recited warnings against the supposed danger presented by "fundamentalism." One "expert" granted generous exposure during this period was Cathy Moses of the Dallas Center for Religious Addiction and Abuse. According to Ms. Moses, fundamentalists are guilty of "religious abuse" and "the religious fanatic takes no responsibility for his words and actions...." Moses directs her efforts toward "healing" the "Adult Child of a Religious Fanatic" — a type which she assures us is plentifully represented among America's adult population.[41]

The federal pogrom against the Branch Davidians was justified in terms similar to those used by Ms. Moses. The public was told both during the siege and following its fiery denouement, were in thrall to "cult leader" David Koresh and incapable of moral initiative. In order to "liberate" the Branch Davidians from their religious beliefs, the federal government made extensive use of the dubious skills of Rick Allen Ross, a "cult deprogrammer" with a criminal background and a dubious psychological history.* Ross has publicly expressed hostility toward all "fundamentalist" denominations, both Christian and Jewish, and has endorsed the notion that "fundamentalist" parents brainwash their children.[42]

So anxious was the federal government to "liberate" the Branch Davidian children from their religious oppression that they assaulted their home with an illegal nerve gas and precipitated a fire which killed nearly all of the denomination's remaining members. In a truly Soviet-style touch, the federal government put the survivors on trial for "conspiracy" to commit murder — after they had undergone "exit therapy" at the hands of another "cult expert."[43] The federal government's attitude regarding the deaths of 80 Americans was captured by former Rep. Jack Brooks (D-TX), who shrugged off criticism of the raid by insisting, "Those people got what they deserved."[44]

Nor was Brooks the only federal official to give voice to such damnable bigotry. The Waco holocaust was seen by President Clinton as an object lesson for those who practice politically incorrect religions. Speaking in the immediate aftermath of the

---

* Documents of the Justice Court of Maricopa County, Arizona demonstrate that Ross was convicted of jewel theft and later violated his probation by committing a second offense, that of Grant Theft by Embezzlement. A psychiatric evaluation performed by a physician at the Arizona State Hospital concluded that Ross "does not seem to identify himself with society and its laws, and believes that punishments are an injustice."

When these aspects of Ross's background were published in the wake of his involvement as a government "advisor" during the Waco siege, he admitted his criminal background but maintained that "No person was hurt or threatened in any way" by his criminal actions and that he has "paid [his] debt to society." (William Norman Grigg, "Good Enough for Government Work?" *The New American*, October 3, 1994, pg. 27; Rick Allen Ross, letter to the editor, *The New American*, November 14, 1994, pg. 2; "Waco Expertise With A Vengeance," Rick Allen Ross, letter to the editor, *The Nation*, January 2, 1995, pg. 2.)

April 19th tragedy, Mr. Clinton declared: "I hope very much that others who will be tempted to join cults and become involved with people like Koresh will be deterred by the horrible scenes they have seen.... There is, unfortunately, a rise in this sort of fanaticism all across the world. And we may have to confront it again."[45] By "fanaticism," Mr. Clinton was not referring to the irrational actions of the Bureau of Alcohol, Tobacco, and Firearms, the FBI, or disreputable anti-"cult" activists like Rick Allen Ross.

Two days after expressing what could be taken as a receptivity to future acts of violent religious persecution, Bill Clinton professed his tireless devotion to religious tolerance, telling an audience at the dedication of the Holocaust Memorial Museum that "We must find in our diversity our common humanity. We must reaffirm that common humanity, even in the darkest and deepest of our own disagreements."[46] Apparently, the creation of a "common humanity" may require the liquidation of those "fundamentalists" — like the Branch Davidians — who practice an unauthorized religion.

The chimera of a monolithic global "fundamentalist" menace has been invoked with increasing frequency during recent years. Perhaps the most labored exposition of this notion is found in "Fundamentalism: The Zeal to Heal — or Kill," a wire service story written by Sharon D. Cohen shortly after the Waco holocaust. Cohen juxtaposed an American pro-life demonstration with a lethal riot between Hindus and Moslems in India and tortured the comparison into surrendering the following lesson:

> Two news events, one common bond: Both are tied to fundamentalism — one of the world's fastest-growing religious movements. For all their differences, they share two goals: They want to change society. And they — and they alone — have the answer.[47]

The "problem" of fundamentalism — specifically, Evangelical Christian conservatives — was memorably addressed in *The Religious Right: The Assault on Tolerance and Pluralism in America*, a 193-page screed published by the Anti-Defamation

League of B'nai B'rith (ADL) which artlessly depicted the "Religious Right" as a menace to American civil society. Although the ADL smear contained criticism for conservative Catholic and Jewish groups, it targeted one particular faith community — Evangelical Christians — for specific condemnation.[48]

The ADL report could be considered a hand-me-down from the global campaign against fundamentalism. The organization's campaign to traduce conservative Evangelicals earned a rebuke from many prominent American Jewish leaders.[49] Nonetheless, the ADL's factually and morally impoverished report was quickly canonized by the Establishment media, enriching the anti-fundamentalist arsenal and helping to prepare the distracted public for further sorties against "fundamentalists."

Attacking Islam

The drive to demonize "fundamentalism" is perhaps best illustrated by the now-common caricature of Moslem "extremism." America's experience with Iran's anti-American regime — a regime installed through the connivance of the same ruling elite which sustains the UN — has had long and bitter after-effects. Events like the bombing of the World Trade Center by anti-Western Moslem extremists have had an impact as well. The residual antipathy toward Moslem fundamentalism has been carefully nurtured by elite opinion molders, who habitually compound the entire Moslem world into an undifferentiated, anti-Western menace.[50]

There are ineradicable differences which separate faithful Christians, Jews, and Moslems, and it must be admitted that history is littered with shameful acts of religious hostility and persecution which have resulted from those differences. But those possessed of a principled attachment to religious freedom must understand that rights inhere in *individuals*, not in *collectives*; one need not endorse or even respect an individual's religious views in order to defend that individual's God-given rights. Indeed, such disinterested defense of the principle of individual liberty is a necessary pre-emptive defense of one's own rights. The demonization of Islam is part of a larger globalist jihad against "fundamentalism" — which for our purposes could be defined as the "sin" of manifesting excessive belief in one's faith.

The only genuine fundamentalist menace can be found among those — of whatever religious background — whose terrestrial god is the all-powerful state. The U.S. Constitution was designed to protect God-given liberties against the ambitions of such people; the UN's "human rights" instruments, however, are designed to facilitate those malevolent ambitions.

No Refuge for the Faithful

The first liberty recognized by the U.S. Bill of Rights is freedom of religion, and the American Founders treasured that liberty enough to provide redundant safeguards for it. Despite the fact that the federal government is not permitted to make impositions beyond those specifically authorized by the Constitution, the Founders sought to protect certain freedoms — including religious liberty — explicitly in the Bill of Rights, thus providing an auxiliary safeguard for them. The UN's founding documents, which are based upon the premise that rights are the conditional gift of the state, offer no similar provision for the protection of individual rights against abuses of a global government or its auxiliaries.

As is the case with all of the other "freedoms" supposedly guaranteed by the UN's founding instruments, the UN's concept of religious liberty is purely utilitarian: It is predicated upon the idea that the individual is free to obey the whims of the governing elite. Article 18 of the UN's *International Covenants on Civil and Political Rights*, an instrument which was ratified in April 1992 by a handful of U.S. Senators, contains the following devious language:

> Everyone shall have the right to freedom of thought, conscience and religion....
>
> Freedom to manifest one's religion or beliefs may be subject only to such limitations as are prescribed by law and are necessary ...."

The First Amendment to the U.S. Constitution limits the power of government to restrict religious liberty; it simply says "Congress shall make no law respecting the establishment of religion, or prohibiting the free exercise thereof...." The various vague exceptions contained in the UN document offer   governments unlimited power to prescribe "necessary" restrictions on religious freedom. Not surprisingly, communist nations which recognized no individual liberties ratified the UN covenants with little difficulty.

In 1964, the UN Human Rights Commission proposed the creation of a declaration on religious toleration, but withdrew the proposal in the face of complaints from communist regimes.[51] When the revised declaration was adopted in 1981, it contained the following language:

> Everyone shall have the right to freedom of thought, conscience and religion. This right shall include freedom to have a religion or whatever belief of his choice, and freedom, either individually or in community with others and in public or private, to manifest his religion or belief in worship, observance, practice and teaching.

These assurances appear solid enough — but wait! The declaration also specified that "no one shall be subject to coercion which would impair his freedom to have a religion or belief of his choice."[52]

The mischief in these assurances is found in the assumption that government enjoys the privilege of parcelling out freedoms to its subjects, rather than the duty to recognize the sovereign, God-given rights of naturally free men. The UN presumes to dictate what religious freedom "shall include." It is also worth noting that while the body would forbid "coercion which would impair [the] freedom to have a religion or belief," it does not forbid coercion which would suppress *expression* of that belief — although the language quoted above might lure the inattentive into thinking otherwise. Furthermore, nothing in the religious "freedom" declaration nullifies the principle contained in the UN covenants on civil and political rights — namely, that government can proscribe individual liberties in the name of the "common good."

Significantly, under the UN's concept of religious freedom, nothing which was done to the Branch Davidians constituted an improper abridgement of rights: Every action taken by the ATF and FBI was justified as "necessary," as is every abuse imposed by dictators throughout history.

However sanguine the UN may be regarding the abuse of power by governments, the world body is not reluctant to demand revisions of religious values when they collide with global "responsibilities." In 1994, the UN Human Rights Commission held that the Sudan was in violation of the Covenant on Civil and Political Rights and the Convention on the Rights of the Child because of punishments which are inflicted under that nation's Islamic law. Gaspar Biro, the UN human rights monitor stationed in the Sudan, told Sudanese authorities that laws derived from the Koran are "irrelevant" when they conflict with UN conventions.[53]

Whatever one may think of the Koran's concept of proportionate punishment, the salient aspect of the Sudan controversy is this: The UN is on record to the effect that codes of behavior rooted in religion must yield to the world body's concept of law. This same assumption was at work in the Australian state of Tasmania, where an anti-homosexuality ordinance derived from Biblical principles was subjected to the scrutiny of the UN's Human Rights Commission. According to the December, 27, 1992 San Francisco Examiner, the UN body believed that it "could oblige the national government to use its powers ... to override Tasmania's state law."

If the UN has the power to compel the Australian national government to bring about the repeal of a Biblically-based state law, it has, in principle, the power to do the same thing anywhere, including the United States. Furthermore, America is slouching toward a similar harmonization with the UN's concept of religious "freedom."

On November 16, 1993, President Clinton signed the so-called Religious Freedom Restoration Act (RFRA), a measure which overturned the 1990 Supreme Court Decision *Employment Services vs. Smith*. The purpose of RFRA was to restore the "compelling interest" test for religious freedom decisions. This means that in order to impinge upon religious freedom, the government would have to declare a "compelling interest" in such an imposition. The problems with this approach should be obvious: The government, after all, would be given the prerogative of defining its own interests. Furthermore, a government which can assert an independent "interest" is no longer the dispassionate protector of individual liberties.

Appropriately, on the same day that President Clinton signed RFRA into law, the Senate took up the Freedom of Access to Clinic Entrances law (FACE), a measure which targets pro-life protesters for fines of up to $250,000 and prison terms of up to three years for obstructing "access" to abortion clinics. As Congressman Jim Bunning (R-KY) lamented during congressional debate over the measure, FACE makes "an individual's pro-life conviction a thought crime and [puts] a congressional stamp of approval on the pro-abortion side of the debate."[54] Rep. Jim Sensenbrenner (R-WI) has observed that "if two people are engaging in identical conduct — i.e., peaceful, non-violent civil disobedience — outside an abortion clinic but for different reasons, only the pro-life person has committed a Federal crime under FACE, and it is only a Federal crime because of the person's belief that abortion is wrong."[55]

Prior to the passage of FACE, proper state and local laws against vandalism, assault, and other crimes which may occur during an abortion protest already existed and were regularly enforced. However, the Administration and its congressional allies decided that the federal government had a "compelling interest" in criminalizing peaceful protests on one side of the most contentious social issue in recent American history. These impositions on freedom of speech, assembly, and religion are perfectly compatible with the UN Covenant on Civil and Political Rights, as they are "prescribed by law" and considered "necessary" by the federal government.

The "Universal Homogenous State"

If, under the UN's principles, a national government can impose upon religious freedom with impunity, what manner of impositions would a unified world government inflict? This is not an idle question, as some of the world's most prestigious thinkers insist that the global state will abide no competition from Biblical faith.

In 1970, Zbigniew Brzezinski, who was then a professor at Colombia University, wrote a book entitled *Between Two Ages: America's Role in the Technetronic Era.* His book was essentially a blueprint for what became the Trilateral Commission; appropriately, when David Rockefeller created the Trilateral Commission three years later, he tapped Brzezinski to be the organization's first director. Brzezinski also went on to serve as National Security Adviser to President Jimmy Carter. According to Brzezinski, we had reached the "end of ideology" and outlived the need for the great Biblical religions:

> The great religions of recorded history were [note the past tense] crucial in establishing a perspective that linked man's individual preoccupation with his inner life to a universal God, who was the source of a standard of behavior binding upon all.[56]

Christianity, according to Brzezinski, had served a historically valuable lesson by universalizing the moral concepts of Judaism and the ethical concepts of Hellenism; however, it was merely a schoolmaster to bring the world to Marxism: "Marxism represents a further vital and creative stage in the maturing of man's universal vision. Marxism is ... a victory of reason over belief...."[57] Stated Brzezinski, "[I]n the second half of the twentieth century, almost everyone — often without knowing it — is to some extent a Christian, a nationalist, and a Marxist."[58]

But now that we have reached the "end of ideology," it is time for a new synthesis — what Brzezinski calls the "emerging global consciousness" through which a "rational humanist world outlook that would gradually replace the institutionalized religious, ideological, and intensely national perspectives that have dominated modern history."[59] In short, once that which is "perfect" — the "global consciousness" — has come, that which is "imperfect" — the sovereign nation-state, doctrinaire Marxism, and supposedly obsolete Biblical religion — will be done away with.

In early 1989, just before the "miraculous" disintegration of the Soviet Bloc, former State Department official Francis Fukuyama — an advisor to the globalist RAND Corporation and a member of the Council on Foreign Relations — published an essay entitled *The End of History?* in a neo-conservative journal called *The National Interest*. Taking up where Brzezinski's "end of ideology" thesis had left off, Fukuyama declared that the Cold War was over: The "final synthesis" prophesied by the German philosopher Hegel was upon us, and doctrinaire Marxism was dead. The essay, which was reportedly read by world leaders including Mikhail Gorbachev, seemed eerily prescient when the Berlin Wall came down on November 9, 1989.

Two years later, Fukuyama embellished upon his argument in *The End of History and the Last Man*. The book, which offered a jacket endorsement from Eduard Shevardnadze, the communist ruler of Soviet Georgia, identifies the "mechanism of history" to be "a kind of Marxist interpretation of history that leads to a completely non-Marxist conclusion."[60] History's conclusion, which Fukuyama declared to be nigh upon us, is the advent of the "universal and homogeneous state" which will destroy the embattled remnants of the biblical worldview.[61] Like Marx and Brzezinski, Fukuyama dismisses Christianity as a "slave ideology" that has outlived its usefulness:

> The problem with Christianity ... is that it remains just another slave ideology, that is, it is untrue in certain crucial respects. Christianity [assumes] the realization of human freedom not here on earth but only in the Kingdom of Heaven.... According to Hegel, the Christian did not realize that God did not create man, but rather that man had created God. He created God as a kind of projection of the idea of freedom, for in the Christian God we see a being who

is the perfect master of himself and of nature. But the Christian then proceeded to enslave himself to this God that he himself created.[62]

These assertions are perfectly compatible with Hegel's thought, given that for him the state represents the "manifestation of god in the world."[63] If man creates "god" in order to serve as a "projection of the idea of freedom," the only acceptable divinity must be the "Universal and Homogenous State" which would be founded upon "liberal democratic" premises. However, in order for the Universal State to prevail, religion must either wither away or be redefined out of existence. Pointing to the example of the French Revolution, Fukuyama states that "Christianity ... had to abolish itself through a secularization of its goals before liberalism could emerge."[64]

Thus the task of the Universal State is to consummate the vision of the French Revolution:

> For Hegel, the French Revolution was the event that took the Christian vision of a free and equal society, and implemented it here on earth.... [I]t constituted a recognition that it was man who had created the Christian god in the first place, and therefore man who could make God come down to earth and live in the parliament buildings, presidential palaces and bureaucracies of the modern state.[65]

By artfully perverting the message of the Bible, Hegel and Fukuyama would make the Universal State the primary agency of salvation — a role in which it would certainly brook no interference from Christianity or any other competing religion. There is no mention in Fukuyama's book of the French revolutionary terror — an unavoidable consequence of the effort to make "god" live through the state. Accordingly, a review of the revolution and its ideological underpinnings may help us understand what the disciples of the Universal State have in mind for recalcitrant believers.

The "Civil Religion"

The religious aspect of the French Revolution was obvious to historian Arnold Toynbee:

> In the Revolution a sinister ancient religion which had been dormant suddenly re-erupted with elemental violence. This revenant was the fanatical worship of collective human power. The Terror was only the first of the mass-crimes that have been committed ... in this evil religion's name.[66]

This religion of "collective human power" — or the "General Will" — once more leads us to Rousseau. It was Rousseau who devised what he referred to as "The Civil Religion" — a doctrine that would enable the masses, in Rousseau's phrase, to "bear with docility the yoke of the public good."[67] According to Rousseau, "There is ... a purely civil profession of faith of which the Sovereign should fix the articles...." The most important of those secular articles of faith was the divinity of the state. The most serious transgression was "intolerance," which was regarded as evil not because it injured the rights of individuals, but because it challenged the authority of the state.[68] Wrote Rousseau, "whoever dares to say, 'Outside the church is no salvation,' ought to be driven from the State, unless the State is the Church, and the prince the pontiff."[69]

Rousseau described his civil religion as a "form of theocracy, in which there can be no pontiff save the prince, and no priests save the magistrates."[70] He recognized that this would be unacceptable to Christians, for whom the covenant to obey Christ enjoys pre-emptive priority in any conflict with civil authority, and for Jews, who define themselves by ancestral covenants with God. But Rousseau gave the state jurisdiction over the minds and souls of its subjects: "The subjects ... owe the Sovereign an account of their opinions *only to such an extent as they matter to the community* [Emphasis added]."[71] This rhetorical sleight of hand — giving "rights" to people and then qualifying them out of existence — is the direct ancestor of the UN's "religious freedom" non-guarantees quoted above.

Under Rousseau's arrangement the state would make belief in its dogmas compulsory, even as it denied it was doing so: "While it can compel no one to believe them, it can banish from the state anyone who does not believe them" — another foreshadowing of the UN's "declaration on religious freedom," which guarantees the freedom of conscience but provides no reliable guarantees against state coercion. Rousseau also maintained that those who resisted exile would find themselves committed to the worship of the state, under penalty of death: "If any one, after publicly recognizing these dogmas, behaves as if he does not believe them, let him be punished by death: he has committed the worst of all crimes, that of lying before the law."[72]

Under the guidance of Rousseau's ideology, the leaders of the French Revolution proclaimed a secular jihad against Christianity — first by seeking to abolish revealed religion in favor of the worship of disembodied "Reason," later by contriving a cult of the "Supreme Being" — which included mandatory worship of nature — as an ersatz religion.[73] Clerics were compelled — upon pain of death — to swear an oath to the "Civil Constitution of the Clergy," which made the church an appendage of the divine state.[74] Those who refused to take that oath were assigned the status of "refractories," persecuted, and often killed.

One region of France, the Vendée, was singled out by the revolutionary government as a hotbed of "refractory" thought; it was populated by traditional Catholics who clung to their traditional beliefs and refused to recognize the religious jurisdiction of the state. Accordingly, the central government sent the revolutionary army in force to subdue what it considered a stronghold of heavily-armed, fanatical fundamentalists. According to historian John Willson, 250,000 people were slaughtered in the Vendée between 1793 and 1799.[75] General Westermann, who presided over this genocidal atrocity, proudly recounted his exploits in a report to the revolutionary Committee on Public Safety:

> The Vendée is no more, my republican comrades! With her women and children she died under our sabers. I have just buried them in

the swamps and forests. As you ordered, the children were trampled to death by our horses, the women butchered so that they no longer give birth to little brigands. The streets are littered with corpses which sometimes are stacked in pyramids. Mass shootings are taking place in Savenay because there brigands keep turning up to surrender. We do not take any prisoners ... [because] pity is incompatible with the spirit of revolution.[76]

The "Tolerance" Trap

Of course, these crimes could not be carried out by the elite alone, and the French public did not suddenly divest itself of its previous convictions. The Terror was the bloodiest battle in a decades-long culture war in France.

Rousseau, it will be remembered, wrote that under the civil religion, there is no sanctuary for freedom of conscience when the "community" decides that it has the right to inspect private opinions. Like his anti-Christian comrades, Rousseau defined freedom of conscience in purely self-serving terms: Only enemies of "reason" were capable of intolerance. Accordingly, one prominent feature of what historians Will Durant and Peter Gay refer to as "the illuminated century"[77] was an unprecedented attack on Christianity which grew to encompass Judaism and Islam as well.

Enemies of Christianity — most of whom, like Voltaire, were also embittered anti-Semites[78] — relentlessly libelled the church in pamphlets. Voltaire himself undertook to protect homosexual friends[79] while loudly accusing Christians of practicing sexual perversions — a tactic not unfamiliar to students of contemporary homo-fascist groups like ACT-UP and Queer Nation.[80] Voltaire and his comrades condemned censorship while urging the government to censor the publications of their critics — another tactic which is familiar to students of "political correctness."[81]

Guillaume Francois Berthier, a capable and respected defender of Christianity, took note of the fashion in which the rules had been written to favor the enemies of Christianity. Writing in the *Journal de Trévoux* for July 1759, he lamented: "The custom has been established to call philosophe those who attack revealed religion, and 'persecutor' those who battle for its defense."[82] To those who insisted that Christianity was a violent, intolerant religion, Berthier offered this telling rebuke: "Unbelievers, you accuse us of a fanaticism which we do not have a semblance of possessing, while the hatred which animates you against our religion inspires in you a fanaticism whose too apparent excesses are inconceivable."[83]

Voltaire and other defenders of "tolerance" took satisfaction in the fact that Berthier and other defenders of the Church were frequently assailed by mobs when they ventured into public.[84] So extensive was the reach of the new gospel of "tolerance" that a tract entitled "The Three Most Famous Impostors: Moses, Jesus, and Mohammed" — an attack on the three monotheistic traditions — became popular in France during the mid-1700s.[85]

These tactics will be familiar to even casual observers of America's contemporary culture war, as well they should be. The same strategy used by 18th-century *illumines* is being followed by their contemporary intellectual descendants, to achieve a similar purpose. Two centuries ago, the objective was to destroy Biblical faith in Europe and replace it with the worship of the state. Today, the goal is to destroy traditional religion — whether through redefinition, adulteration, regulation, or overt persecution — as a prelude to the construction of a global superstate.

Reviewing the labors of the 18th-century *illumines*, the Durants state:

> This dream of "enlightened despots" as the leaders of human advance was the precarious [thesis] upon which most of the philosophes rested their vision of progress... And what is our faith in government but that hope revived?[86]

The wages of that faith have been murderous. In this century alone, calculates political scientist R.J. Rummel, governments have killed more than 119,400,000 people during times of "peace" — a number four times greater than the combat casualties of this century's wars and easily eclipsing the combined total of all the victims killed in acts of religious persecution in history.[87] If the disciples of "progress" realize their ambitions, government — the most sanguinary idol in human history — will enjoy a monopoly on devotion, and the UN will be the citadel of that barbaric faith.

CHAPTER 9

Ending the "Experiment on our liberties": Get *US* Out!

The most potent weapon in the collectivist arsenal is fatalism. Those who seek to destroy liberty labor to persuade free men that their problems are intractable and that "history" — which is supposedly an abstract, impersonal force — is on the side of despotism. This is perhaps the most important reason why it is necessary to understand the "conspiratorial view of history." There is ironic comfort to be found in a realization that the most destructive political developments of the past two centuries have been the product of the combined willful actions of individuals, rather than the result of the inscrutable workings of indifferent fortune. Tyranny enjoys no privileged status with respect to futurity; it is not preordained to prevail.

Although we should not underestimate the assets or the determination of the collectivist Conspiracy, we should also remember that the enemies of freedom labor beneath insurmountable disadvantages — beginning with the fact that it is easier to explain and defend the principles of liberty than it is to devise elaborate rationales for tyranny. The desire for liberty resonates with the noblest impulses of the human soul, and — as survivors of the Soviet gulag can testify — those impulses cannot be suffocated from without; rather, they must be extinguished from within. This is why we have nothing to fear from the arguments of collectivists.

Furthermore, the oligarchs who preside over the collectivist Conspiracy are aware of the tenuous hold they have on power. No better illustration of this can be found than this anxious statement from Richard Hahnen of the UN Association of the USA: "If we had a cultural revolution in this country, and the NRA replaces the Council on Foreign Relations as the leading thought... we're really in trouble."[1] The conspiratorial elites whom Hahnen serves cannot prevail by argument, nor can they ultimately prevail by force — unless honorable men and women abdicate their responsibility to learn and defend the principles of freedom.

The Resilient American Character

Fortunately, our plight is not yet terminal. As Edmund Burke wrote of the traditionalists who opposed the murderous French Revolution two centuries ago, "Thanks to our sullen resistance to innovation, thanks to the cold sluggishness of our national character, we still bear the stamp of our forefathers."[2] The same may still be said of contemporary America, despite decades of subversive efforts undertaken by a well-entrenched, conspiratorial elite.

The single greatest impediment to the ambitions of the globalist elite is the Constitution of the United States of America, which — however battered and abused — remains the indispensable bulwark of individual liberties.

In 1984, Professor James MacGregor Burns lamented:

> Let us face reality. The framers have simply been too shrewd for us. They have outwitted us. They designed separate institutions that cannot be unified by mechanical linkages, frail bridges, tinkering. If we are to "turn the founders upside down" — to put together what they put asunder — we must directly confront the constitutional structure they erected.[3]

Burns was a co-director of Project '87 and a board member of the Committee on the Constitutional System, two organizations which sought to dismantle the U.S. Constitution in favor of a more "modern" system of government. His frustration is an eloquent tribute to the Founders' handiwork, which — although embattled — remains a formidable obstacle to tyrannical ambitions. The drive to centralize government at the national and global level simply cannot succeed as long as Americans understand the basic nature of Constitutional government.

As summarized by Madison in *Federalist Paper* #45:

> The powers delegated by the proposed Constitution to the federal government are few and defined. Those which are to remain in the State governments are numerous and indefinite. The former will be exercised principally on external objects, as war, peace, negotiation, and foreign commerce.... The powers reserved to the several States will extend to all the objects which, in the ordinary course of affairs, concern the lives, liberties and properties of the people, and the internal order, improvement, and prosperity of the State.

Once these basic principles are understood, it becomes clear that the federal government has neither the right nor the responsibility to dispense foreign aid, to subsidize population control, or to participate in any of the other UN-related initiatives which have been described in this book. Furthermore, it is in the recognition that the federal government possesses only those "few and defined" powers specifically delegated to it by the Constitution that we find the key to defeating the entrenched globalist oligarchy and restoring American independence.

During the 1994 UN population control conference in Cairo, this author was able to ask U.S. delegation leader Timothy Wirth (a CFR member with an impeccable Establishment pedigree) to identify the provision of the Constitution which authorizes American involvement in population control activities. Wirth replied:

> I think the Constitution very clearly says that the powers are left to the government except that which is in interstate and foreign commerce, and in the issue of foreign commerce, the Congress has clearly over and over again authorized funding for this....[4]

Like Professor Burns, Wirth seeks to "turn the founders upside down." He apparently believes that the purpose of the Constitution is to reserve all powers to the federal government, except those specifically given to other entities. Furthermore, he contradicted himself immediately by saying that U.S. involvement in population control is authorized in the name of "interstate and foreign commerce" — which he had just said was among the powers not given to Congress.

This anecdote provides a useful representative specimen of the intellectual powers of the elite which seeks to destroy our freedom; surely Mr. Wirth and his ilk could not last long in a debate with a reasonably well-informed High School student. Furthermore, alarm over the blatant abuse of power by the federal government has helped catalyze opposition to the corrupt oligarchy which infests Washington. During a 1994 year in review program on PBS's *MacNeill-Lehrer NewsHour*, political commentator Jim Fisher pointed out that "Waco was a huge thing in Mid-America" and that there was a "Waco thread through the election" in which the semi-permanent Democratic majority was evicted from Congress.[5]

In 1994, many Americans rediscovered the truth of George Washington's oft-quoted observation, "Government is not reason; it is not eloquence; it is force! Like fire, it is a dangerous servant and a fearful master." The healthy rebellion of the American electorate may yet give rise to a new generation of statesmen who will refuse to compromise on matters of American independence and constitutional principle. A splendid example of such statesmanship was offered by the "irreconcilables" — the Senators who refused to ratify the League of Nations Covenant — whose stalwart patriotism frustrated the designs of Colonel House and his conspiratorial allies. Some Senators who were less devoted to constitutional principle suggested that the Covenant could be amended to minimize the damage it would do to American independence. However, Idaho Senator William Borah dismissed this spineless temporizing by declaring: "You can't amend treason!"[6]

The rejection of the League of Nations Covenant illustrates that although the Insiders are tenacious, *they have been beaten before, and they can be beaten again*. But statesmen of William Borah's caliber do not arise spontaneously; they are created by an educated electorate and — more importantly — they are diligently monitored by an electorate which is jealous of its God-given liberties.

Education and Activism

Edward Gibbon recalls that when the Roman Emperor Julian, a humanist with occultic affiliations, sought to restore paganism as the state religion in Rome, he forbade Christian instructors to teach grammar and rhetoric in Roman schools, insisting that "men who exalt the merit of implicit faith are unfit to claim or enjoy the advantages of science." Because the education of youth in the Roman world was entrusted to the masters of grammar and rhetoric, Julian's plan was to create "the unrivalled dominion of the Pagan sophists":

> Julian invited the rising generation to resort with freedom to the public schools, in a just confidence that their tender minds would receive the impressions of literature and idolatry. If the greatest part of the Christian youth should be deterred by their own scruples, or by those of their parents, from accepting this dangerous mode of instruction, they must, at the same time, relinquish the benefits of a liberal education. Julian had reason to expect that, in the space of a few years, the church would relapse into its primaeval simplicity, and that the theologians, who possessed an adequate share of the learning and eloquence of the age, would be succeeded by a generation of blind and ignorant fanatics, incapable of defending the truth of their own principles, or of exposing the various follies of Polytheism.[7]

Gibbon observes that the Christians of Julian's era "had much more to fear from his power than from his arguments." This is why the Emperor sought to use his power to create an intellectual monopoly.

As we have seen, a similar situation exists today. Beginning with the French Revolution, modern pagans have resumed the crusade to destroy Biblical faith and the culture which is rooted in that faith. The anti-religious efforts of the Soviet, Maoist, and National Socialist regimes are well-known and require no elaboration here. As previous chapters have sought to illustrate, this project now has its focus in the efforts of the UN, which is itself protected by the CFR's political and cultural hegemony.

But, as was the case with the embattled Church of Julian's time, we have more to fear from the Conspiracy's power than from its arguments. With relatively minimal exertion, Americans can learn enough about our constitutional system and the evils of collectivism to uproot the embedded axioms and pry open the closed premises of the Conspiracy. The Founding Fathers dealt with the challenge of establishing America's intellectual foundation while wresting our nation's independence from a vast empire, and then defending our independence from foreign predators. Granted, Providence is parsimonious in dispensing abilities of the sort which the Founders enjoyed. However, we have one advantage they were denied — the strength of their own example.

Reclaiming Our Rights

Among the most important political developments in 1994 was the passage of Tenth Amendment resolutions in California, Missouri, Hawaii, and Illinois. These resolutions, the product of grassroots activism on the part of motivated Americans, reasserted the constitutional principles expressed by Madison above, namely that the federal government's powers are "few and defined" and are merely the serviceable residue of the powers exercised by the people at the state and local level. The passage of such a resolution in California — a state containing 12 percent of the country's population — is particularly noteworthy.[8]

Furthermore, the 1994 voter revolt was, to a significant extent, a testimony to the influence of TRIM, an education project of The John Birch Society. TRIM — Tax Reform IMmediately — provides voters in all 435 Congressional districts with brief summaries of the spending votes cast by their respective Congressmen, along with basic truths about the proper role of government. One measure of TRIM's potential can be seen in the program's impact in 22 Congressional races in 1994. The educational efforts conducted in those districts helped inform electorates who then evicted 16 of the most notoriously liberal incumbents (including House Speaker Thomas Foley, a longtime member of both the

CFR and the Trilateral Commission). Four other similarly liberal Congressmen whose Districts were blanketed by TRIM bulletins declined the run for re-election, and four others eked out re-election by a margin of less than three percent.[9]

Significantly, at least one major media outlet was aware of the impact of TRIM. When *Newsweek* magazine became aware of the TRIM program, it contacted the Appleton office of The John Birch Society to ask about the program. However, the magazine elected not to mention TRIM in its coverage of the conservative electoral revolt of 1994.

Why is this? One possible answer is that *Newsweek*, like the rest of the "prestige press," seeks to persuade the public that The John Birch Society is dead, or at least irrelevant to contemporary concerns. The standard media profile of the JBS begins with some variation of this opening sentence: "The Berlin Wall has collapsed, Moscow now has a McDonald's, and the Cold War has disappeared. However, the ultra-right John Birch Society still soldiers on ..."

The assumptions here are that the collectivist threat to American liberty has ceased because the custodians of respectable opinion have declared that the Cold War is over, and that only monomaniacal eccentrics would claim otherwise.

The case offered by this book is meant to demonstrate that the threat to America's liberties remains dreadfully alive. Beginning in the 1960s, The John Birch Society organized a campaign of education and activism to help Americans understand the dangers represented by the UN and act upon that understanding. When President George Bush announced on September 11, 1990 that the UN-directed Gulf War was intended to create a "new world order," many Americans recognized that the JBS had warned, literally for decades, that a UN-dominated new world order was under construction. For their part, leaders and members of the JBS felt the dreadful vindication that comes from the fulfillment of an ominous prophecy.

As the drive to collectivize the world under the aegis of the United Nations has accelerated, the recognition of the unalloyed evil the world body represents has grown substantially among the American public. Now, at long last, Americans have the opportunity to end the "experiment on our liberties" by getting the U.S. out of the UN, and the UN out of the U.S.

Living Beyond Politics

To preserve political freedom, it is necessary to attend to the essential business of free life — the maintenance of stable homes, the preservation of a cultural heritage, the reverent recognition of God through worship. This is how free men and women have always lived; this is how they will continue to live. For this reason, the "bunker mentality," which is also sometimes described as the "guns and groceries" mindset, should be avoided. If we allow the oligarchical conspirators who seek to rule us to dictate radical dislocations in our lives, priorities, and values, they win. After all, *this is exactly what patriots should be seeking to prevent.*

Furthermore, freedom cannot be preserved through the use of sensationalism, which is one of the Conspiracy's most useful weapons. The growing anti-UN sentiment in this country is a good and healthy thing, as is the mounting public awareness of the evils of intrusive government. The Clinton Administration, a dismal collection of power-intoxicated socialists who literally defy parody, has provided a constant supply of outrages to freedom. Its craven embrace of UN-directed "multilateralism" in foreign policy and the frankly fascist nature of many of its domestic initiatives have created appropriate alarm among sober people.

However, there are — and always have been, and always shall be — those who wish to make themselves distinctive by getting ahead of the factual curve. Regrettably, it is not uncommon to see a rhetorical bidding war develop in which professional alarmists seek to exceed each other in inventiveness and factual irresponsibility. Such tactics belong in the arsenal of the left, and they always redound to the benefit of the left. Generating panic over exaggerated or fabricated "crises" — whether the subject in question is poverty, racism, environmental pollution, child abuse, or whatever — is a time-tested socialist routine. Of course, leftists always insist that even if they have misrepresented or misunder-stood the facts of an issue, their lies have "raised the public's awareness" of a "larger truth" — in short, that even when they lie they're doing a public service by advancing "progressive" causes. Friends of freedom who know and understand the designs of the elites which seek world government cannot take refuge in such tactics. Freedom cannot flourish among falsehoods.

Unlike the left, patriots cannot embrace the tactics of expediency and situational ethics. Since the 18th century, socialists have in-sisted that their oracular insight into history's unfolding design "empowers" them to do whatever is necessary to secure the tri-umph of "social justice." Thus they could lie, cheat, steal, murder, oppress, despoil, and desecrate with impunity, as their labors are all consecrated for the "greater good." This mentality is a consis-tent feature of the left, whether it is on display in the forest of guil-lotines which sprang up in Revolutionary France or in the chaotic streets of Los Angeles during the "Rodney King" riots of 1992.

One of the noblest examples of principled freedom in action was provided by Frederic Bastiat during France's communist upris-ing in 1848. For his entire adult life, Bastiat had labored to learn and disseminate sound principles of political economy; with equal assiduity he had tried to prevent the debacle being created by the French government's collectivist policies. When armed violence erupted in February 1848, Bastiat acted on his knowledge that the struggle for freedom requires more than the ability to ex-pound sound principles. In his biography of Bastiat, President George Roche of Hillsdale College recalls:

> One early clash between the people and the National Guard had resulted in 52 deaths from a single fusillade. Bastiat was in the streets throughout the night after the "massacre." He had immedi-ately summoned two assistants and spent his time giving medical aid to the wounded, whatever their role in the Revolution.[10]

This decision, which required no small amount of courage, dis-played a sound commitment to the principles which Bastiat acknowledged must undergird a free society. When the inevitable consequences of political foolishness befell his nation, Bastiat did not retreat into a bunker, nor did he take triumphant, vindictive pleasure in the misfortune of the less enlightened. Rather, he attended to the needs of the injured with Christian indifference to their political philosophies. As a free man, Bastiat understood that politics is not the measure of all things.

Unless the power of the UN and its sponsors is checked, the horrors which will descend upon humanity will fill the measure of the world body's despicable pedigree. The key to the preservation of freedom resides in the creation of a Congress which is faithful to its oath to protect the Constitution, and that can only be brought about through the propagation of sound constitutional principles which are embraced by a sober and principled electorate.

We must be prepared to make sacrifices, if necessary. Although the hour is late, we can yet preserve a nation worthy of America's blessed pedigree.

Notes

Chapter 1
Welcome to the
"Global Neighborhood"

1. Edward Gibbon, *The History of the Decline and Fall of the Roman Empire*, from *Great Books of the Western World*, Robert Maynard Hutchins, editor-in-chief (Encyclopedia Britannica/University of Chicago, 1952), vol. 40, p. 34.

2. Answer to a question posed by the author during a press conference at the International Conference on Population and Development in Cairo, Egypt, September 7, 1994. See *The New American*, October 3, 1994, p. 13.

3. "Withdrawing U.N. support an idea worth rejecting," *Deseret News*, February 13, 1995, p. A6.

4. Thomas Molnar, "Justice and Its Harvesters: The National Conference of Catholic Bishops," *Chronicles*, December 1994, p. 21.

5. *Tibet: Environment and Development Issues 1992* (Dharamsala, India: Department of Information and International Relations, Central Tibetan Administration of His Holiness the XIV Dalai Lama, 1992), pp. 41-42. See also William F. Jasper, "UNICEF Wants Your Children," *The New American*, October 31, 1994, p. 20. The author has also interviewed Tibetan refugees for first-hand accounts of the actions described, and the UN's complicity in those actions.

6. Lain Christie, "UN troops had sex with kids," *Washington Times*, February 26, 1994, p. A6.

7. Robert Kozak, "Canadian Regiment Disbanded," *Washington Times*, January 24, 1995, p. A13.

8. Ben Barber, "GOP Win has U.N. seeking support," *Washington Times*, December 22, 1994, p. A1.

9. Charles Krauthammer, "Let It Sink: Why the U.S. Should Bail out of the UN," *The New Republic*, August 24, 1987, p. 23.

10. "Achieving Global Human Security," Address by Sir Shridath Ramphal, Co-Chairman of the Commission on Global Governance, January 16, 1995, p. 5.

11. *Global Security Programme, Final Report*; Gorbachev Foundation/Moscow, Gorbachev Foundation/USA, and Rajiv Gandhi Foundation, October 1994, pp. 10-15.

12. St. Augustine, *The City of God*, IV:4; from *Great Books of the Western World*, vol. 18, p. 190.

13. Taylor Caldwell, *Captains and the Kings* (Garden City, NY: Doubleday and Company, Inc., 1972), foreword page.

14. Will and Ariel Durant, *The Age of Voltaire* (New York: Simon and Schuster, 1965), p. 335.

15. Ibid., p. 336.

16. Ibid.

17. Ibid.

18. Ibid., p. 335.

19. Will and Ariel Durant, *Rousseau and Revolution* (New York: Simon and Schuster, 1967), p. 19.

20. Grace G. Roosevelt, *Reading Rousseau in the Nuclear Age*, With full translations of Jean-Jacques Rousseau's "Etat de guerre" and of his "Extrait" and "Judgement" of the Abbe de Saint-Pierre's *Project de paix perpetuelle* (Philadelphia, PA: Temple University Press, 1990), p. 204.

21. William Shakespeare, *King Richard III*, Act V, Scene II; from *The Works of William Shakespeare* (Roslyn, NY: Blacks Readers Service, 1937), p. 710.

22. Grace G. Roosevelt, p. 229.

23. James H. Billington, *Fire in the Minds of Men: Origins of the Revolutionary Faith* (New York: Basic Books, 1980), p. 87.

24. Will and Ariel Durant, *Rousseau and Revolution*, p. 507.

25. Gary Allen, "Illuminism: The Great Conspiracy 1776-1848," *American Opinion*, June 1976, p. 49.

26. Anton Szandor LaVey, *The Satanic Rituals* (New York: Avon Books, 1974), p. 78.

27. Charles William Heckethorn, *The Secret Societies of all Ages and Countries* (New Hyde Park, New York: University Books, 1965), vol. I, p. 306.

28. Heckethorn, vol. I, pp. 308-309.

29. Ibid., vol. I, p. 310.

30. John Robison, A.M.: *Proofs of a Conspiracy* (Boston, MA: Western Islands/ Americanist Classics ed., 1967), pp. 204-205.

31. Billington, p. 96.

32. Ibid., p. 94.

33. Heckethorn, vol. I, p. 312.

34. Billington, pp. 19-20.

35. Ibid., p. 20.

36. Heckethorn, vol. I, p. 313.

37. Ibid., vol. I, pp. 313-314.

38. The Marquis de Jouffroi, *Dictionary of Social Errors*, summarized in Heckethorn, vol. I, p. 314.

39. Billington, pp. 28-29.

40. Ibid., p. 31.

41. Ibid., pp. 38-39.

42. John Emerich Edward Dalberg-Acton, First Baron Acton, *Lectures on the French Revolution*, John Neville Figgis and Reginald Vere Laurence, eds. (New York: The Noonday Press, 1959), p. 97.

43. Robison, p. 242.

44. George Washington, letter to Reverend G.W. Snyder, September 25, 1798; from *The Writings of George Washington from the original manuscript sources, 1745-1799*; John C. Fitzpatrick, ed. (Washington, DC: U.S. Government Printing Office) vol. 36, pp. 452-453.

45. Fisher Ames, *The Works of Fisher Ames as published by Seth Ames*, W.B. Allen, ed. (Indianapolis, IN: Liberty Classics, 1983), vol. I., p. 214.

46. Ibid., p. 218.

47. Ibid., p. 240.

48. Ibid., pp. 197-198.

49. George Washington to Reverend G.W. Snyder, October 24, 1798, quoted in Fitzpatrick, pp. 518-519.

50. See Seth Payson, A.M., *Proofs of the Real Existence and Dangerous Tendency of Illuminism, containing An Abstract of the most interesting parts of what Dr. Robison and the Abbé Barruel have published on the subject, with collateral proofs and general observations* (printed by Samuel Etheridge for the Author, 1802).

51. James Madison, *The Mind of the Founder* (Indianapolis, IN: Babbs Merrill Co., 1973), p. 250.

52. Ibid., pp. 252-253.

53. Paul Johnson, *The Birth of the Modern: World Society 1815-1830* (New York: Harper Collins Publishers, 1991) p. 115.

54. Ibid.

55. Allen, p. 110.

56. See Richard Wurmbrand, *Marx & Satan* (Westchester, IL: Crossway Books, 1986), pp. 1-19, particularly 17-18. Reverend Wurmbrand, a cleric who suffered at the hands of Romanian Communists, presents a well-documented and tightly-argued case for the proposition that Marx and other significant Communist figures have been conscious Satanists.

57. Heckethorn, *The Secret Societies*, vol. II, p. 115; see also Leopold Schwartzschild, *Karl Marx: The Red Prussian* (New York: Grosset and Dunlap, 1947), p. 93. Regarding the League's descent from the Illuminati, see Billington, pp. 182-187.

58. Schwartzschild, p. 162.

59. George Charles Roche III, *Frederic Bastiat: A Man Alone* (New Rochelle, New York: Arlington House, 1971), p. 116.

60. Heckethorn, vol. I, p. 306.

61. Charles Seymour, *The Intimate Papers of Colonel House* (New York: Houghton Mifflin Company, 1926), vol. I: Behind the Political Curtain, 1912-1915, p. 114.

62. Ibid., p. 115.

63. Ibid., p. 155.

64. Ibid., p. 158.

65. Ibid., p. 156.

66. Billington observes that the "Black Hand" conspirators responsible for the

assassination of Archduke Franz Ferdinand — the event which triggered WWI — were disciples of Mazzini as well. (Billington, *Fire in the Minds of Men*, p. 334.)

67. Edward Mandell House, *Philip Dru: Administrator — A Story of Tomorrow, 1920-1935* (New York, 1912), p. 95.

68. Ibid., p. 45.

69. Ibid., p. 160.

70. Ibid., p. 154.

71. Seymour, pp. 160-161.

72. Ibid.

73. George Sylvester Viereck, *The Strangest Friendship in History: Woodrow Wilson and Colonel House* (New York: Liveright Inc., 1932), p. 28.

74. This synopsis is taken from William F. Jasper, *Global Tyranny ... Step by Step* (Appleton, WI: Western Islands, 1992) pp. 50-53.

75. Ron Chernow, *The House of Morgan: An American Banking Dynasty and the Rise of Modern Finance* (New York: Atlantic Monthly, 1990), pp. 485-486.

76. Jasper, p. 63.

77. For an excellent overview of the Wall Street/Bolshevik axis, see James Perloff, *The Shadows of Power: The Council on Foreign Relations and the American Decline* (Appleton, WI: Western Islands, 1988), chapter 3. For more information about this evil symbiosis, see the following books by Antony C. Sutton: *Western Technology and Soviet Economic Development*, three vols. (Stanford University, Stanford, California: Hoover Institution, 1968, 1971, 1973); *The Best Enemy Money Can Buy* (Billings, MT: Liberty House Press, 1986).

78. Jasper, p. 57.

79. See, for instance, *The Insiders* by John F. McManus; *Shadows of Power*, by James E. Perloff; *None Dare Call It Conspiracy*, by Gary Allen and Larry Abraham; and *The Invisible Government*, by Dan Smoot; all of which are available through the American Opinion Book Services, P.O. Box 8040, Appleton, Wisconsin, 54913.

80. Richard Harwood, "Ruling Class Journalists," *Washington Post*, October 30, 1993, p. A21.

81. "Gorbachev wants to reduce nukes, boost peacekeeping," *Atlanta Journal and Constitution*, October 20, 1994, p. A9.

82. "Gorbachev, Meet Jefferson," by George F. Will, *Newsweek*, December 19, 1988, p. 76.

83. *Weekly Compilation of Presidential Documents*, Volume 27, Number 39; Monday, September 30, 1991, p. 1327.

84. "Lenin Aims Like U.N.'s, Thant Says," *Los Angeles Times*, April 7, 1970.

85. Johann Wolfgang von Goethe, *Faust, Pt. I*; from *Great Books of the Western World*, Robert Maynard Hutchins, editor in chief (Encyclopedia Britannica/University of Chicago, 1952), vol. 47, p. 33.

86. Wurmbrand, p. 33.

87. Ibid., p. 55.

88. Leo Gershoy, *Bertrand Barere: A Reluctant Terrorist* (Princeton, NJ: Princeton University Press, 1962), p. 84.

89. Anton LaVey, undated letter to The John Birch Society, circa 1970, p. 2. The letter, which was printed on Church of Satan letterhead and over LaVey's signature, contains the date "20 October V Anno Satanas."

90. Those who wish to examine the evidence that the UN's masters seek to create a new "golden age of the political police" should examine the November 29, 1993 issue of *The New American* magazine, entitled "American troops are being conscripted into a New World Army," and the Fall/Winter 1994 edition, entitled "Toward a Police State." They may both be obtained for $2.50 postpaid by writing the American Opinion Book Services, P.O. Box 8040, Appleton, WI. 54913.

91. Gibbon, p. 464.

92. See note number two above.

93. James Madison, "Memorial and Remonstrance Against Religious Assessments" (1785); quoted in *James Madison*, Neal Riemer, editor (New York: Washington Square Press, 1968), p. 165.

— Chapter 2 —
**UNESCO: School Board
of the New World Order**

1. George Orwell, *1984* (New York: Signet Classics; 1961). p. 210.
2. Bertrand Russell, from the UNESCO quarterly journal *The Impact of Science on Society*, quoted in "Analysis of the Ray Murphy Committee Report on UNESCO by Americanism Committee," The American Legion, 8th District Department of Texas, Houston, Texas, p. 5.
3. Daniel J. Shepard, "Plugging away in the United States," *Earth Times*, January 15, 1995, p. 13.
4. Ibid.
5. Gerald O. Barney, et al., *Global 2000 Revisited: What Shall We Do?* (Arlington, VA: The Millennium Institute, 1993), p. 90.
6. George F. Will, *The Morning After: American Successes and Excesses 1981-1986* (New York: The Free Press, 1986), p. 289.
7. "US to pull out of UNESCO: Calls UN group 'Politicized;' withdrawal set for 1984," *Boston Globe*, December 30, 1983.
8. Stanley Meisler, "Task Force Urges U.S. to Rejoin Controversial UNESCO," *Los Angeles Times*, August 31, 1993, p. A8.
9. "Don't Rush Back to UNESCO," *New York Times*, February 23, 1994, p. A16.
10. "The Climate of Freedom," *The Saturday Review*, July 19, 1952, p. 22.
11. UNESCO Constitution, London, November 11, 1945; preamble.
12. Richard Hoggart, *An Idea and Its Servants: UNESCO From Within* (New York: Oxford University Press, 1978), p. 25.
13. Samuel L. Blumenfeld, *N.E.A.: Trojan Horse in American Education* (Boise, ID: The Paradigm Company, 1984), p. 193.
14. Walter H.C. Laves and Charles A. Thomson, *UNESCO: Purpose, Progress, Prospects* (Bloomington, IN: Indiana University Press, 1957) p. 19.
15. Ibid., p. 21.
16. Ibid., p. 6.

17. G. Edward Griffin, *The Fearful Master: A Second Look at the United Nations* (Boston, MA: Western Islands, 1964) p. 141.
18. Ibid., p. 142.
19. Julian Huxley, *UNESCO: Its Purpose and Philosophy* (Washington, DC: Public Affairs Press, 1948), p. 32.
20. Ibid., p. 6.
21. Ibid., p. 18.
22. Ibid., p. 46.
23. Lin Mousheng, "Human Rights For A World Society," in *Education For A World Society: Promising Practices Today*, Christian O. Arndt and Samuel Everett, eds. (New York: Harper & Brothers, 1951), p. 19.
24. Ibid.
25. Blumenfeld, p. 194.
26. Blumenfeld, pp. 194-195.
27. *Towards World Understanding, Vol. I: Some Suggestions on Teaching about the United Nations and Its Specialized Agencies*, Paris, France, 1948, p. 3.
28. Huxley, p. 36.
29. *Towards World Understanding*, vol. I, p. 18.
30. Ibid., pp. 19-20.
31. *Towards World Understanding, Vol. V: In The Classroom With Children Under Thirteen Years of Age*, Paris, France, 1949, pp. 7, 54-55.
32. Ibid., p.8.
33. Ibid., p. 9, 54.
34. Ibid, p. 58.
35. *Teaching About the United Nations In The United States*, U.S. Department of Health and Human Services (Washington, DC: The United States Government Printing Office, 1964), p. v.
36. Ibid., p. 1.
37. Arndt and Everett, p. 59.
38. T.W. Adorno, et al., *The Authoritarian Personality* (New York: John Wiley and Sons, Science Editions, 1964), Part one, p. 225.
39. Adorno, et al, p. 228.
40. Christopher Lasch, *The True and Only Heaven: Progress and its Critics* (New York: W.W. Norton and Company, 1991), p. 447.
41. *The Radical Right: The New American*

Right expanded and updated, Daniel Bell, editor (Garden City, New York: Doubleday/Anchor Books, 1964), pp. 76, 93.

42. Claire Chambers, *The SIECUS Circle: A Humanist Revolution* (Boston, MA: Western Islands, 1977), pp. 11-12.

43. Ibid., p. 12.

44. Ibid., p. xiii.

45. Judith A. Reisman, et al., *Kinsey, Sex and Fraud: The Indoctrination of a People* (LaFayette, LA: Lochnivar-Huntington House Publishers, 1990), p. 226.

46. Robert W. Lee, "Sweden's Second Thoughts," *The New American*, November 30, 1992, p. 23.

47. Reisman, et al., p. 129.

48. Steven Waldman, *The Bill* (New York: Viking, 1995), pp. 7, 19.

49. David S. Richie, "Working Together in International Camps," in Arndt and Everett, pp. 106-107.

50. Ibid.

51. Ibid., p. 107.

52. Ibid., p. 109.

53. Ibid., p. 118.

54. "Draft Declaration and Draft Programme of Action of the World Summit for Social Development Preparatory Committee," executive summary, p. 7.

55. B.F. Skinner, *Beyond Freedom and Dignity* (New York: Bantam/Vintage Books, 1971), Acknowledgements page.

56. Skinner, pp. 22-23.

57. Skinner, p. 216.

58. William F. Jasper, "Outcome-Based Education: Skinnerian Conditioning in the Classroom," *The New American*, August 23, 1993, p. 7.

59. USCEFA Conference Report, p. 4.

60. Ibid., p. 23.

61. *Linking Progress to People: An AED Policy Paper for the World Summit for Social Development* (Academy for Educational Development, 1995), p. vii.

62. *Teaching About the United Nations*, p. v.

— Chapter 3 —
Whose Children?

1. Sheldon Richman, *Separating School & State: How to Liberate America's Families* (Fairfax, Virginia: The Future of Freedom Foundation, 1994), p. xv.

2. Dolores Barclay, "The Family: It's Surviving and Healthy ..." *Tulsa World*, August 21 1977.

3. Paul Lewis, "Sex Scandal Roils UNICEF Unit," *New York Times*, June 25, 1987; "Staff of U.C. Children's Fund Sentenced in Child Sex Case," Reuters news service, March 7, 1988; and "Former Belgian UNICEF Boss Wins Appeal in Child Sex Case," Reuters news service report, October 27, 1988.

4. Ibid.

5. Ibid.

6. Judith Reisman, "GATT and the Drugs and Children Trade: Some Moral Reconsiderations," The Institute for Media Education, 1994, p. 1.

7. Jasper, "UNICEF Wants Your Children," *The New American*, October 31, 1994, p. 20.

8. James P. Grant, written remarks delivered on his behalf at awards ceremony at the 1995 International Development Conference in Washington, D.C., transcribed from audiotape.

9. "Keynote Address by Mrs. Graca Machel, Expert, Study on the Impact of Armed Conflict on Children, to the International Development Conference, January 16-18, 1995."

10. See, for instance, Michael Ryan, "It Takes An Entire Village To Raise A Child," *Parade* magazine, October 9, 1994, a report about the Children's Defense Fund-sponsored "Children's Sabbath."

11. "US to sign UN convention of rights of children," *Boston Globe*, February 12, 1995, p. A4.

12. Ibid.

13. Allan Carlson, "Uncle Sam's Child," *Chronicles*, January 1993, p. 14.

14. G.K. Chesterton, *Brave New Family: Chesterton on Men and Women, Children, Sex, Divorce, Marriage and the Family*, Alvaro de Silva, ed. (San Francisco: Ignatius Press, 1990) pp. 34-35.

15. John Locke, "Concerning Civil Government, Second Essay," in *Great Books of the Western World*, vol. 35, pp. 37-39,

43.

16. Plato, *The Republic*, V:460; from *Great Books of the Western World*, vol. 7, p. 362.

17. Ibid., p. 360.

18. Ibid., p. 364.

19. Aristotle, *The Politics*, Book II, 3:35; *Great Books*, vol. 9, p. 456.

20. Jean-Jacques Rousseau, "On The Origin of Inequality," from *Great Books of the Western World*, vol. 38, p. 357.

21. Ibid., p. 372.

22. Ibid., pp. 372-373.

23. Ibid., p. 375.

24. Ibid., p. 376.

25. Ibid.

26. Dennis L. Cuddy, Ph.D., *Chronology of Education with Quotable Quotes* (Highland, FL: Pro Family Forum, 1994) pp. 1, 3.

27. Gershoy, pp. 225-226.

28. Karl Marx, *The Communist Manifesto* (Appleton, WI: The John Birch Society, 1990), p. 22.

29. H.G. Wells, *New Worlds For Old* (New York: The Macmillan Company, 1919) p. 122.

30. Ibid., p. 124.

31. Ibid., pp. 124-125.

32. Arthur W. Calhoun, *A Social History of The American Family: From Colonial Times to the Present* (Cleveland, OH: The Arthur H. Clark Company, 1919) pp. 162-163.

33. Ibid., p. 171.

34. Ibid., pp. 326-327.

35. Wells, p. 128.

36. Laura Fermi, *Mussolini* (The University of Chicago Press, 1961), p. 272.

37. Chesterton, *Brave New Family*, p. 192.

38. C.W. Guillebaud, *The Social Policy of Nazi Germany*, quoted in William P. Hoar, "Supplanting Mom and Dad," *The New American*, August 8, 1994, p. 43.

39. Frederick L. Schulman, *The Nazi Dictatorship: A Study in Social Pathology and the Politics of Fascism* (New York: Alfred A. Knopf, 1935), p. 372.

40. William L. Shirer, *The Rise and Fall of the Third Reich: A History of Nazi Germany* (New York: Crest Books, 1961), p.

343.

41. Ibid.

42. A.S. Makarenko, *The Collective Family: A Handbook for Russian Parents* (Garden City, NY: Doubleday and Company Inc., 1967), p. xi.

43. Ibid., p. xii.

44. Ibid., p. 156.

45. Ibid., p. 26.

46. Ibid., p. 320.

47. Ibid., pp. xvii-xix.

48. Ibid., p. 31.

49. Ibid., p. 364.

50. Ibid., p. 42.

51. *Who's Who in America 1995*, vol. 1, p. 27.

52. Mortimer J. Adler, *Haves Without Have-Nots: Essays for the 21st Century on Democracy and Socialism* (New York: Macmillan Publishing Company, 1991), p. 251.

53. Mortimer J. Adler (On behalf of the members of the Paideia Group), *The Paideia Proposal: An Educational Manifesto* (New York: MacMillan Publishing Co., Inc, 1982), pp. 38-39.

54. "Our Babies, Our Future," *Carnegie Quarterly*, Spring 1994, pp. 2-3.

55. Ibid., p. 6.

56. Ibid., p. 12.

57. *The Unfinished Agenda: A New Vision For Child Development and Education*, A Statement by the Research and Policy Committee of the Committee for Economic Development, 1991, pp. 21, 25, 28.

58. Office of Management and Budget, *Budget of the United States Government*, Fiscal Year 1995 (Washington, DC: United States Government Printing Office, 1994), book 1, p. 90.

59. Hugh LaFollette, "Licensing Parents," *Philosophy and Public Affairs*, Winter 1980, pp. 182-183.

60. Ibid., p. 187.

61. Ibid., pp. 196-197.

62. Gene Stephens, "Crime in the Year 2000," *The Futurist*, April 1981 p. 50.

63. Dr. Jack C. Westman, interview with author.

64. Jack C. Westman, M.D. *Licensing Parents: Can We Prevent Child Abuse and*

Neglect? (New York and London: Insight Books, 1994) pp. xii-xiii.

65. Ibid., pp. 159-160.
66. Ibid., pp. 239-240, 242. See also p. 261.
67. Jack C. Westman, quoted in PR Newswire (syndicated feature), October 4, 1994.
68. Westman, *Licensing Parents*, pp. 123-124.
69. Ibid., p. 252.
70. Jack C. Westman, interview with author.
71. Westman, *Licensing Parents*, p. 164.
72. Ibid., pp. 196-197.
73. Ibid., p. 29.
74. Westman, interview with author.
75. "His say: Should we license parents?" Jack C. Westman, *Chicago Tribune*, November 27, 1994 sec. 6. p. 4.
76. Westman, *Licensing Parents*, p. 256.
77. Ibid., pp. vii-viii.
78. Judge Charles D. Gill, interview with author.
79. Ibid.
80. Ibid.
81. Alix Boyle, "Judge Charles D. Gill: 'We Look at Children as Property,'" *New York Times*, November 24, 1991.
82. Kurt Chandler, "Should being a parent require a license?" Minneapolis *Star-Tribune*, December 17, 1994, pp. 1A, 12A.
83. LaFollette, pp. 187-188.
84. William Aiken and Hugh LaFollette, *Whose Child?* (Totowa, NJ: Rowman and Littlefield, 1980).
85. Westman, *Licensing Parents*, p. 220.
86. Ibid., p. 161.
87. Ibid., p. 153.
88. Judge Gill, interview with author.
89. Undated NTFCCR Pamphlet.
90. Ibid.
91. Honorable Charles D. Gill, "Essay On The Status of the American Child, 2000 A.D.: Chattel or Constitutionally Protected Child-Citizen?" *Ohio Northern University Law Review*, vol. XVII Number 3, 1991, p. 578.
92. Ibid., Cohen & Naimark, *United Nations Convention on the Rights of the Child: Individual Rights Concepts and Their Significance for Social Scientists,*

46 American Psychologist 60, 60 (Jan. 1991); Quoted in Charles Gill, supra.
93. Undated NTFCCR pamphlet.
94. Transcription of Welcoming Address, United Nations General Assembly, Earth Day 1991 — Concert For Peace, March [sic] 20, 1991, Monica Getz, co-chair; transcript provided by Judge Charles Gill.
95. Charles Gill, *New York Law School Journal of Human Rights*, 1992, p. 593.
96. Ibid., p. 594.
97. Charles Gill, "Essay," pp. 556-557.
98. 1994 International Year of the Family: Building the smallest democracy at the heart of society," United Nations, Vienna 1991, p. 14.
99. Ibid.
100. Ibid., p. 23.
101. Ibid., p. 15.
102. Ibid., p. 20.
103. "First Presidency Supports International Year of the Family," The Church of Jesus Christ of Latter-Day Saints, press release, December 31, 1993.
104. Nancy Hobbs, "UN Year of the Family Coordinator Checks S.L.'s Preparations for Global Conference," *Salt Lake Tribune*, June 23, 1994, p. D3.
105. Transcript of Committee on Rights of the Child, fifth session, Geneva, January 10-18, 1994; Federal Information Service, January 7, 1994.
106. Brenda Scott, *Out Of Control: Who's Watching our Child Protection Agencies?* (Lafayette, LA: Huntington House, 1994), p. 136.
107. Ibid., p. 170.
108. Ibid.
109. Ibid., p. 166.
110. Ibid.
111. "U.S. May Reverse U.N. Vote over NAMBLA Ties," *Lambda Report*, November, 1993, p. 1.
112. "Families around the world: Universal in their diversity," *UN Chronicle*, March 1994, pp. 46-47.
113. Celeste McGovern, "Social engineers get a new tool," *British Columbia Report*, August 8, 1994, p. 27.
114. Shafer Parker Jr., "The second childrens' crusade," *British Colombia Re-*

port, December 19, 1994, p. 30.

115. Dr. Bryce J. Christensen, interview with author.

116. Ibid.

117. Richard Ebeling, interview with author.

— Chapter 4 —
"Empowerment" or Enslavement?

1. Heckethorne, vol. I, p. 310.

2. "Sugar and Spite: Radical feminists begin a new drive to pass the ERA," by John Kenneth Weiskittel, *The New American*, March 16, 1987, p. 36.

3. Johanna Dohnal, presentation at the 1995 International Development Conference, "Achieving Global Human Security," January 17, 1995.

4. Seble Dawit, presentation at the 1995 International Development Conference, "Achieving Global Human Security," January 17, 1995, transcribed from audiotape.

5. Shulamith Firestone, *The Dialectic of Sex: The Case for Feminist Revolution* (New York: Bantam Books, 1970), pp. 11-12.

6. Uli Schmetzer, "Show trial offers hope for women's rights in China," *Chicago Tribune*, January 6, 1995, p. A1.

7. "Towards A Women's Development Agenda for the 21st Century: United Nations Development Fund for Women (UNIFEM) as a vehicle of change for sustainable livelihoods and women's empowerment," Noeleen Heyzer, Director, UNIFEM (undated), p. 8.

8. Charlotte Bunch and Niamh Reilly, *Demanding Accountability: The Global Campaign and Vienna Tribunal for Women's Human Rights* (New Jersey and New York: Center for Women's Global Leadership and the United Nations Development Fund for Women, 1994), pp. 10-12.

9. Ibid., pp. 30-31.

10. Ibid., p. 82.

11. Ibid., pp. 85-86.

12. Ibid., p. 85.

13. Ibid., p. 55.

14. Jim Hyde, "Changing Concepts of the Family: Responses to HIV/AIDS and Development," *Development — Journal of SID*, 1993:4, pp. 22-23.

15. Ibid., p. 23.

16. Wendy Harcourt, "Women, Sexuality and the Family," *Development*, 1993:4, pp. 26-27.

17. *Draft Outcome of the World Summit for Social Development: Draft Declaration and Draft Programme of Action*, Preparatory Committee for the World Summit for Social Development, New York, 16-27 January, 1995, pp. 10-11.

18. Ashali Varma, "Women demand stronger support for local concerns," *Earth Times*, January 15, 1995 p. 4.

19. "Towards a Women's Development Agenda for the 21st Century," p. 7.

20. "Perspectives Related to Families in the Regional Platforms for Action for the Fourth World Women's Conference," undated, distributed at the 1995 International Development Conference in Washington D.C. on January 18, 1995; p. 1.

21. Steven Mosher, *A Mother's Ordeal: One Woman's Fight Against China's One-Child Policy* (New York: Harcourt, Brace, and Company, 1993). "Ying Chi An" is a pseudonym given to a woman who had worked as a nurse and birth control official in communist China.

22. Mosher, p. 117.

23. It is interesting to note that the idea of "escorts" or "guards" who shuttle women into abortion clinics has migrated from Communist China to the United States. "Clinic Escorts" at American abortion clinics claim to protect women from harassment, but their primary concern is to shield equivocal women from information about the health risks of abortion in general and the specific risks which may be associated with a particular clinic. See "Meet the 'J Street Five'" by this author, *The New American*, May 16, 1994, p. 41.

24. John F. McManus, "A Global Attack on Women," *The New American*, November 28, 1994, p. 44.

25. Robison, *Proofs of a Conspiracy*, pp. 262-263.

— Chapter 5 —
A Covenant With Death:
Population Control in the
Brave New World Order

1. Huxley, p. 21.
2. Garrett Hardin, "Parenthood: Right or Privilege?" *Science*, vol. 169:427.
3. Programme of the International Conference on Population and Development, Cairo (final draft, September 13, 1994), Chapter 1:20, p. 6.
4. Cairo Programme, Chapter 2.
5. Timothy Wirth, Under-secretary of state for global affairs, interview with author.
6. Steven W. Mosher, *A Mother's Ordeal*, p. 213.
7. Hardin, op. cit.
8. Jasper, pp. 159-160.
9. Donella H. Meadows, "We Already Number Too Many," *Los Angeles Times*, April 5, 1994.
10. Jasper, *Global Tyranny*, p. 168. Cousteau also made a perfunctory appearance at the Cairo population control summit.
11. William F. Jasper, "The Population Controllers: Their Coercive Agenda," *The New American*, June 27, 1994 p. 7.
12. Gro Harlem Brundtland, plenary address to ICPD conference.
13. Cairo Programme, Chapter 4:1.
14. Johanna Dohnal, plenary address to ICPD conference, September 6, 1994.
15. Cairo Programme, op. cit.
16. Helen Simons, "Repackaging Population Control," *CovertAction*, Winter 1994-95, p. 33.
17. Cairo Programme, Chapter 5:1.
18. Paul R. Ehrlich, *The Population Bomb* (New York: Ballantine Books, 1968), pp. 45-77.
19. Paul R. Ehrlich and Anne H. Ehrlich, *Population, Resources, Environment: Issues in Human Ecology* (San Francisco, CA: W.H. Freeman and Company, 1970) p. 146.
20. Ibid., pp. 147-148.
21. Paul R. Ehrlich and Anne H. Ehrlich, *The Population Explosion* (New York: Simon and Schuster, 1990) p. 17.
22. Paul R. Ehrlich and Anne H. Ehrlich,

Population, Resources, Environment, pp. 251-252.
23. Ibid., p. 256.
24. Ibid., p. 254.
25. Ibid., pp. 256-257.
26. Robert Whelan, *Choices In Childbearing: When Does Family Planning Become Population Control?* (London: The Committee on Population & The Economy, 1992), p. 4.
27. Ibid.
28. Ibid.
29. Ibid., pp. 54-55.
30. Ibid.
31. Ibid., pp. 5-7.
32. Ehrlich and Ehrlich, *Population, Resources, Environment, Environment: Issues in Human Ecology*, p. 255.
33. For a first-hand account of the events at the Cairo conference, see William Norman Grigg, "A Covenant With Death," *The New American*, October 17, 1994.
34. Ibid.
35. Ibid.
36. Edgar R. Chasteen, *The Case for Compulsory Birth Control* (Englewood Cliffs, NJ: Prentice-Hall, Inc, 1971) pp. 194-195.
37. Ibid., p. 195.
38. Ibid., p. 197.
39. Ibid., p. 204.
40. Ibid., p. 206.
41. Ibid., p. 211.
42. Ehrlich and Ehrlich, *Population, Resources, Environment: Issues in Human Ecology*, p. 255.
43. Robert J. Anglin, "Scientist Says Government May Have to Control Births," *Boston Globe*, August 10, 1968.
44. Ehrlich and Ehrlich, *Population, Resources, Environment: Issues on Human Ecology* p. 256.
45. Ibid., p. 196.
46. Norman Myers, *The Gaia Atlas of Future Worlds* (New York: Anchor Doubleday, 1990), p. 46.
47. Ibid., p. 148.
48. Anne Johnstone, "Future in the Balance," *Glasgow Herald*, August 31, 1994, p. 13; Tim Radford, "Education Is Key to Population Crisis," *Manchester*

Guardian, August 18, 1994, p. 13; Liz Hunt, "Tax parenthood to save the world says top surgeon," *London Independent*, August 10, 1994, p. 2; and "Below the belt," *London Daily Telegraph*, July 15, 1994, p. 19.

49. Robert Whelan, interview with author.
50. Lesley White, "Will the Pope listen to this man?" *The Sunday Times* of London, August 14, 1994.
51. Claire Chambers, *The SIECUS Circle* (Boston, MA: Western Islands, 1977), p. 330.
52. Louis B. Fleming, "More Aggressive U.N. Birth Control Role Due," *Los Angeles Times*, April 20, 1965. Appropriately, this item was published on the anniversary of Adolf Hitler's birth.
53. Whelan, p. 28.
54. Ibid., pp. 28-29.
55. Ibid., p. 29.
56. Ibid., p. 35.
57. Sharon L. Camp, *Conscience*, Autumn, 1993, p. 11.
58. See William Norman Grigg, "A Covenant With Death," *The New American*, October 17, 1994, p. 7.
59. Whelan, p. 34.
60. *Ford Foundation Report*, Fall, 1994, p. 43.
61. Ibid., p. 40.
62. "Rwanda: Post-Genocide Population Planning," *ICPD Watch*, September 12, 1994 p. 7; 'War wiped out 20% of Rwanda's population," *The Egyptian Gazette*, September 14, 1994, p. 3.
63. Vice President Al Gore, remarks made at the "NGO Forum" of the UN International Conference on Population and Development in Cairo, Egypt. See Grigg, "A Covenant With Death," op cit.
64. Alexander Cockburn, "Real U.S. Policy in the Third World: Sterilization," *Los Angeles Times*, September 8, 1994.
65. Timothy Wirth, interview with author.
66. Camp, *Conscience*, p. 8.
67. Nesta H. Webster, *The French Revolution*, p. 424.
68. Ibid., p. 425.
69. Mikhail Heller and Aleksandr M. Nekrich, *Utopia in Power: The History of the Soviet Union from 1917 to the Pres-*

ent (New York: Summit Books, 1986), p. 235.
70. Ibid., p. 236.
71. Valentin Chu, *Ta Ta, Tan Tan ("Fight fight, talk talk...")* (New York: W.W. Norton and Company, 1963), p. 55.
72. "The Human Cost of Communism in China," Report of the U.S. Senate Subcommittee on Internal Security, 1971, p. 16.
73. See William Norman Grigg, "A Covenant With Death," *The New American*, October 17, 1994, p. 7.

— Chapter 6 —
Multiculturalism and the UN Assault on American Nationhood

1. Richard Bernstein, *Dictatorship of Virtue: Multiculturalism and America's Future* (New York: Alfred A. Knopf, 1994) p. 283.
2. Gail Burry, interview with author.
3. *Global Security Programme* (The Gorbachev Foundation, October 1994), p. 14.
4. "McCarthy, Seneca Falls and History," the *Wall Street Journal*, December 30, 1994, p. A8.
5. Ibid.
6. "San Jose Learning Equal Treatment for All Deities," *Los Angeles Times*, December 9, 1994.
7. Florida State statute, 91-226.
8. Rep. Tom Feeney, interview with author.
9. Pat Hart, interview with author.
10. "Voters Defeat Proponents of America-First Curriculum," *New York Times*, October 7, 1994.
11. Bernstein, p. 53.
12. Ibid., pp. 55-56.
13. Ibid., p. 52.
14. Ibid., p. 56.
15. *Chronicles*, February 1993, p. 50.
16. "But Can Juanito Really Read?" by Tom Bethell, *National Review*, September 30, 1983, p. 1197.
17. William Bigelow, "Rereading the Past," in *Confronting Columbus: An Anthology*, John Yewell, Chris Dodge, and Jan DeSirey, eds. (Jefferson, NC: McFar-

land and Company, 1992), pp. 73-75.

18. Bernstein, p. 58.

19. "Fear of Violence Derails Denver Columbus Day Parade," *Salt Lake Tribune*, October 11, 1992.

20. "American Indians Seize Columbus Day Spotlight," *Salt Lake Tribune*, October 13, 1992, p. D10.

21. Bernstein, p. 58.

22. Philip Wayne Powell, *Tree of Hate: Propaganda and Prejudices Affecting United States Relations with the Hispanic World* (Vallecito, CA: Ross House Books, 1985), p. 34.

23. Ibid., p. 93.

24. Ibid., p. 109.

25. George Hills, *Franco* (New York: Mac-Millan Company, 1967) p. 46.

26. Ibid.; and Will and Ariel Durant, *Rousseau and Revolution* pp. 280-281.

27. Hills, p. 47.

28. Will and Ariel Durant, *Rousseau and Revolution*, p. 281.

29. Will and Ariel Durant point out that atheism and "utilitarian morality" were rampant within certain clerical circles in France and Spain in the mid-1700s; Durants, *Rousseau and Revolution*, p. 901.

30. Arthur Schlesinger, "Was America a Mistake?" *Atlantic Monthly*, September 1992, p. 22.

31. Will and Ariel Durant, *The Age of Voltaire*, p. 693.

32. Gershoy, *Bertrand Barere: A Reluctant Terrorist*, pp. 14-15.

33. Abbe Guillaume Raynal, *A Philosophical and Political History of the Settlements and Trade of the Europeans in the East and West Indies*, J.O. Justamond, F.R.S., trans. (London, 1798), vol. VI, p. 491.

34. Schlesinger, p. 22.

35. Will and Ariel Durant, *The Age of Voltaire*, p. 694.

36. Kirkpatrick Sale, *The Conquest of Paradise: The Columbian Legacy and its Aftermath* (New York: Alfred A. Knopf, 1990), p. 367.

37. Ibid., p. 368.

38. Ibid., pp. 368-369.

39. Schlesinger, pp. 20, 27.

40. *Revolutionary Activities Within the United States: The American Indian Movement*, Report of the U.S. Senate Judiciary Committee Subcommittee on Internal Security, September 1976, p. 38.

41. Ibid., p. 20.

42. Ibid., p. 35.

43. "Revolutionary Activities Within The United States: The American Indian Movement," Hearing before the U.S. Senate Judiciary Subcommittee on Internal Security, April 6, 1976; p. 71.

44. Ibid., pp. 188-189.

45. Ibid., pp. 194-195.

46. Ibid., pp. 195-199.

47. Ibid, p. 199.

48. Ibid., p. 202.

49. Reuters Business Report, October 18, 1994.

50. *The Gaia Atlas of First Peoples: A Future for the Indigenous World* (London: Anchor Doubleday, 1990), foreword page.

51. Ibid., pp. 178-179.

52. "Civil and Political Rights in the United States," *Department of State Dispatch*, September 19, 1994.

53. Bill Simmons, Treaty Study Coordinator for the Indian Treaty Council, interview with author.

54. Ibid.

55. Tony Gonzales, ITC official in San Francisco, interview with author; Andrea Carmen, ITC Executive Director, interview with author.

56. Andrea Carmen, interview with author.

57. Ibid.

58. Richard Grenier, "Curious Credentials for the Nobel Peace Prize," *Washington Times*, October 25, 1992, p. B4.

59. Tony Gonzales, interview with author.

60. Andrea Carmen, interview with author.

61. *The Gaia Atlas of First Peoples*, p. 167.

62. Terry L. Anderson, *Sovereign Nations or Reservations? An Economic History of the American Indian* (Unpublished galley copy of forthcoming book), p. 10.

63. Hugh Thomas, *Conquest: Montezuma, Cortes and the Fall of Old Mexico* (New York: Simon and Schuster, 1993) p. 189.

64. Jonathan Kandell, *La Capital: The Biography of Mexico City* (New York: Random House, 1988), pp. 53-54.
65. Thomas, *Conquest*, p. 25.
66. Mario Vargas Llosa, "Questions of Conquest: What Columbus Wrought and What He Did Not," *Harper's*, December 1990, p. 49.

— Chapter 7 —
One World Under Gaia

1. Dennis L. Cuddy, *Now is the Dawning of the New Age New World Order* (Oklahoma City, OK: Hearthstone Publishing, 1991), p. 312.
2. Matthew Fox, *The Coming of the Cosmic Christ: The Healing of Mother Earth and the Birth of a Global Renaissance* (San Francisco, CA: Harper & Row, Publishers, 1988), pp. 145, 149.
3. Gerald O. Barney, *Global 2000 Revisited: What Shall We Do? The Critical Issues of the 21st Century* (Arlington, VA: The Millennium Institute, 1993), p. 13.
4. Will and Ariel Durant, *Rousseau and Revolution*, p. 175.
5. Tal Brooke, *When the World Will Be as One* (Eugene, OR; Harvest House Publishers: 1989), p. 207.
6. Cuddy, *Now is the Dawning*, p. 272.
7. Ibid., p. 272.
8. Edith Kermit Roosevelt, "Temple of Understanding," The Freedom Press, November 5, 1962.
9. "World Unity The Only Road To World Peace," pamphlet of The Temple of Understanding, p. 5.
10. Claire Chambers, *The SIECUS Circle*, p. 33.
11. Don Shannon, "'Silent' Room: Tranquil Center at U.N.'s Heart," *Los Angeles Times*, May 15, 1974.
12. Eunice S. Layton and Felix Layton, *Theosophy: Key To Understanding* (Wheaton, IL: The Theosophical Publishing House, 1967), pp. 12-13.
13. Column Lynch, "At UN, lobbyists seek to open world body to other worlds," *Boston Globe*, December 12, 1993 p. 4.
14. Ibid.

15. Vaclav Havel, "What The World Needs Now," *New Age Journal*, September/October 1994, pp. 45, 161.
16. Ibid.
17. Ibid., p. 162.
18. Monte Leach, interview with author; see William Norman Grigg, "The 'Master' On Earth: New Age Messiah Makes an Appearance," *The New American*, February 20, 1995, p. 16.
19. Aart Jurriaanse, "The New World Religion," *Share International*, December 1994, p. 19.
20. Monte Leach, interview with author.
21. Robison, *Proofs of a Conspiracy*, pp. 24-25.
22. Robert Ellwood, *Theosophy: A Modern Expression of the Wisdom of the Ages* (Madras, India/London, England: Quest Books [The Theosophical Publishing House], 1986), p. 211.
23. Helena Petrovna Blavatsky, *Collected Writings (Miscellaneous)* (Wheaton, IL: The Theosophical Publishing House, 1985), p. xv.
24. Helena Petrovna Blavatsky, *Collected Writings, 1877: Isis Unveiled* (Wheaton, IL: The Theosophical Publishing House, 1972), vol. I, p. 11.
25. Ibid., vol. I, p. 21.
26. Ibid., vol. I, p. 189.
27. Ibid., vol. I, p. 435.
28. Ibid., vol. I, p. 307.
29. Ibid., vol. II, p. 544.
30. Ibid., p. 613.
31. Ibid., p. 217.
32. Ibid., p. 448.
33. Robert Ellwood, *Theosophy: A Modern Expression of the Wisdom of the Ages* (Madras, India/London, England: Quest Books [The Theosophical Publishing House], 1986, pp. 133, 135.
34. Ibid., p. 11.
35. Ibid., p. 137.
36. Blavatsky, *Isis Unveiled*, vol. II, p. 481.
37. Helena Petrovna Blavatsky, *An Abridgement of The Secret Doctrine*, Elizabeth Preston and Christmas Humphreys, eds. (Wheaton, IL: Theosophical Publishing House, 1966), p. 38.
38. Blavatsky, *Isis Unveiled*, vol. I, p. 17.
39. Blavatsky, *The Secret Doctrine*, p. 192.

40. Geoffrey A. Barborka, *H.P. Blavatsky, Tibet and Tulku* (Wheaton, IL: Theosophical Publishing House, 1974), p. 156.

41. Chambers, p. 33.

42. Joscelyn Godwin, *The Theosophical Enlightenment* (New York: State University of New York Press, 1994), p. 378.

43. Blavatsky, *The Secret Doctrine*, p. xx.

44. Godwin, p. 379.

45. Ibid.

46. Ibid., pp. 24, 115, 131, 167.

47. Ibid., p. xi.

48. Jasper, *Global Tyranny*, p. 224.

49. Sylvia Cranston, *HPB: The Extraordinary Life and Influence of Helena Blavatsky, Founder of the Modern Theosophical Movement* (New York: G. P. Putnam's sons, 1993), p. 522.

50. Jasper, *Global Tyranny*, p. 223.

51. Cranston, pp. 523-524.

52. Michael Piller, who has produced and written for *Star Trek: The Next Generation* and *Star Trek: Deep Space Nine*, describes his approach as a "Zen writing outlook." The latter series in particular offers an apparently unending stream of Hindu, Taoist, and Buddhist/Theosophical references and allusions. In *Deep Space Nine's* pilot episode, "The Emissary," the hero undergoes a New Age initiation during an encounter in a "celestial temple" with an unseen alien race called "The Prophets." The parallels to HPB's "Occult Brotherhood" are obvious and probably intentional.

George Lucas is an unabashed New Age adept, and the evolution of his *Star Wars* trilogy illustrates the way in which New Age evangelism can be quite insidious. The first *Star Wars* film was little more than a "space western," except for one thing: the introduction of an undefined element called "The Force," which is expounded by an elderly teacher named Obi-Wan Kenobi. The film's all-American hero is named Luke Skywalker — an interesting choice, given that HPB taught each of her disciples that he should aspire to become a "Walker of the sky" (HPB, *The*

Voice of Silence [Pasadena, California: The Theosophical University Press, 1976] p. 9).

In *The Empire Strikes Back*, the second installment, Skywalker is initiated into the mysteries of The Force by "Yoda," a diminutive guru; the hero's ambition is to become a "Jedi Knight" — a prelude to becoming a "Jedi Master" like Yoda.

Skywalker also discovers that the saga's Lucifer figure — the fallen Jedi Knight Darth Vader — is really his father: In other words, his "Serpent" and his "father" were the same. The parallels to HPB's doctrine are consummated when the Vader, the Lucifer surrogate, becomes Skywalker's savior in *The Return of the Jedi*, the trilogy's final chapter. One more interesting parallel: Although Obi-Wan, Yoda, and Vader are all killed, they return as shimmering, illuminated beings, and — like HPB's "Masters," perhaps? — they can intervene in political and spiritual matters. (For a more detailed analysis of the philosophical content of this pop culture staple, see Richard Grenier, *Capturing the Culture: Politics, Art, and Popular Culture* [Ethics and Public Policy Center, 1991] pp. 3-15.)

53. Cranston, p. 524.

54. David Spangler, *Reflections On the Christ* (Scotland: Findhorn Books, 1981) pp. 44-45.

55. Spangler, *Reflections On the Christ*, dust cover.

56. The Greenhouse Crisis Foundation and the Eco-Justice Working Group of the National Council of Churches of Christ, *101 Ways to Help Save the Earth With Fifty-Two Weeks of Congregational Activities to Save the Earth*, 1990 pp. 27-35.

57. *Earth Prayers From Around the World: 365 Prayers, Poems, and Invocations for Honoring the Earth*, Elizabeth Roberts and Elias Amidon, eds. (San Francisco, CA: HarperSanFrancisco books, 1991) p. xxi.

58. Ibid., p. 94.

59. "Excerpts From Remarks By Vice Presi-

dent Gore At Partnership Inaugura-
tion, October 4 1993," released by the
National Religious Partnership for the
Environment.

60. "Religious Groups Announce Environmental Campaign And Plans To Mobilize 53,000 Congregations," press
release from the National Religious
Partnership For the Environment.
61. *Washington Times*, May 14, 1994.
62. Paul Gorman, interview with author.
63. "History And Organization Background," National Religious Partnership on the Environment press release.
64. Jasper, pp. 225-226.
65. Excerpts from remarks by Vice President Gore, op cit.
66. All of these accounts are taken from an
undated Religious Partnership press
release.
67. *Los Angeles Times*, April 9, 1994 pp.
B4-B5.
68. Al Gore, *Earth In The Balance: Ecology
and the Human Spirit* (New York:
Houghton Mifflin, 1992), p. 238.
69. Ibid., p. 255.
70. Ibid., pp. 258-259.
71. Ibid., p. 14.
72. Ibid., p. 269.
73. For those who are concerned about
individual freedom but who are not
particularly religious, the infiltration of
the churches may not seem to be a
matter of great moment. However,
earth worship has tangible deleterious
effects upon individual rights, particularly property rights. Canada, a country considered by the UN to be an
exemplary nation-state, offers an illustration of earth worship's political
ramifications.

In Canada, environmentalist groups
have direct access to policy-making
bodies at the provincial and federal levels. The story of British Colombia's
"singing trees" offers a remarkable example of "environmentally correct"
Christianity in the service of pagan
environmentalism. On at least one occasion, a provincial land use agency has
used quasi-theosophist language in a
defense of what could be called "tree
rights." This curious episode began in
the spring of 1990 when an organic
farmer named Gladys McIntyre experienced a pantheist epiphany while
planting trees near Duncan Lake in
British Colombia. According to
McIntyre, she received a message from
a nearby grove of old cedar trees: "I interpreted it as a hymn to the joy of
creation."

As it happened, McIntyre was a director of an environmental group called
the Applied Ecological Stewardship
Coalition, which is a component of the
B.C. Commission on Resources and Environment (CORE), a regulatory body
which supervises land-use decisions. In
May 1994, CORE issued guidelines for
future development of the area which
contained McIntyre's "sacred" grove.
Among CORE's recommendations was
the desire to preserve the "spiritual
continuity" of the region inhabited by
the "singing trees." According to the
body, land use strategy should "identify
and conserve physical conditions necessary to the superphysical life-force renewal function."

To provide a quasi-biblical chaser to
this potent shot of New Age spiritualism, CORE enlisted the support of Rev.
Peter Hamel, an Anglican parish Priest
and founder of the Ecumenical Stewards of Creation Council. According to
Rev. Hamel, "People who are close to
the land, the forest, the trees — they
do have spiritual gifts and a sensitivity
to nature that others don't have. I
doubt they are in spiritual error." In
other words, radical environmentalists
are a specially illuminated elite — the
spiritual betters of the working class
hoi-polloi. Hamel underwent some con-
tortions to shoehorn McIntyre's pantheism into a biblical framework:
"Christ died for all of creation. We need
to recognize that's not only humans."
Other species, according to Hamel,
have rights "to have living space, a vi-
able food habitat and food." Those who
seek to take away nature's rights, according to Hamel, will reap retribution

from the "creator" — perhaps in the form of fines or property confiscation imposed by the creator's supposed vicar, the omnipotent state. (Rick Hibbert, "But do they take requests? CORE recognizes the 'spiritual value' of 'singing trees,'" *British Colombia Report*, October 31, 1994, p. 16.)

74. Jasper, *Global Tyranny*, pp. 226-227.

75. Cranston, p. 548.

76. Ibid., p. 552.

77. John T. Flynn, *The Roosevelt Myth* (New York: Devin-Adair, 1956), p. 227; Cranston, p. 551.

78. Cranston, p. 551.

79. Chief Oren Lyon, interview with author.

80. Christopher Story, "Soviet 'Convergence' Strategy & The 'New World Social Order'," *International Currency Review*, Autumn 1994, p. 14.

81. *Los Angeles Times*, October 18, 1994, p. B1.

82. Reuters business report, October 18, 1994.

83. Michael S. Coffman, "The Pagan Roots of Environmentalism," *21st Century Science and Technology*, Fall 1994, pp. 63-64.

84. Tony Perry: "Rangers Kill Cougar After Girl Is Attacked"; *Los Angeles Times*, September 19, 1993; see also William Norman Grigg, "A Problem of Priorities," *The New American*, December 27, 1993.

85. Paul Ciotti, "Cat Fight," *National Review*, December 19, 1994, p. 26.

86. Wayne Pacelle, "We have to learn to live with the mountain lions" (letter to the editor), *Washington Times*, January 6, 1995, p. A20.

87. Fox, p. 15.

88. Norman Myers, *The Gaia Atlas of Future Worlds*, p. 12.

89. Ibid., p. 181.

90. William F. Jasper, "Shackling Planet Earth," *The New American*, Fall 1993 "The Resilient Earth" reprint edition, p. 50.

91. Blavatsky, *The Key to Theosophy* (Madras, India: The Theosophical Publishing House, 1953), p. 262.

— Chapter 8 —
The Coming Persecution of the Faithful?

1. Gerald Barney with Jane Blewett and Kristen R. Barney, *Global 2000 Revisited: What Shall We Do?* Executive Summary (Arlington, VA: The Millennium Institute, 1993) p. 2.

2. Hans Küng, *Global Responsibility: In Search of a New World Ethic* (New York: Crossroad, 1991) p. 23.

3. J. Brian Atwood, address to the "NGO Forum" at the International Conference on Population and Development in Cairo, Egypt, September 5, 1994, transcribed from audiotape.

4. Harold Stassen, *United Nations: A Working Paper for Restructuring* (Minneapolis, MN: Lerner Publications Company, 1994), p. 111.

5. Richard Kirby and Earl D.C. Brewer, "Temples of Tomorrow: Toward a United Religions Organization," *The Futurist*, September-October 1994, pp. 26-28.

6. Larry Witham, "Religions asked to come together for world peace," *Washington Times*, November 9, 1991, p. B11.

7. Ibid., p. 30.

8. Ibid., p. 35.

9. Ibid., p. 69.

10. Witham, op cit.

11. David Neff, "The Supermarket of the Gods: What we should and shouldn't learn from the Parliament of the World's Religions," *Christianity Today*, September 13, 1993, pp. 20-21.

12. William Metzger, "A Theosophical Revival?", *The Quest*, Spring 1995, p. 8.

13. David Briggs, Associated Press wire service, August 23, 1993.

14. Sylvia Cranston, *HPB: The Extraordinary Life and Influence of Helena Blavatsky, Founder of the Modern Theosophical Movement* (New York: G. P. Putnam's sons, 1993), p. 425.

15. Michael McAteer, "In Search of Tolerance World Religions Get Set for Summit to Promote World Peace," *Toronto Star*, August 21, 1993, p. J14.

16. *The World's Parliament of Religions*, Rev. John Henry Barrows, D.D., editor (Chicago, IL: The Parliament Publish-

ing, 1893), p. 171.

17. Cranston, pp. 427-428.

18. Michael Hirsley, "World's religions heading this way," *Chicago Tribune*, June 4, 1993, p. 9N.

19. Gerald Barney, keynote address to 1993 Religious Parliament, p. 2.

20. Jasper, pp. 223, 225-226.

21. Barney et al., *Global 2000 Revisited: What Shall We Do?*, author page.

22. Barney, *Global 2000 Revisited* Executive Summary, pp. 2-3; see also Barney's keynote address.

23. Gerald O. Barney, keynote address to Parliament of World Religions, pp. 31, 34.

24. Barney, *Global 2000* Executive Summary, pp. 10-15.

25. Barney, *Global 2000 Revisited*, appendix beginning on p. 87.

26. Ibid., p. 92.

27. Ibid., p. 95.

28. This was explained to the author by an Icelandic delegate to the 1994 International Conference on Population and Development in Cairo, Egypt.

29. *Deseret News*, September 5, 1993 p. A3.

30. David Briggs, "A U.N. of Religions? Spiritual Leaders Dream of Bringing Peace on Earth," Associated Press wire service, August 16, 1993.

31. *The Declaration of a Global Ethic*, distributed at the Parliament of the World's Religions, August 28-September 5, 1993, Chicago, IL, p. 1.

32. Ibid. The phrase "authentically human" appears regularly throughout the document.

33. Ibid., p. 5.

34. Ibid., p. 6.

35. Ibid.

36. Ibid., p. 7.

37. John West, "Christian, Jewish Clergy Flock to Jerusalem Talks," Reuters World Service, February 1, 1994.

38. Larry Witham, "Extremists draw criticism from religious leaders," *Washington Times*, February 7, 1994, p. A11.

39. Ibid.

40. For two definitive, factually sound accounts of the Waco massacre, see Robert W. Lee, "Truth and Cover-up:

Sorting out the Waco Tragedy," *The New American*, June 14, 1993, p. 23-30; and James Bovard, *Lost Rights: The Destruction of American Liberty* (New York: St. Martin's Press, 1994) pp. 250-255.

41. Cathy Moses, pamphlet published by the Dallas Center for Religious Addiction and Abuse.

42. "Parents Who Brainwash Children With Their Beliefs," The *Donahue Show*, July 6, 1993 (transcript), p. 6.

43. For details of the post-holocaust treatment of the Branch Davidians at the hands of the federal government, see William Norman Grigg, "Christianity as a 'Cult,'" *The New American*, August 23, 1993, pp. 33-35.

44. *Rothbard-Rockwell Report*, January 1995, p. 4. Rep. Brooks' remark was captured on tape and was replayed incessantly in a campaign commercial run by Steve Stockman, who defeated Brooks during the 1994 Congressional campaign.

45. "The President's News Conference, April 20, 1993"; *Weekly Compilation of Presidential Documents*, vol. 29, Number 16, pp. 623, 625.

46. Ibid., p. 645.

47. Sharon D. Cohen, "Fundamentalism: The Zeal to Heal — or Kill," *Salt Lake Tribune*, May 15, 1993, p. A1.

48. *The Religious Right: The Assault on Tolerance and Pluralism in America* (New York: The Anti-Defamation League, 1994), p. 8.

49. See William Norman Grigg, "ADL Campaign Against Tolerance," *The New American*, September 19, 1994.

50. For a thoughtful examination of this trend see Charles Carlson, "Attacking Islam," *The New American*, March 21, 1994.

51. "UN Council Will Not Discuss Religious Liberty," wire service report, July 31, 1964.

52. Anthony Goodman, "UN Adopts religious freedom statement," *Boston Globe*, December 25, 1981, p. A3.

53. Paul Lewis, "U.N. Monitor and the Sudan In Dispute Over Islamic Law,"

New York Times, March 8, 1994 p. A4.

54. Congressman Jim Bunning (R-KY), *Congressional Record*, May 5, 1994, pp. H3117-18.

55. Congressman Jim Sensenbrenner (R-WI), *Congressional Record*, May 5, 1994, pp. H3123-24.

56. Zbigniew Brzezinski, *Between Two Ages: America's Role in the Technetronic Era* (New York: Penguin Books, 1970), p. 64.

57. Ibid., p. 72.

58. Ibid., p. 75.

59. Ibid., pp. 308-309.

60. Francis Fukuyama, *The End of History and the Last Man* (New York: The Free Press, 1992), p. 131.

61. Ibid., p. 204.

62. Ibid., p. 197.

63. Ibid., p. 199.

64. Ibid., p. 216.

65. Ibid., p. 199.

66. John Willson, "The Gods of Revolution," (essay) in *Reflections on the French Revolution: A Hillsdale Symposium*, Stephen J. Tonsor, ed. (Washington, DC: Regnery Gateway, 1990), p. 22.

67. Will and Ariel Durant, *Rousseau and Revolution*, p. 175.

68. Rousseau, *The Social Contract*, Book VIII: "Of The Civil Religion," *Great Books of the Western World*, vol. 38, p. 439.

69. Ibid.

70. Ibid., p. 437.

71. Ibid., p. 438.

72. Ibid., p. 439.

73. Billington, *Fire in the Minds of Men*, pp. 67-71.

74. Willson, pp. 23-25.

75. Willson, p. 28.

76. Erik Ritter Von Kuhnelt-Leddihn, "The Age of the Guillotine (Sade, Robespierre and the Consequences)," in *Reflections on the French Revolution*, p. 77.

77. Will and Ariel Durant, *Rousseau and Revolution*, p. 322; Peter Gay, *The Enlightenment, An Interpretation: The Rise of Modern Paganism* (New York: W.W. Norton and Company, 1966), p. 21.

78. Gay, ibid., p. 93.

79. Ibid., p. 385.

80. Will and Ariel Durant, *The Age of Voltaire*, pp. 760, 768; see also Peter Gay, pp. 24, 200, 355, 388.

81. Will and Ariel Durant, *The Age of Voltaire*, p. 497.

82. Ibid., p. 605.

83. Ibid., p. 757.

84. Ibid., p. 768.

85. Ibid., p. 611.

86. Ibid., p. 776.

87. R.J. Rummel, *Lethal Politics* (New Brunswick, NJ: Transaction Publishers, 1990), p. xi.

— Chapter 9 —
Ending the "Experiment on our liberties": Get *US* Out!

1. Richard Hahnen, remarks at the International Development Conference, workshop entitled "Financing Global Human Security," transcribed from audiotape.

2. Edmund Burke, *Reflections of the Revolution in France* (New York: Penguin Books, 1969) p. 181.

3. *Reforming American Government: The Bicentennial Papers of the Committee on the Constitutional System*, Donald C. Robinson, ed. (Boulder, CO: Westview Press, 1985), p. 160.

4. Timothy Wirth, reply at a press conference during the International Conference on Population and Development, September 7, 1994. See *The New American*, October 3, 1994, p. 12.

5. Paul Craig Roberts, "Cover-up from Idaho to Waco? Role For Congress," *Washington Times*, January 18, 1995, p. A15.

6. Bill Kauffman, "Alice of Malice," *Chronicles*, February 1995, p. 27.

7. Gibbon, p. 355.

8. William F. Jasper, "Victory for the Tenth," *The New American*, October 17, 1994, p. 14.

9. *The John Birch Society Bulletin*, December 1994, pp. 9-11.

10. Roche, *Frederic Bastiat: A Man Alone*, p. 77.

Index

101 Ways to Help Save the Earth,
170, 229
1984, 208, 220
21st Century Science and Technology, 231
21st World Conference of the
Society for International
Development, 151
"365 Prayers, Poems, and Invocations for Honoring the Earth,"
171, 229

Abarca, Pedro Pablo (see also
Aranda), 141-142, 146
Aberdeen, South Dakota, 147
Abraham, Larry, 219
*An Abridgement of The Secret
Doctrine*, 165-166, 228-229
Academy for Educational Development (AED), 53, 221
Academy of Lyons, 143
"Achieving Global Human
Security," 217, 224
ACT-UP, 203
Acton, Lord, 15, 218
ADL (see Anti-Defamation
League)
Adler, Mortimer J., 68, 222
Adorno, Theodor W., 44-45, 220
Africa, 6
The Age of Voltaire, 217, 227, 233
Agency for International Development (AID), 23-24, 34, 56, 64,
98, 122, 124-127, 181, 209, 215
"Agenda 21," 127, 179, 185
Agriculture Ministry, 124
Aid to Families with Dependent
Children, 64
AIDS, 98, 126, 224
Aiken, William, 223
AIM (see American Indian
Movement)
Akenaton, 174
al-Quadir, Abd, 133
Alexandria, Virginia, 52
Allen, Gary, 218-219
Allen, W. B., 218
America 2000, 53
America First (curriculum), 135
American Academy of Child and
Adolescent Psychiatry, 83
American Association for the
Advancement of Science, 109
The American Crime Factory, 79
American Federation of Teachers,
52
American Indian, 146, 148, 153-
154
*American Indian Culture: Traditionalism and Spiritualism in
a Revolutionary Struggle*, 148
American Indian Movement
(AIM), 7, 38, 65, 135, 146-148,
150-153, 227
American Legion, 220
American Library Association

(ALA), 136
American Opinion, 218
American Psychologist, 82, 223
"American troops are being conscripted into a New World Army," 219 AmeriCorps, 48
Ames, Fisher, 15, 218
Ames, Seth, 218
Amidon, Elias, 229
Anderson, Terry L., 153, 227
Anglin, Robert J., 225
"Anthropic Cosmological Principle," 160
Anti-Defamation League of B'nai B'rith (ADL), 192-193, 232
AP (see Associated Press)
Applied Ecological Stewardship Coalition, 230
The Aquarian Conspiracy, 168
Aranda, Count (Pablo Pedro Abarca), 141-142, 146
Aristide, Jean-Bertrand, 2
Aristotle, 61, 222
Arizona State Hospital, 191
Arlington, Virginia, 185
Arndt, Christian O., 220-221
Arone, Shidane, 3
Ascended Masters, 161
Aspen Institute for Humanistic Studies, 10, 68, 174
Associated Press (AP), 231-232
ATF (Bureau of Alcohol, Tobacco, and Firearms), 147, 196
Atlanta Journal and Constitution, 219
Atlantean era, 162
Atlantic Monthly, 219, 227
Atwood, J. Brian, 125-126, 181, 185, 231
Augustine (see St. Augustine)
Aurangzeb, 133
The Authoritarian Personality, 44,

220
Aztec, 133-134, 154-155, 177

Babel, Tower of, 164
Babeuf, Gracchus, 128
Babur, 133
Baca Grande, 174
Baghdad, 2
Bailey, Alice, 162
Balkans, 2
Baltic, 15
Bane, Mary Jo, 55
Bank of England, 22
Barber, Ben, 217
Barborka, Geoffrey A., 229
Barclay, Dolores, 221
Barere, Bertrand, 62, 219, 227
Barney, Gerald O., 157, 181, 185, 220, 228, 231-232
Barney, Kristen R., 231
Barrows, John Henry, 184, 231
Barruel, Abbé, 218
Bassus, Baron, 91
Bastiat, Frederic, 18, 23, 215-216, 218, 233
Bastille, 14
BATF (Bureau of Alcohol, Tobacco, and Firearms), 147, 196
Bavarian Illuminism, 11
Beethoven, Ludwig von, 17
Beijing, 53, 94-96, 100, 102, 124
Beijing Women's Research Institute, 94
Belgian Congo, 2
Belgian UNICEF, 3, 221
Bell, Daniel, 44-45, 221
Benedict (see Spinoza)
Bennet, Douglas, 35
Bennett, William J., 79
Berelson, Bernard, 114-115
Berkeley, California, 138
Bernstein, Richard, 138-139, 226-

227

Berthier, Guillaume Francois, 203-204

Bertrand Barere: A Reluctant Terrorist, 219, 227

Besant, Annie, 165, 171, 184

Besharov, Douglas, 74

The Best Enemy Money Can Buy, 219

Bethell, Tom, 226

Between Two Ages, 198, 233

Beyond Freedom and Dignity, 51, 221

Bible (Holy), 27, 164, 200

Bigelow, William, 138, 226

The Bill, 221

Bill of Rights, 194

Billingsley, K. L., 74

Billington, James H., 10-11, 13-14, 217-219, 233

Biro, Gaspar, 196

The Birth of the Modern: World Society 1815-1830, 218

Black Hand, 218

Black Legend, 140-143

Blanc, Louis, 18-19

Blavatsky, Helena Petrovna, 162-167, 171, 173-175, 180, 184, 228-229, 231

Blewett, Jane, 231

Blumenfeld, Samuel L., 220

Bolshevik, 23, 65, 219

A Book for Parents, 66

Borah, William, 210

Bosnia, 2

Bosphorous, 15

Boston Globe, 58, 159, 220-221, 225, 228, 232

Boulding, Kenneth, 116

Boutros-Ghali, Boutros, 160

Bovard, James, 232

Boyle, Alix, 223

Bradshaw, John, 173

Branch Davidians, 76, 147, 189-192, 196, 232

Brave New Family, 221-222

Brave New World, 42

Brewer, Earl D. C., 182, 231

Brezhnev, Leonid, 23

Briggs, David, 231-232

Britain, 120-121

British Colombia, 223, 230

British Colombia Report, 231

Bronfenbrenner, Urie, 67-68

Brooke, Tal, 228

Brooks, Jack, 191

Brotherhood of the Masters of Wisdom, 164

Brundtland, Gro Harlem, 110, 225

Brussels, 3, 55

Brzezinski, Zbigniew, 198-199, 233

Buddhism, 159, 162, 166, 171, 188, 229

Budget of the United States Government, 222

Bunch, Charlotte, 224

Bund der Gerechten (see League of Just Men)

Bunning, Jim, 197, 233

Bureau of Alcohol, Tobacco and Firearms (BATF, ATF), 147, 192, 196

Bureau of Indian Affairs, 147

Burgess, Ann, 79

Burke, Edmund, 208, 233

Burning Reichstag Gambit, 77

Burns, James MacGregor, 82, 208-209

Burry, Gail, 131, 226

Bush, George, 26, 133, 213

Bush Administration, 79

"But Can Juanito Really Read?," 226

Caesar, Julius, 1
Cain, 164
Cairo, Egypt, 2, 53, 100, 106-107,
    110-111, 115, 120, 122-128,
    130, 181, 185, 217, 225-226,
    231-232
Cairo Conference (see also Int'l
    Conf. on Pop. & Develop.), 106,
    110, 115, 120, 122-128, 130,
    209, 225
Cairo Programme of Action, 2,
    110, 125, 225
Calderone, Mary, 46-47
Caldwell, Taylor, 7, 217
Calhoun, Arthur W., 64-66, 72,
    222
Callahan, Sonny, 4
Calne, Roy, 120-121
Cambridge University, 120
Camp, Sharon L., 48-49, 66, 123,
    127-128, 226
Canada, 87-88, 230
"Canadian Regiment Disbanded,"
    217
cannibalism, 154
Capra, Fritjof, 168
Captains and the Kings, 217
*Capturing the Culture: Politics,
    Art, and Popular Culture*, 229
Cardenal, Ernesto, 171
Carey, George, 189-190
Carlson, Allan, 221
Carlson, Charles, 232
Carlsson, Ingvar, 5
Carmen, Andrea, 151-152, 227
Carnegie, Andrew, 23, 69, 222
Carnegie Corporation, 69
Carnegie Quarterly, 222
Carter, Jimmy, 23, 168, 198
Carter Administration, 185
*The Case for Compulsory Birth
    Control*, 117, 225

Castel, Charles Irénée (see also
    Saint-Pierre), 8
Castelreagh, 16
Castro, Fidel, 148
Cathedral of St. John the Divine,
    58, 167, 172
Catholicism, 141
CED (see Committee for Economic
    Development)
CEDAW (see Convention on the
    Eradication of All Forms of
    Descrimination Against
    Women)
Central Intelligence Agency (CIA),
    25
Centre for Information on Chil-
    dren and Sexuality (CRIES), 56
CFCCA (see New York State
    Council of Family and Child
    Caring Agencies)
CFR (Council on Foreign Rela-
    tions), 10, 21-26, 33, 35, 53, 70,
    106, 122-123, 125, 146, 158,
    182, 199, 208-209, 212-213, 219
CGG (see Commission on Global
    Governance)
Chambers, Claire, 46, 221, 226,
    228-229
Chandler, Kurt, 223
change agents in human evolu-
    tion, 51
change agents, women as, 224
Chapel Hill, North Carolina, 137
Charles III, 141-142
Charter of the United Nations, 5,
    26, 39, 182
Chasteen, Edgar R., 117-119, 225
Chavez, Cesar, 134
Chernow, Ron, 21, 219
Chesterton, G. K., 59-60, 62-63,
    65, 221-222
Chiapas, Mexico, 151

Chicago Public School System, 50
Chicago Tribune, 94, 223-224, 232
child abuse, 47, 72, 74, 76, 85-86, 214, 222
Child Protective Services (CPS), 86
China, 2-3, 42, 89, 94-97, 100-102, 107, 120-124, 127, 129-130, 133-134, 224, 226
China Women's Health Network, 124
Chinese Academy of Social Sciences, 124
Chinese Cultural Revolution, 134
Chinese Family Planning Association, 123
Chinese State Statistical Bureau, 102
Chinese Women's Federation, 101
Choices in Childbearing: When Does Family Planning Become Population Control?, 225
"The Christ," 162, 169
Christ Jesus, 158, 201, 230
Christ the Good Shepherd Eastern Orthodox Church in St. Louis, 172
Christensen, Bryce J., 88-89, 224
Christianity, 2, 9, 11-12, 103, 131, 136-138, 141-143, 145, 149, 151, 159, 164, 166, 170-171, 181, 186-187, 189-192, 198-200, 202-204, 211, 216, 220, 230-232
Christianity Today, 231
Christians, 76, 131-132, 172, 187, 193, 201, 203, 211
Christie, Lain, 217
Christmas, 170
Chronicles, 217, 221, 226, 233
Chronology of Education with Quotable Quotes, 222
Chu, Valentin, 129, 226

Church of Jesus Christ of Latter-Day Saints, 85, 223
Church of Satan, 28, 219
Cicero, 1
Ciotti, Paul, 231
The City of God, 7, 217
Civil Constitution of the Clergy, 202
civil religion, 157, 201, 203, 233
Civilian Conservation Corps, 48
Clinton, Bill, 48, 52, 77, 191-192, 196-197
Clinton, Hillary Rodham, 58
Clinton Administration, 33-35, 49, 58, 70, 119, 124, 126, 214
Club of Rome, 108-109
Cockburn, Alexander, 126-127, 226
Coffman, Michael S., 176, 231
Cohen, Sharon D., 192, 223, 232
Cold War, 23, 199, 213
Colgate University, 165
Collected Writings, 1877: Isis Unveiled, 163, 228
Collected Writings (Miscellaneous), 228
The Collective Family: A Handbook for Russian Parents, 67, 222
Colombian Exposition of 1893, 184
Colombian Quincentennial, 136, 139
Colorado, 138, 146, 174
Columbia University, 44
Columbus, Christopher, 136-139, 143-146, 226-228
Columbus Day, 137-139, 146, 227
The Coming of the Cosmic Christ, 228
Commission for the Prevention and Resolution of Conflicts, 6, 132 Commission on Global

Governance, 1, 5, 29, 217

Commission on Resources and Environment (CORE), 230

Committee for Economic Development (CED), 70, 222

Committee on Population and the Economy, 121

Committee on Public Safety, 62, 202

Committee on the Constitutional System, 208, 233

Communism, 3, 7, 24, 149, 226

The Communist Manifesto, 7-8, 17, 63, 222

Communist Party, 27, 37, 55, 101, 107

compulsory abortion, 2, 94, 105, 114, 122

compulsory birth control, 30, 113, 118

compulsory sterilization, 114, 122

Concert For Peace, 223

Concert of Europe, 16

Conference of Allied Ministers of Education (CAME), 9, 11, 13, 35, 37, 52, 66, 102, 112, 124, 135, 147, 158, 162, 199

Confronting Columbus: An Anthology, 226

Confucianism, 159

Congress of Vienna, 16-17

Congressional Research Service, 5

Connecticut Superior Court, 77

Conquest: Montezuma, Cortes and the Fall of Old Mexico, 227

Conquest of Paradise: Christopher Columbus and the Colombian Legacy, 144

Conquest of Paradise: The Columbian Legacy and its Aftermath, 227 *Conscience*, 123, 226

conspiracy, 7, 12, 14, 24, 168, 191, 207, 212, 214, 218-219, 224, 228

Consultation on the Environment and Jewish Life, 171

Continous Progress-Mastery Learning (CP-ML), 50

Contras, 152

Copenhagen, Denmark, 34, 49, 53, 99-101

Copenhagen Declaration, 99

Copenhagen Summit (see also World Summit on Social Development), 53, 101

Corneille de Pauw, Abbe, 142

Cornell University, 109

Corporation for National and Community Service, 48

Cortez, Hernando, 145, 154, 227

Cosmic Christ, 157, 228

Cousteau, Jacques, 109, 225

Covenant on the Rights of the Child, 57

"A Covenant With Death," 225-226

Covention on the Eradication of All Forms of Descrimination Against Women (CEDAW), 92-94, 97, 100

CovertAction, 225

Cranston, Sylvia, 229, 231-232

Cravath, Paul, 21

Creme, Benjamin, 161-162

CRIES (see Centre for Info on Children and Sexuality)

"Crimes Against Women Related to Population Policies," 115

Cuba, 137, 150

Cuddy, Dennis L., 222, 228

cults, 3, 20, 22, 30, 33, 36, 41, 43, 49, 51, 53, 67-68, 76, 80, 93, 95, 97, 99, 102-103, 110-111, 131,

133-135, 137, 139, 142, 145,
148, 153, 157-158, 160, 167,
169, 175-176, 180-182, 188,
191-192, 202-204, 208, 211-212,
214, 229, 232
Custer, South Dakota, 147

d'Alembert, 11
Daddy's Roommate, 86
Dalai Lama, 217
Dalberg-Acton, John Emerich
    Edward, 15, 218
Dallas Center for Religious
    Addiction and Abuse, 190, 232
Davis, John W., 21
Davis, Kingsley, 113-114, 117
Dawit, Seble, 92, 224
de Cuellar, Javier Perez, 88, 123
de Sade, Marquis, 14, 132, 233
de Silva, Alvaro, 221
de Toqueville, Alexis, 15
"Declaration of Continuing
    Independence of the First
    National Indian Treaty"
    Council, 148
The Declaration of a Global Ethic,
    188, 232
Declaration of the Sacred Earth,
    180
Declaration on the Prohibition of
    Violence Against Women, 97
Defense for Children Interna-
    tional, 83
*Demanding Accountability: The
    Global Campaign and Vienna
    Tribunal for Women's Human
    Rights*, 224
democide, 128
Democracy, 14, 19, 44, 68, 75-76,
    78, 150, 222-223
Democratic Societies, 15
Denver, 138, 146, 227

Department of Health, Education,
    and Welfare (HEW), 43
Department of Information and
    International Relations, 217
Department of State Dispatch, 227
Deseret News, 1, 217, 232
DeSirey, Jan, 226
Detroit News, 56
Development — Journal of SID,
    224
Dewey, John, 44
*The Dialectic of Sex: The Case for
    Feminist Revolution*, 93, 224
*Dictatorship of Virtue: Multi-
    culturalism and America's
    Future*, 9, 11, 143, 166
Dictionary of Social Errors, 218
Dodge, Chris, 226
Dohnal, Johanna, 91, 110, 224-
    225
Donahue, Phil, 232
*Draft Outcome of the World
    Summit for Social Develop-
    ment*, 224
Dru, Philip, 19-22, 219
DuBois, W. E. B., 171
Duke of Orleans (Phillip), 14
Duncan Lake, British Columbia,
    230
Durant, Will and Ariel, 8-9, 11,
    142-144, 203-204, 217, 227-228,
    233
Durham, Doug, 147-148
Durham, Jim, 148, 152

"Earth Charter," 6, 149, 174-176
Earth Day, 83, 170, 173, 223
Earth Flag, 173
*Earth In The Balance: Ecology
    and the Human Spirit*, 173,
    230
Earth Mother, 161

Earth Prayers From Around the World, 171, 229

Earth Summit, 107, 127, 149, 174, 179

Earth Times, 220, 224

East West Journal, 167

Eastern Europe, 23, 49

Ebeling, Richard, 89, 224

Eco-Justice Working Group of the National Council of Churches, 170, 229

Economic and Social Council (ECOSOC), 86-87

Ecuador, 151

Ecumenical Stewards of Creation Council, 230

Eddlem, Thomas R., 5

Education For A World Society: Promising Practices Today, 220

Education for International Understanding in American Schools, 41 Education Summit (1989), 133

The Egyptian Gazette, 226

Ehrlich, Anne H., 112, 225

Ehrlich, Paul R., 112-113, 115-117, 119-120, 130, 225

Eisenhower Administration, 24

Elder Brethren, 164

Eleventh International Conference on Public Education, 42

Ellis, Lee, 131

Ellwood, Robert, 228

Emille, 62

The Empire Strikes Back, 229

Enabling Act, 28

Encyclopedia Britannica, 217, 219

Encyclopedists, 11, 142

The End of History and the Last Man, 199, 233

Engels, Friedrich, 63, 79

The Enlightenment, An Interpreta-
tion, 233

Enough is Enough, 77

Environmental Media Association, 149, 176

Environmental Sabbath, 170-171

Equal Rights Amendment (ERA), 4, 7, 15, 26, 40, 60-61, 63, 92-93, 133, 144, 162, 186-187, 198, 211, 224, 233

Essay on the Status of the American Child, 2000 A.D., 82, 223

Etheridge, Samuel, 218

eugenic, 64, 72, 80, 105, 108, 118

European Union, 8

Evangelic Environmental Network, 171

Everett, Samuel, 220-221

Fabian Socialist, 44, 63-65, 165, 171

FACE (see Freedom of Access to Clinic Entrances)

Family Planning Perspectives, 114

Family Preservation and Support Funds, 70

Faust, 27, 219

FBI (see Federal Bureau of Investigation)

FEA (see Florida Education Association)

The Fearful Master: A Second Look at the United Nations, 210, 220 Federal Bureau of Investigation (FBI), 147-148, 192, 196

Federal Income Contributory Act (FICA), 118

The Federalist, 209

Feeney, Tom, 135, 226

Felu, Michel, 56

Ferdinand, Franz, 219

Ferguson, Marilyn, 168

Fermi, Laura, 222
FICA (Federal Income Contributory Act), 118
Figgis, John Neville, 218
Findhorn Community, 167
Finland, 26
Fire In the Minds of Men: Origins of the Revolutionary Faith, 10, 217, 219, 233
Firestone, Shulamith, 93, 224
First Amendment, 82, 195
Fisher, Jim, 15, 210, 218
Fitzpatrick, John C., 218
Fleming, Louis B., 226
Florida Education Association (FEA), 131, 135
Flynn, John T., 175, 231
Foley, Thomas, 212
Ford Foundation, 122, 124
Ford Foundation Report, 226
Foreign Affairs, 22-24
Foreign Intelligence Advisory Board, 25
Fourth of July, 170
Fox, Matthew, 157, 178, 228
Framework for Action to Meet Basic Learning Needs, 52
France, 13-15, 18, 28, 128, 143, 202-204, 215, 220, 227, 233
Franco, 227
Frederic Bastiat: A Man Alone, 218, 233
Freedom of Access to Clinic Entrances (FACE), 24, 36, 64, 177, 195, 197, 208
Freire, Paulo, 137-138
French National Assembly, 13
French Revolution, 13-15, 17-18, 25, 40, 62, 103, 128, 140, 157, 200-202, 208, 211, 218, 226, 233
The French Revolution, 226

Freud, Sigmund, 86
Friends Social Order Committee, 48
Fukuyama, Francis, 199-200, 233
"Fundamentalism: The Zeal to Heal — or Kill," 192, 232
Fundamentalism, 128, 184, 189-194, 202, 232
"Fundamentals of Abiding Peace," 41
The Futurist, 182, 222, 231

Gael, Ann, 148
The Gaia Atlas of First Peoples, 149-150, 152, 227
The Gaia Atlas of Future Worlds, 116, 119, 179, 225, 231
Gaia Day, 170
Gaia, 116, 119-120, 149-150, 152, 157, 161, 163, 169-171, 175-176, 179-180, 186-187, 225, 227-228, 231
Gaia, 157, 161, 163, 169-171, 175-176, 179-180, 186-187, 228
Gaia Hypothesis, 161, 163, 179
Gandhi, Indira, 122
Gandhi, Rajiv, 217
Garbage Mass, 173
Garden of Eden, 165
Gay, Peter, 86, 98, 203, 233
Gay Men's Health Centre, 98
Genesis, 116
Geneva, 42, 85, 223
Genocide Convention, 148
Gerety, Pierre, 38
German National Socialism, 28, 72, 77
Gershoy, Leo, 143, 219, 222, 227
Getz, Monica, 83, 223
Gibbon, Edward, 1, 29, 211, 217, 219, 233
Gill, Charles D., 77-84, 88, 223

Glasgow Herald, 225
Global 2000, 168, 185, 187, 220, 228, 231-232
Global 2000 Revisited: What Shall We Do?, 185, 187, 220, 228, 231-232
Global Campaign for Women's Human Rights, 95
global cooling, 112
global culture, 3, 131
Global Ethos, 183
Global Forum of Spiritual and Parliamentary Leaders for Human Survival, 175
"Global Human Security," 5, 34, 99, 217, 224, 233
Global Responsibility: In Search of a New World Ethic, 183, 231
Global Security Programme (GSP), 6, 132, 217, 226
Global Security Programme Final Report, 217, 226
Global Tribunal on Violations of Women's Human Rights, 95
Global Tyranny ... Step by Step, 22, 219, 225, 229, 231
global village, 3
God, 9, 11-12, 27, 60, 76, 81, 103, 130, 157, 164-165, 174, 186, 188, 194, 199-201, 214
Godwin, Joscelyn, 165-166, 229
Goethe, Johann Wolfgang von, 27, 219
Gomez-Ibanez, Daniel, 185
Gonzales, Tony, 152, 227
"Good Enough for Government Work?," 191
Good Shepherd Eastern Orthodox Church, 172
Goodman, Anthony, 232
Goodrick-Clarke, Nicholas, 187
Gorbachev, Meet Jefferson, 219

Gorbachev, Mikhail, 6, 25, 132, 149, 174-176, 199, 217, 219, 226 Gorbachev, Raisa, 175
Gorbachev Foundation, 6, 217, 226
Gore, Al, 125-126, 171-174, 181, 226, 230
Gorman, Paul, 172, 230
Gould, Stephen Jay, 171
Grant, James P., 56, 58-59, 221
"The Great Blessing of the Waters," 172
Great Books of the Western World, 217, 219, 221-222, 233
Green Crescent, 175
Green Cross, 175
Green lobby, 177-178
Greenhouse Crisis Foundation, 170, 229
Grenier, Richard, 152, 227, 229
Griffin, G. Edward, 220
Grigg, William Norman, 191, 225-226, 228, 231-232
GSP (see Global Security Programme)
Guillebaud, C. W., 222
Guines, James T., 50-51
Gulf War, 2, 213
Gupta era, 133
Guttmacher, Alan, 121

H.P. Blavatsky, Tibet, and Tulku, 229
Hahnen, Richard, 207-208, 233
Haiti, 2, 34, 125-127
Hamel, Peter, 230
Hammarskjold, Dag, 53, 159
Hanoi, 56
Harcourt, Wendy, 99, 224
Hardin, Garrett, 105, 108, 110, 117, 225
Harman, Willis, 168

Harold Pratt House, 24-25
Harper's, 228
Hart, Pat, 135-136, 226
Harwood, Richard, 24, 219
Havel, Vaclav, 160-161, 163, 167, 228
Haves Without Have-Nots, 68, 222
Head Start, 67, 70
Heather Has Two Mommies, 86
Heckethorn, Charles William, 12-13, 18, 218
Hegel, Georg Wilhelm Friedrich, 199-200
Heilongjiang, 94
Heinl, Robert, 56
Hellenism, 198
Heller, Mikhail, 129, 226
Helms, Jesse, 4
HEW (see Department of Health, Education, and Welfare)
Hewlett, Sylvia, 83
Heyzer, Noeleen, 100, 224
Hibbert, Rick, 231
Hills, George, 141, 227
Hillsdale College, 89, 215, 233
Hinduism, 159, 165-166, 173, 184, 192, 229
Hirsley, Michael, 232
Hiss, Alger, 22
The History of the Decline and Fall of the Roman Empire, 217
Hitler, Adolf, 28, 59, 65-66, 70, 139, 154, 226
Ho Chi Minh, 171
Hoar, William P., 222
Hobbs, Nancy, 223
Hoggart, Richard, 220
Hollywood, 149, 176
Holocaust Memorial Museum, 192
"Holy Alliance," 16
Homophobia, 98-99
Hoomi, Koot, 162

House, Edward Mandell, 18, 22, 210, 218-219
The House of Morgan: An American Banking Dynasty and the Rise of Modern Finance, 219
Howland, Charles, 22
HPB: The Extraordinary Life and Influence of Helena Blavatsky, 229
HSUS (see Humane Society of U.S.)
Huitzilopochtli, 154, 177
The Human Cost of Communism in China, 226
Humane Society of U.S. (HSUS), 178
humanist, 33, 44, 61, 188, 198, 211, 221
Hunt, Liz, 177, 226
Hussein, Saddam, 2
Hutchins, Robert Maynard, 217, 219
Huxley, Aldous, 42
Huxley, Julian, 38, 45, 51, 105, 108, 220
Hyde, Jim, 98, 218, 224

I, Rigoberta Menchu, 151
Ibarra, Tony, 151
Iceland, 187, 232
ICPD (see Programme of Action of the UN Conference on Population and Development.)
ICPD Watch, 226
IDC (International Development Conference), 92, 100, 221, 224, 233
An Idea and Its Servants: UNESCO From Within, 220
ILGA (International Lesbian and Gay Association), 86-87
Illuminati, 10-13, 15-16, 18-19,

163, 166, 218
illumines, 11, 14, 20, 141-143, 204
Illuminism: The Great Conspiracy, 218
IMF (International Monetary Fund), 98
The Impact of Science on Society, 220
Incas, 155, 177
An Incomplete Guide to the Future, 168
Indian Treaty Council (ITC), 148, 151-152, 227
Indigenous Peoples Day, 139
Indochina, 56
infanticide, 101-102, 105, 122
Ingolstadt (University of), 11
The Inquiry, 21
Insiders, 7, 21, 210
The Insiders, 219
"Instances of Use of United States Armed Forces Abroad," 5
Institute of International Affairs, 21
International Symposium on Health Education, Sex Education and Education for Home and Family Living, 45
interdependent, 3, 41
International Conference on Population and Development, 2, 91, 105, 217, 225-226, 231-233
International Covenant on Civil and Political Rights, 150
International Criminal Court for Women, 97
International Currency Review, 231
International Decade of Indigenous Peoples, 131
International Development

Conference (IDC), 92, 100, 221, 224, 233
International Indian Treaty Council, 148
International Institute for Intellectual Cooperation, 37
International Lesbian and Gay Association (ILGA), 86-87
International Monetary Fund (IMF), 98
International Organizations Employees Loyalty Board, 38
International Planned Parenthood Fed. (IPPF), 121-124
International Relations Committee, 37
International Symposium on Health Education, Sex Education ..., 45
International Treaty Office (ITO), 148
International Tribunal for Children's Rights (ITCR), 88
International Women's College in China, 124
International Year of Blavatsky, 174
International Year of the Family, 84-85, 87, 98, 223
The Intimate Papers of Colonel House, 218
The Invisible Government, 219
IPPF (see International Planned Parenthood Fed.)
Iran, 193
Irrevocable Directives, 188
Isaiah, 105, 130
Isis Unveiled, 163, 228
Islam, 159, 166, 181, 189, 193-194, 196, 203, 232
ITC (Indian Treaty Council), 148, 151-152, 227

ITCR (International Tribunal for Children's Rights), 88
ITO (see International Treaty Office)
IUDs, 102
IYF (see International Year of the Family)

Jaffe, Frederick, 114-115
James Madison, 219
Jasper, William F., 22, 69, 109, 217, 219, 221, 225, 229-233
Jehovah, 165
Jerusalem, 189, 232
Jesuits (Society of Jesus), 11, 141
Jesus, 134, 164, 204
Jews, 76, 129, 132, 172, 193, 201
Jing Zhiping, 94
Job, Book of (Holy Bible), 27
The John Birch Society (JBS), 212-213, 219, 222, 233
The John Birch Society Bulletin, 233
John of Plano Carpini, 133
Johnson, Paul, 16, 218
Johnstone, Anne, 225
Jomtien, Thailand (Conference), 52-53
Jouffroi, Marquis de, 218
Journal de Trévoux, 203
Journal of Human Rights, 83, 223
Judaism, 159, 166, 189, 198, 203
Judeo-Christian, 173
Julian, Roman Emperor, 38, 45, 51, 105, 108, 211-212, 220
Jurriaanse, Aart, 162, 228
Justamond, J. O., 227
"Justice and Its Harvesters: The National Conference of Catholic Bishops," 217
Justice Court of Maricopa County, 191

Kandell, Jonathan, 228
Karl Marx: The Red Prussian, 218
Katanga, 2
Katme, Kajid, 130
Kauffman, Bill, 233
Kennedy, John F., 146
Kennedy Administration, 24
Kenobi, Obi-Wan, 229
Ketchel, Melvin, 119
The Key to Theosophy, 180, 231
King, Rodney, 215
King Richard III, 217
Kingdom of Heaven, 199
Kinsey, Alfred Charles, 221
Kinsey, Sex and Fraud: The Indoctination of a People, 221
Kirby, Richard, 182, 231
Kirkpatrick Sale, 144, 152, 176, 227
Klinberg, Otto, 44
Koran, 196
Koresh, David, 191-192
Kornfeder, Joseph Z., 37
Korten, David C., 151
Kozak, Robert, 217
Krauthammer, Charles, 4, 217
Kulaks, 129
Küng, Hans, 181, 183, 188, 231

La Capital: The Biography of Mexico City, 228
LaFollette, Hugh, 71, 80, 222-223
Lake County, Florida, 134-135
Lambda Report, 223
Lane, Franklin K., 20
Las Casas, Bartolomé De, 140-141
Lasch, Christopher, 44, 220
Latin America, 6
Laurence, Reginald Vere, 218
"Lavender Lobby," 87
Laves, Walter H. C., 37, 220

LaVey, Anton Szandor, 28, 218-219

Layton, Eunice S. and Felix, 159, 228

Leach, Monte, 161-162, 228

League of Just Men (*Bund der Gerechten*), 7-8, 17

League of Nations Covenant, 21, 210

League of Nations, 20-21, 23, 37, 116

Learning For All: Bridging Domestic/International Education, 52

Lectures on the French Revolution, 15, 218

Lee, Robert W., 221, 232

Leffingwell, Russell, 21

Lenin, V. I., 26, 149, 154, 219

"Lenin Aims Like U.N.'s, Thant Says," 219

"Let It Sink: Why the U.S. Should Bail out of the UN," 217

Lethal Politics, 233

Lewis, John, 122

Lewis, Paul, 221, 232

liberation theology, 142, 151

Liberty, Equality, and Fraternity, 17, 143

licensing parents, 73-74, 76-77, 80, 121

"Licensing Parents," 71, 222

Licensing Parents: Can We Prevent Child Abuse and Neglect?, 72, 222-223

The Limits to Growth, 108-109

Lin Mousheng, 39, 220

Lindisfarne Association, 157, 172, 174

Lindisfarne Institute, 167

Linking Progress to People: An AED Policy Paper for the World

Summit for Social Development, 53, 221

Linowitz, Sol M., 53

Llosa, Mario Vargas, 155, 228

Locke, John, 60, 221

London Daily Telegraph, 226

London Independent, 226

"Lords of Wisdom," 165

Los Angeles Times, 109, 219-220, 225-226, 228, 230-231

Lost Rights: The Destruction of American Liberty, 232

Lucas, George, 168, 229

Lucifer, 165

Lucifer, 166-169, 172, 185, 229

Lucifer Press, 165

Luciferian Theosophical Society, 168

Lucis Trust, 159, 165

Lykken, David, 79-80

Lynch, Column, 228

M'Bow, Amadou Mahtar, 34-36

Machel, Graca, 57, 221

Machel, Samora, 57

MacNeill-Lehrer NewsHour, 210

Madison, James, 16, 26, 30, 73, 209, 212, 218-219

Magna Carta, 58

Magus degree, 12

Mahatmas, 164

Maitreya (Lord), 161-162

Makarenko, A. S., 66-68, 222

Malesherbes, Chretien-Guillaume de Lamoignon de, 9

Manchester Guardian, 121, 225

Mao Tse-Tung, 91, 94, 97, 129, 136, 211

Marburg, Theodore, 23

Marcellus, 1

Martinez, Miguel Alfonzo, 150-152

Marx & Satan, 218

Marx, Karl, 2, 7-8, 17, 19-20, 23, 27, 37, 44, 63, 65, 79, 93, 133, 137-138, 142, 148-152, 170, 175-176, 198-199, 218, 222
Marxism, 23, 149, 151-152, 198-199
Marxism-Leninism, 149
Masada (ancient Palestine), 190
Masters of Wisdom, 164
Mastery Learning, 50
Maya, 133
Mayor, Federico, 36
Mazimuka, Patric, 124-125
Mazzini, Giuseppe, 19, 219
McAteer, Michael, 231
McCarthy, Tom, 173
McDonald's restaurant, 213
McGovern, Celeste, 223
McIntyre, Gladys, 230
McManus, John F., 219, 224
McNamara, Robert S., 122, 158
Mead, Margaret, 117
Meadows, Donella H., 109, 225
Means, Russell, 138, 146
Meisler, Stanley, 220
Melbourne, Australia, 98
Memorial and Remonstrance Against Religious Assessments, 219
Menchu, Rigoberta, 151-152
Mephistopheles, 27
Mercier, Louis-Sebastien, 14, 18
Metternich, Prince Klemens Wenzel Nepomuk Lothar von, 16
Metzger, William, 231
Mexico, 150-151, 227-228
Mexico City, 151, 228
Millennium Institute, 34, 157, 181, 185, 220, 228, 231
The Mind of the Founder, 218
Minneapolis *Star-Tribune*, 80, 223

Mirabeau, Honoré Gabriel Victor Riqueti, 13
Miwetok, 137
Mohammed, 204
Molnar, Thomas, 2, 217
Mongella, Gertrude, 95-96
Mongols, 133
Montana State University, 153
Montezuma, 154, 227
Montreal, Canada, 88
Morgan, J. P., 20-22, 219
Morgan, Joy Elmer, 37, 40
The Morning After: American Successes and Excesses 1981 - 1986, 220
Morse, Jedediah, 16
Morse, Samuel, 16
Morya, 162
Moses, Cathy, 190, 232
Moses, 204
Mosher, Steven W., 101, 224-225
Moslems, 132, 192-193
Mother Earth, 157, 179, 228
Mother's Day, 170
A Mother's Ordeal: One Woman's Fight Against China's One-Child Policy, 101, 224-225
Mozambique, 3, 57
MTV, 77
Mughal, 133
Muller, Robert, 158, 160
multiculturalism, 131-136, 138-140, 142, 144-145, 148, 151, 153-155, 164, 178, 185, 226
Murphy, Ray, 220
Muslims, 106, 126, 130
Mussolini, Benito, 65, 95
Mussolini, 222
"Muter Und Kind," 65, 70
Myers, Norman, 119-120, 179, 225, 231
Mysticism, 163, 165-166, 173, 184

N.E.A. Trojan Horse in American Education, 220
NAMBLA (see North American Man-Boy Love Association)
Nance, Bud, 4
Napoleon, 11, 16
Nash, Gary, 134
The Nation, 191
National Center for the Prevention of Child Abuse, 74
National Center on Child Abuse, 74
National Committee for the Rights of the Child, 83
National Conference of Catholic Bishops 217
National Council of Churches of Christ, 136, 170-171, 229
National Council of Education Activists, 136
National Education Association (NEA), 37, 40-41, 52, 83, 131, 136 National Endowment for the Humanities, 133
The National Gazette, 16
National Guard, 215
National Institutes of Mental Health, 51
The National Interest, 199
National Religious Partnership for the Environment (NRPE), 171-173
National Review, 226, 231
National Rifle Association (NRA), 208
national service, 48-49
National Socialism, 7, 28, 65-66, 72, 77, 108, 139, 211
National Standards for World History, 133
National Standards project, 134
National Task Force for

Children's Const. Rights, 77, 81-82, 223 Nationalizing U.S. Education, 69
NATO, 68
Nazi, 28, 65, 89, 105, 118, 129, 187, 222
The Nazi Dictatorship: A Study in Social Pathology and the Politics of Fascism, 222
Nazi Germany, 65, 89, 105, 129, 222
NEA (see National Education Association)
NEA Journal, 37, 40
NEA Today, 136
Neff, David, 231
Nekrich, Aleksandr M., 129, 226
Network of Educators on Central America, 138
New Age, 167
New Age, 144, 157, 162, 166-169, 171, 173-174, 185, 228-230
New Age Journal, 228
New Age University, 144
The New American, 69, 191, 217, 219-222, 224-226, 228, 231-233
The New American Right, 44
New Covenant, 182-183
New Deal, 22, 48
The New Republic, 4, 217
New World Army, 219
New World Church, 162
New World Economic Order, 35
New World Information Order, 35
New World Order, 63
New World Order, 3, 8, 14, 26, 30, 33, 36, 105, 155, 182-183, 213, 220, 225
New World Religion, 162, 180, 190,
New Worlds For Old, 63-64, 222
New York Green Party, 144

New York Law School, 83, 223
New York Law School Journal of Human Rights, 223
New York Native American Solidarity Committee, 148
New York State Council of Family and Child Caring Agencies (CFCCA), 85
New York Times, 35, 79, 102, 138, 220-221, 223, 226, 233
Newsweek, 48, 213, 219
NGO Forum, 226, 231
Nicaragua, 137, 151-152
Nicaraguan Indians, 152
Nobel Peace Prize, 151, 227
Non-Governmental Organizations (NGOs), 34, 151, 161, 226, 231
None Dare Call It Conspiracy, 219
Norplant, 80, 115-116, 126
North American Man-Boy Love Association (NAMBLA), 87, 223
Now is the Dawning of the New Age New World Order, 228
NRA (National Rifle Association), 208
NRPE (National Reglious Partnership for the Environment), 171-173 NTFCCR (see National Task Force for Children's Const. Rights)

O'Brien, Big Brother's (*1984*) agent, 33
OBE (see Outcome-Based Education)
"Observations on the Continuous Progress of Universal Reason," 8
Occult Brotherhood, 163-165, 229
The Occultic Roots of Nazism, 187
Odio, Elizabeth, 96

Office of Economic Opportunity, 147
Office of Management and Budget, 222
Office of National Drug Control Policy, 79
Ohio Northern University Law Review, 82, 223
Olcott, Henry Steel, 163, 165
On Political Economy, 62
one-child policy, 101, 122, 224
"Operation Restore Hope," 3
The Order, 12-14
Ortega, Daniel, 152
Orwell, George, 33, 220
Out Of Control: Who's Watching our Child Protection Agencies?, 223
Outcome-Based Education (OBE), 50-53
Oxford University, 121

Pacelle, Wayne, 178, 231
PAI (see Population Action International)
The Paideia Proposal: An Educational Manifesto, 68, 222
Pakistan, 3, 113
Palais-Royal, 14
Panama Canal Treaties, 53
Pantheism, 176, 230
Parade, 221
Paris Commune, 128
Parker, Shafer Jr., 223
Parliament of World Religions, 184, 189, 232
Patron Cities Conference, 85
Pax Americana, 26
Pax Universalis, 26
Payson, Seth, 15, 218
PBS (see Public Broadcasting System)

Peace Altar, 185
Peace Corps, 48
Peace Through Culture, 175
People's University in Beijing, 102
People-Centered Concensus, 151
People-Centered Development
    Forum, 151
Perfektibilisten, 11
Perloff, James E., 219
Perry, Tony, 231
Philip Dru: Administrator — A
    Story of Tomorrow, 19, 22, 219
Philosophical and Political
    History of the Settlements and
    Trade of the Europeans in the
    East and West Indies, 143, 227
Philosophy and Public Affairs,
    222
Piller, Michael, 229
Pimentel, David, 109
"Plan for Perpetual Peace," 8, 10
Planetary Citizens, 166-167
Planned Parenthood, 69, 114, 117,
    121
Plato, 8, 61-63, 70-71, 222
Platonic Guardians, 8
Plaza de Cesar Chavez, 134
"Plugging away in the United
    States," 220
Pluralism, 183, 192, 232
Podebrady, Czechoslovakia
    (seminar), 42
The Politics (Aristotle), 61, 222
Polytheism, 211
The Pope, 226
Population, Resources, Environ-
    ment: Issues in Human Ecol-
    ogy, 112, 225
Population Action International
    (PAI), 123, 127-128
The Population Bomb, 112, 225
Population Crisis Committee, 123

The Population Explosion, 112-
    113, 225
Population Fund, 33, 122
Powell, Philip Wayne, 140-142,
    227
Pratt, Harold, 24-25
Preston, Elizabeth, 228
Programme of Action (UN Intl
    Conf on Pop & Devlop —
    ICPD), 105-106, 110, 123, 125,
    221, 224-226
Project '87, 208
Project de paix perpetuelle, 217
"A Project to Perfect the Govern-
    ments of States," 8
Proofs of a Conspiracy, 218, 224,
    228
Proofs of the Real Existence and
    Dangerous Tendency of
    Illuminism, 218
Proposition 117, 177
Public Broadcasting System
    (PBS), 210
public education, 42, 62, 127, 136
Pyle, Cassandra A., 53

Qian Xinzhong, 123
Quebec, Canada, 88
Queer Nation, 203
The Quest, 38, 184, 231
Quetzalcoatl, 134, 154

Radford, Tim, 225
The Radical Right: The New
    American Right expanded and
    updated, 45, 220
Ramadan, Mohammed, 159
Ramage, David, 188
Ramey, Paul, 46-47
Ramphal, Shridath, 1, 5-6, 29,
    182, 217
RAND Corp, 199

Raynal, Abbe Guillaume, 143-145, 149, 227
Reading Rousseau in the Nuclear Age, 217
Reagan, Ronald, 34-35, 148
Reagan Administration, 35
Red China (see also China), 2-3, 89, 101
Reflections on the Christ, 168, 229
Reflections on the French Revolution, 233
Reflections on the Revolution in France, 233
Reforming American Government: The Bicentennial Papers, 233
Reichstag, 28, 77
Reilly, Niamh, 224
Reisman, Judith A., 56, 221
Religious Freedom Restoration Act (RFRA), 196-197
"Religious Leadership in Secular Society," 189
The Religious Right: The Assault on Tolerance and Pluralism in America, 192, 232
Reno, Janet, 89
The Republic, 70, 222
"The Resilient Earth," 231
Rethinking Columbus, 136
The Return of the Jedi, 229
Reuters Business Report, 227, 231
reversible fertility immunization, 118
Revolutionary Activities Within the United States: The American Indian Movement, 227
Rex degree, 12
RFRA (see Religious Freedom Restoration Act)
Rhodes, Cecil, 10, 21
Rhodes Scholar, 10
Richie, David S., 48-49, 221

Richman, Sheldon, 221
Riemer, Neal, 219
RIIA, 21
Rio Earth Summit, 100, 107, 109, 127, 149, 174, 179
The Rise and Fall of the Third Reich: A History of Nazi Germany, 222
"The Road from Cairo to Copenhagen to Beijing," 53
Roberts, Elizabeth, 229
Roberts, Paul Craig, 233
Robespierre, Maximilien de, 128-129, 233
Robinson, Donald C., 233
Robison, John, 218, 224, 228
Roche, George, 215, 218, 233
Rockefeller, David, 198
Rockefeller, John D. IV, 158
Rockefeller, John D., 23
Rockefeller Brothers Fund, 181, 185
Rockefeller foundations, 122
Rockford Institute, 88
Roerich, Nicholas, 175
Roerich Fund, 175
Romania, 42
Romberg, Alan, 35
Rome, 108-109, 211
Roosevelt, Edith Kermit, 23, 228
Roosevelt, Franklin Delano, 22, 48, 175, 231
Roosevelt, Grace G., 217
Roosevelt, Theodore, 23
Roosevelt Administration, 22
The Roosevelt Myth, 175, 231
Ross, Rick Allen, 191-192
Rothbard-Rockwell Report, 232
Rousseau, Jean-Jacques, 9-11, 13, 16, 25, 61-63, 66, 89, 141, 143, 149, 157, 201-203, 217, 222, 227-228, 233

Rousseau and Revolution, 217, 227-228, 233

Royal Institute of International Affairs (RIIA), 21

Ruffo, Andree, 88

"Ruling Class Journalists," 219

Rummel, R. J., 204, 233

Rusk, Dean, 53

Russell Sage Foundation, 116

Russell, Bertrand, 21, 33, 50, 116, 138, 146, 220

Russia, 89, 120, 174-175

Russian Revolution, 25

Rwanda, 124, 151, 226

Ryan, Michael, 221

Sabbah, Michael, 189

Sacramento Bee, 178

Sagan, Carl, 171

Sage, Russell, 116

Saint Augustine, 7, 217

Saint-Pierre, Abbé de, 8-10, 16, 25, 217

Salas, Rafael, 123

Salt Lake City, 85

Salt Lake Tribune, 223, 227, 232

San Francisco Examiner, 196

San Jose, California, 134, 226

San Luis Valley, California, 174

Sandinistas, 137, 152

Satan (The Accuser), 27

Satan, 13, 26-28, 165, 218-219

The Satanic Rituals, 218

Saturday Review, 36, 220

Savenay (France), 203

Schiff, Jacob, 23

Schlesinger, Arthur Jr., 146, 227

Schmetzer, Uli, 224

Schoener, Barbara, 177-178

Schulman, Frederick L., 222

Schwartzschild, Leopold, 218

Science, 113, 225

Scotland, 167, 229

Scott, Brenda, 85, 223

The Secret Doctrine, 165-166, 228-229

The Secret Societies of all Ages and Countries, 218

secularists, 141, 144

Security Programme (GSP), 6, 132, 217, 226

Senate Judiciary Committee, 38, 227

Sensenbrenner, Jim, 197, 233

Separating School & State: How to Liberate America's Families, 221

sex education, 45-47, 92-93

Sex Information and Education Council of the United States (SIECUS), 46-47, 221, 226, 228

Seymour, Charles, 19-20, 218-219

SFPC (see State Family Planning Commission of China)

The Shadows of Power, 219

Shakespeare, William, 10, 217

Shalala, Donna, 70, 72

Shannon, Don, 228

Share International, 161-162, 228

Shattuck, John, 150

Shenon, Philip, 102

Shepard, Daniel J., 220

Sheraton Maria Isabel Hotel, 151

Shevardnadze, Eduard, 199

Shirer, William L., 222

Shultz, George, 35

SID (see Society for International Development)

The SIECUS Circle: A Humanist Revolution, 46, 221, 226, 228

Simmons, Bill, 151, 227

Simons, Helen, 111, 225

Singapore, 100, 120

Skinner, B. F., 50-51, 221

Skywalker, Luke, 229
Smoot, Dan, 219
Snyder, G. W., 218
The Social Contract, 233
Social Development Summit (Copenhagen, 1995), 34, 49, 99, 221, 224
Social Errors, 218
A Social History of The American Family: From Colonial Times to the Present, 64, 222
The Social Policy of Nazi Germany, 222
Social Security Administration, 118
Socialist International, 110
Society for International Development (SID), 98-99, 151, 224
Society for the Scientific Study of Sex (SSSS), 46-47
Society of Jesus (see also Jesuits), 11, 141
Somalia, 3
South Africa, 162
Souza de Farias, Marie, 115
Sovereign Nations or Reservations?, 227
Soviet Ministry of Education, 38
Soviet Union (USSR), 6, 22-23, 68, 174, 226
Spain, 140-142, 146, 227
Spangler, David, 167-169, 185, 229
Spanish Empire, 140
Sparta, 128
Special Committee to Investigate Tax-Exempt Foundations, 69
Special Rapporteur, 97, 150
Spinoza, Benedict de, 12
"Spiritual Hierarchy," 161
Spiritualism, 149, 173, 230
SSSS (see Society for the Scientific Study of Sex)
St. John the Evangelist Roman Catholic Church, 173
St. Leonard's Roman Catholic Church, 173
Stalin, Josef, 23, 27, 59, 129
Star Trek, 168, 229
Star Trek: Deep Space Nine, 229
Star Trek: The Next Generation, 115, 229
Star Wars, 168, 229
Starting Points: Meeting the Needs of Our Youngest Children, 69-70
Stassen, Harold, 182, 231
State Department, 22, 35, 60, 150, 199
State Department for Education and Universal Social Adjustment, 60
State Family Planning Commission (SFPC) of China, 123
Stephens, Gene, 71-72, 222
sterilization, 2, 94, 114-115, 118-119, 122, 125-126, 226
Stewart, Michael, 85
Stockman, Steve, 232
Story, Christopher, 231
The Strangest Friendship in History, Woodrow Wilson and Colonel House, 219
Strong, Maurice, 149, 152, 174, 180
Studies for the 21st Century, 34
Sudan, 196, 232
Sunday Times of London, 121, 226
Supreme Court, 197
"Sur le Système de la Dépopulation," 128
sustainable development, 87, 99-100, 106-107, 109, 124-125, 128-130, 153, 170, 181, 185-186

"Sustainable Societies and Global Governance: The People-Centered Concensus," 151
Sweden, 5, 221
Swindler, Leonard, 183
Switzerland, 183

Ta Ta, Tan Tan ("Fight, fight, talk talk..."), 226
Talleyrand-Perigord, Charles Maurice de, 13
Tao Teh Ching, 164, 188, 229
Taoism, 188, 229
Tasmania, 196
Tax Reform IMmediately (TRIM), 212-213
TC (Trilateral Commission), 24, 26, 70, 198, 213
The Teacher and World Government, 40
Teachers College (Columbia University), 44
Teaching About the United Nations, 43, 220-221
Temple Emmanuel, 172
"Temple of Understanding," 158-159, 165-166, 172, 185, 228
"Temples of Tomorrow: Toward a United Religions Organization," 182, 231
Ten Commandments, 176
Tenochtitlan, 154
Tenth Amendment, 212
terror, 2, 17, 57, 89, 128, 137, 200-201, 203
The Terror, 201, 203
Thanksgiving, 136, 170
The Theosophical Enlightenment, 166, 229
Theosophical Publishing House, 228, 231
Theosophical Society, 163, 165-

166, 168, 180, 184
The Theosophist, 159, 161-165, 171, 175
Theosophy: A Modern Expression of the Wisdom of the Ages, 228
Theosophy: Key To Understanding, 228
Theosophy, 159, 161-166, 168, 171, 174-176, 180, 184, 228-229, 231
Thingvellir, Iceland, 187
Thingvellir Oath, 187
Thomas, Hugh, 227
Thomas, Norman, 158
Thompson, William Irwin, 157
Thomson, Charles A., 37, 220
"Three Most Famous Impostors: Moses, Jesus, and Mohammed," 204
Tibet, 163, 217, 229
Tibet: Environment and Development Issues 1992, 217
Tlacaelel, 154
Tonsor, Stephen J., 233
Too Many People, 77, 120-121
Toronto Star, 231
Torres, Esteban E., 35
"Toward a Police State," 219
Toward International Understanding, 50, 132
Towards World Understanding, 41-42, 132, 220
Towards World Understanding, Vol. I: Some Suggestions on Teaching, 41-42, 220
Towards World Understanding, Vol. V: In The Classroom, 42, 220
Tower of Babel, 164
Toynbee, Arnold, 201
trade, 143, 193, 221, 227
Transnational Network of Citizen

Action Groups, 132
"Tree of Hate," 142
Tree of Hate: Propaganda and Prejudices Affecting United States Relations with the Hispanic World, 227
Trilateral Commission (TC), 24, 26, 70, 198, 213
TRIM (see Tax Reform IMmediately)
Trudell, John, 153
True and Only Heaven: Progress and its Critics, 220
Tufts University School of Medicine, 119
Tulsa World, 221
Turkey, 135
The Turning Point, 168
Twentieth Century Fund, 22

U Thant, 26, 219
U.S. Catholic Conference, 171
UFO, 159
Ukraine, 129
Ukraine depopulation, 129
UN Charter, 5, 26, 39, 182
UN Children's Fund (UNICEF), 3, 55-59, 98, 217, 221
UN Chronicle, 87, 223
UN Commission Against Torture, 96
UN Convention on the Rights of the Child, 39, 57-59, 71, 77-83, 85, 87-88, 118, 196, 221, 223
UN Copenhagen Summit (see Social Development Summit)
UN Economic Security Council, 6
UN General Assembly, 25-26, 83
UN Genocide Convention, 148
UN Human Rights Commission, 195-196
UN Human Rights Committee,

150
UN Population Fund, 33, 122
UN's Convention on the Eradication of All Forms of Discrimination, 92
UN's Environmental Sabbath, 170-171
UN's International Covenants on Civil and Political Rights, 194
UN's Temple of Understanding, 165-166, 185
UN's World Conference on Human Rights, 95
UN Society for Enlightenment and Transformation, 159
UN World Conference on Women (1995), 94-96, 100
UN World Summit on Social Development, 34, 49, 99, 221, 224
UNDP (see United Nations Development Programme)
UNESCO, 26, 33-54, 57, 105, 108-109, 132, 135, 183, 220
UNESCO: Its Purpose and Philosophy, 220
UNESCO: Purpose, Progress, Prospects, 220
UNESCO Courier, 109
The Unfinished Agenda: A New Vision For Child Development and Education, 70, 185, 222
UNFPA (see United Nations Fund for Population Activities)
"United Nations General Assembly Commission for the Prevention and Resolution of Conflicts," 6, 132
UNICEF, 3, 55-59, 98, 217, 221
"UNICEF Wants Your Children," 217, 221
UNIFEM (see United Nations

Development Fund for Women)
Union of Concerned Scientists, 171
United Lodge of Theosophists of
New York, 159
*United Nations: A Working Paper
for Restructuring*, 231
United Nations Association, 125
United Nations Bureau of Education, 37
*United Nations Convention on the
Rights of the Child: Individual
Rights Concepts ...*, 223
United Nations Department of
Public Information, 161
United Nations Development
Fund for Women (UNIFEM),
95, 100, 224 United Nations
Development Programme
(UNDP), 33, 98
United Nations Economic and
Social Council (ECOSOC), 87
United Nations Environment
Program, 170
United Nations Fund for Population Activities (UNFPA), 3, 98,
122-124
"The United Peoples of the
World," 37
United Religions Organization
(URO), 182, 231
United Species Conference, 179
United States Coalition for
Education For All (USCEFA),
52, 221
Universal Brotherhood of Humanity, 165
Universal Church, 162
Universal Declaration of Human
Rights, 39, 183
Universal Mystic Brotherhood,
164
Universal State, 200

University of Minnesota, 79
University of South Carolina, 71
University of Wisconsin-Madison,
72
URO (United Religions Organization), 182, 231
USCEFA (see United States
Coalation for Education For
All)
USCEFA Conference Report, 221
Utah, 1, 85
*Utopia in Power: The History of
the Soviet Union From 1917 to
the Present*, 226

Vader, Darth, 229
Vance, Cyrus, 23
Vanderlip, Frank, 20
Varma, Ashali, 224
Vendée (France), 128, 202
Verbeek, Jos, 55-56
Victorian AIDS Council, 98
Vienna, 16-17, 95, 100, 223-224
Viereck, George Sylvester, 219
Vietnam, 56
Vivikenanda, Swami, 184-185
The Voice of Silence, 229
Voltaire, 11, 141-143, 166, 203-
204, 217, 227, 233
Volunteers in Service to America,
48
von Kuhnelt-Leddihn, Erik Ritter,
233
von Mises, Ludwig, 89
Vonnegut, Kurt, 166

Waco, Texas, 76, 147, 189-192,
210, 232-233
"Waco Expertise With A Vengeance," 191
Waite, Terry, 121
Waldman, Steven, 48, 221

"Walker of the sky," 229
Wall Street Journal, 226
Wallace, Henry, 175
Warburg, Paul, 20, 23
Warren Court, 178
Warsaw Pact, 68
Washington, George, 15, 210, 218
Washington Post, 24, 51, 219
Washington Times, 189, 217, 227, 230-233
WCEFA (see World Conference on Education For All), 52
Webster, Nesta H., 226
Weekly Compilation of Presidential Documents, 219, 232
Weishaupt, Adam, 11-13, 24-25, 166
Weiskittel, John Kenneth, 224
Wells, H. G., 63, 65, 79, 222
West, John, 232
West Indies, 143, 227
Westerman, General, 202
Western Technology and Soviet Economic Development, 219
Westman, Jack C., 72-80, 88-89, 118, 222-223
WFDY (see World Federation of Democratic Youth)
Whelan, Robert, 121-122, 225-226
When the World Will Be as One, 228
White, Lesley, 226
Who's Who in America 1995, 222
Whose Child?, 80, 223
Will, George F., 219-220
Willson, John, 202, 233
Wilson, E. O., 171
Wilson, Woodrow, 18-22, 219
WIPC (see World Indigenous Peoples Council)
Wirth, Timothy, 33, 106-107, 111, 127-128, 209-210, 225-226, 233

Witham, Larry, 189, 231-232
Wolfgang, Johann, 219
Women, Infants, and Children Program, 70
The Works of Fisher Ames as published by Seth Ames, 218
The Works of William Shakespeare, 217
World Bank, 98, 119, 122, 179
World Conference on Education For All (WCEFA), 52
World Court, 148
"The World Declaration on Education for All," 52
World Environment Day, 170
World Federation of Democratic Youth (WFDY), 49
World Indigenous Peoples Council (WIPC), 150-151
World Network of Religious Futurists, 182
World Resources Institute, 119
The World's Parliament of Religions, 231
World Summit on Social Development (Copenhagen, 1995), 34, 49, 99, 221, 224
World Trade Center, 193
World War I, 18, 21-22, 48, 219
World War II, 22-23, 37, 52, 108
Worldwide Conference of Religions, 182
Wotanism, 187
Wounded Knee, South Dakota, 147, 151
The Writings of George Washington, 218
Wurmbrand, Richard, 218-219

Yaacov's Lantern, 173
Year of Inter-religious Cooperation, 185

Yewell, John, 226
Ying Chi An, 101, 224
Yoda, 229
Yugoslavia, 98

Zen, 229
Zoroastrian, 165

Personal Acknowledgements

Writing a book offers an author a guided tour through the dismal landscape of his own inadequacies. Gary Benoit, G. Vance Smith, William F. Jasper, Tom Gow, Thomas R. Eddlem, Tom Burzynski, Paul Smith, and Sharilyn Stanley all served as perceptive and sympathetic tour guides.

Steve DuBord's virtuosity with a computer easily met and overcame the challenges of a nearly impossible production schedule, and his indefatigable good humor made that schedule tractable. Alan Scholl's labors as a despotic — yet personable — supervisor were also indispensable.

Were it not for an off-handed suggestion from Virginia Goverdare, my seventh-grade English teacher, I would not be a writer. I am similarly indebted to Lee Allen, who wrote the first check I earned as a journalist and offered invaluable advice regarding politics and many other much more important matters. Earl Biederman, my editor at the Provo *Daily Herald*, earned my gratitude by offering me a column — and then cheerfully ignoring the wrath of the "tolerance" gestapo for four years.

No expression of gratitude is adequate to the task of thanking my mother and father for their love, patience, generosity, and example, and no language can encompass my debt to the Lord Jesus Christ, whose sacrifice is mankind's sole claim upon salvation and whose teachings offer mankind's only hope for freedom and peace.

About the Author

William Norman Grigg was born in Idaho and educated at Ricks College and Utah State University. While studying at the National Journalism Center in Washington, D.C., he worked as a research assistant to Fred Barnes, the White House correspondent for *The New Republic* magazine. He has also worked on the staff of the National Right to Life Committee. From 1989 to 1993, Mr. Grigg wrote an award-winning column for the Provo *Daily Herald* newspaper in Provo, Utah. His first book, *The Gospel of Revolt: Feminism vs. The Family*, was published in 1993.

Mr. Grigg has reported from five foreign countries and covered the 1994 UN International Conference on Population and Development in Cairo, Egypt for *The New American* magazine. He is presently a senior editor at *The New American* magazine.

Recommended Reading

Global Tyranny ... Step By Step .... **pb $12.95**
WILLIAM F. JASPER — A counterpart to *Financial Terrorism*. Thoroughly documents the plan to build the United Nations into a world tyranny. Extremely compelling. (1992 ed., 350 pp.)

The Shadows Of Power .... **pb $10.95**
JAMES PERLOFF — An exposé of the Council on Foreign Relations and its tragic impact on American foreign policy. Compiled from the group's own documents. Highly recommended. (1988 ed., 266 pp.)

The Insiders .... **pb $3.00**
JOHN F. MCMANUS — A look at the powerful few who really dictate America's policies. Spotlights the Council on Foreign Relations and Trilateral Commission. (1995 ed., 152 pp.)

Changing Commands .... **pb $8.95**
JOHN F. MCMANUS — Carefully documents the plans of many U.S. leaders to convert America's military from defender of the nation to enforcer of the New World Order. (1995 ed., 240 pp.)

The Law .... **pb $3.95**
FREDERIC BASTIAT — Arguably the best essay ever written on the proper role of government. Bastiat, a French statesman and economist, confronted socialist tyranny in the middle 1800s. (75 pp.)

The Fearful Master .... **pb $4.95**
G. EDWARD GRIFFIN — An early criticism of the UN, including the backgrounds of its founders and their intentions. (1964 ed., 256 pp.)

John Birch Society Introductory Packet............... **$5.00**
Numerous pamphlets analyzing current events, a sample *JBS Bulletin*, and a sample of *The New American* magazine.

The New American .... **(see below)**
The New American magazine, a biweekly publication affiliated with The John Birch Society, is must reading for those who would be truly informed about the plans and programs of the Insiders.

- **Six-months subscription**.................... **$22.00**
- **One-year subscription**...................... **$39.00**
  (Please contact *The New American* for foreign rates.)

Except for subscriptions to *The New American*, please add 15 percent for postage and handling ($2.00 minimum).

American Opinion Book Services
P.O. Box 8040 • Appleton, WI 54913
(Credit card orders accepted at 414–749–3783.)